NEW TOWNS FOR OLD

LALH

NEW TOWNS FOR OLD

Achievements in Civic Improvement in Some

American Small Towns and Neighborhoods

JOHN NOLEN

New Introduction by Charles D. Warren

Library of American Landscape History / Amherst, Massachusetts

Library of American Landscape History
P.O. Box 1323
Amherst, MA 01004
www.lalh.org

Cloth edition published by University of Massachusetts Press and
Library of American Landscape History, 2005
Paperback edition published by Library of American Landscape History, 2021

Printed in the United States by Porter Print Group, LLC

Library of Congress Control Number: 2021934465
ISBN: 978-1-952620-31-7

Designed by Jonathan D. Lippincott
Set in Old Style 7

This volume is reprinted from the first edition of *New Towns for Old* by John Nolen.
Published by Marshall Jones Incorporated. Copyright 1927.

Distributed by
National Book Network
nbnbooks.com

The Library of Congress has cataloged the hardcover edition as follows:
Nolen, John, 1869–1937.
New towns for old : achievements in civic improvement in some American small towns
and neighborhoods / by John Nolen ; [new introduction by Charles D. Warren].
p. cm. — (American Society of Landscape Architects centennial reprint series)
Originally published: Boston, Mass. : Marshall Jones Company, 1927. Includes
bibliographical references and index. ISBN 1-55849-480-4 (cloth : alk. paper)
1. City planning. 2. Civic improvement. 3. New towns—United States. 4. Cities and
towns—Designs and plans. I. Warren, Charles D. (Charles Davock), 1953– II. Title. III.
Centennial reprint series.
NA9105.N6 2005
711'.4'0973—dc22
2005000058

Publication of the paperback edition was supported by a generous gift
from Evelyn and Michael Jefcoat and by the Nancy R. Turner Fund.

CONTENTS

PREFACE

John Nolen (1869–1937) published *New Towns for Old* in 1927, at the height of his career as America's preeminent town planner. Although modest in size, Nolen's illustrated text is breathtaking in scope—it outlines the collective goals of city planning in the United States, many of which were formulated by Nolen himself. Over the course of his lifetime, the practitioner completed nearly four hundred planning projects from his office in Cambridge, Massachusetts. He also wrote and lectured extensively to promote the new profession of city planning. *New Towns for Old*, long out of print and increasingly rare, is avidly sought by today's planners, architects, landscape architects, historians, and developers as a catalog of Nolen's remarkable built accomplishments. Here, with a new, sweeping introduction by the architect Charles D. Warren, Nolen's classic work assumes broader significance.

Warren's introduction provides far-ranging insight into the roots of Nolen's professional vocation, the forces that shaped it, and the complex circumstances behind the publication of Nolen's book, including the Boston-based journalist Sylvester Baxter's role as ghostwriter of some sections of it. Warren portrays Nolen as one of the vanguard of Progressive activists, whose work encompassed social as well as physical reform. "Both Nolen and Baxter spent much of their lives proselytizing for the new civic ideals," writes Warren, "but Nolen did more than persuade and convert. . . . His idea of reform was pragmatic, accommodating plans to realities without losing sight of sometimes elusive ideals."

Nolen spent his formative years at a nonsectarian boarding school for orphaned boys in Philadelphia, where he finished at the head of his class. In 1891 he entered the Wharton School of Finance and Economy at the University of Pennsylvania, where he absorbed the German *verein* model, which dissolved barriers between academia, political activism, and government initiatives. Nolen's first published work, on the beneficial effect of city control over the Philadelphia Gas Works, presaged his lifelong interest in the betterment of society through public policy. After Nolen visited the World's Columbian Exposition in 1893 and witnessed the spectacle of Olmsted and Burnham's grandly unified scheme—open to all—he expressed "a deep desire to do *something* in this great universe."

Warren's richly contextual biography follows Nolen to the University of Munich, where he studied European art and history and viewed the fruits of modern city planning at close hand, marveling over "hygienic innovations, zoning, and novel land development techniques, as well as new artistic approaches to urban design." Nolen returned to the United States to attend Harvard, where he studied under Frederick Law Olmsted Jr., heir to the distinctly American approach to city planning pioneered by his father and shaped by the geography, politics, and personalities of Massachusetts at the end of the nineteenth century. Warren's essay traces the commingling influences of Charles W. Eliot, Charles Eliot, Edward Everett Hale, and the often-overlooked Baxter, and how these forces coalesced in the young planner.

The new introduction also presents an overview of

Nolen's far-flung practice and, in its final sections, covers the projects discussed in Nolen's book, supplying rich background information and perspective on disparate places, from the rail town of Kingsport, Tennessee, to the company town of Kistler, Pennsylvania, to the elegant suburb of Myers Park, North Carolina. The reprint edition contains a list of all of Nolen's projects and provides an index for the new as well as the original text. In 1912, Nolen described the goal of town planning as the endeavor "to establish the individuality of a city—to catch its peculiar spirit, to preserve its distinctive flavor, to accent its particular physical situation." *New Towns for Old* gives tangible form to these ideals.

We are pleased to publish a paperback edition of Nolen's influential book, supported by a generous gift from Evelyn and Michael Jefcoat and by the Nancy R. Turner Fund.

Robin Karson
Executive Director
Library of American Landscape History

JOHN NOLEN AND THE NEW SYNTHESIS
IN AMERICAN CITY PLANNING
Charles D. Warren

As the nineteenth century turned to the twentieth, civic leaders, businessmen, and intellectuals joined together in a complex effort to improve urban life in the United States. The Boston journalist Sylvester Baxter, writing in the *Century* magazine, called it the "Great Civic Awakening," and he enumerated the major participants in the movement he described. These included village beautifiers, housing reformers, and park advocates aiming to ameliorate the degrading effects of rapid growth and rampant industrialization in American towns and cities. They came together in local and mostly voluntary organizations to improve and beautify the physical environment, but many also worked to address the underlying social, economic, and political causes of the chaos and misery of impoverished neighborhoods and congested streets. These reformers relied on the work of journalists, experts, and emerging professionals to inspire and abet their efforts to cleanse and revive the American city. Baxter's title alludes to the hope for enlightenment and communal redemption that had characterized earlier American awakenings and captures the evangelical fervor of the movement. The new century's reformers were motivated by an urban darkness filled with nightmares of poverty, disease, and disorder, and they envisioned a new morning lighted with promise, energy, and more than a few dreams.[1]

In his first book, *Replanning Small Cities* (1912), John Nolen wrote:

> The form of this civic awakening that is most signif-
> icant and promising is the recognition of the need of
> comprehensive planning and replanning, especially
> of the smaller cities, where so much is practicable.
> Town planning, let it be understood, is not a move-
> ment to make towns beautiful in a superficial sense.
> Its purposes are fundamental. It aims consciously to
> provide those facilities that are for the common good,
> that concern everybody. . . . It endeavors to estab-
> lish the individuality of a city,—to catch its peculiar
> spirit, to preserve its distinctive flavor, to accent its
> particular physical situation.[2]

Both Nolen and Baxter spent much of their lives proselytizing for the new civic ideals, but Nolen did more than
persuade and convert. His idea of reform was pragmatic,
accommodating plans to realities without losing sight of
sometimes elusive ideals. Nolen worked at a time of great
technological advances and huge movements of population;
as the United States shifted from a rural to an urban society and wave after wave of immigrants arrived, a complex
social urgency unfolded. He concentrated on smaller cities
where urban growth had not produced the intractable politics, the frightening, gargantuan scale, and the accompanying despair of their larger counterparts. Planning there
could anticipate the future, not just ameliorate the present.
Though many of Nolen's concrete achievements are fragmentary—we see them in a street corner, a village green, a
parkway, or an urban district, often subsumed now by the
growth that he foresaw—the land, the architecture, and in
some ways the structure of our society record the impact of

his work on the complicated ongoing encounter between culture and nature.

Nolen's life and work encompassed both the physical and social reform of towns and cities—indeed, his productive activism personifies the myriad concerns of the Great Civic Awakening. Born in 1869, Nolen lived the first half of his life in Philadelphia, and from 1903 until his death in 1937 he lived in Cambridge, Massachusetts. While he was still an infant, the violence and political corruption that later goaded Americans to seek reform entered his life in an event that left him suddenly without a father. Yet soon thereafter the bleak prospect for his future was transformed by one of Philadelphia's remarkable charitable institutions, an exemplar of the voluntary civic culture of America prior to the Great Depression. As Nolen reached adulthood he was drawn to those giving direction to the broad movement for urban reform, and after a protracted and often self-directed education, he began to assume the leadership of efforts to improve American cities. As the profession of city planning emerged in the early twentieth century, Nolen was in the vanguard—in important ways he was its inventor—and he devoted his career not only to nearly four hundred planning projects (see Appendix) but to formulating the profession's collective goals and nurturing its institutional development.[3] He was always looking forward, and his adult life became something of a mission to redeem the besmirched promise of the City Upon a Hill.

New Towns for Old was published in 1927 at the high point of Nolen's career. It offers a glimpse of his mature work, and it should be seen in the context of the career that preceded it and its ten-year aftermath. The book chronicles some of his greatest efforts and those of others too; civic leaders, businessmen, land developers, architects, and engineers—who were Nolen's clients and collaborators—all played a role in his achievements. Especially important are those who worked with Nolen, his associates Philip Foster, Justin Hartzog, and Hale Walker, whose names grace his firm's plans. But credit is due to many others whose names appear less prominently, or not at all. Among them is the great, neglected Sylvester Baxter, whose part in the present volume was crucial.

CHILDHOOD AND EARLY EDUCATION

John Nolen was born on June 14, 1869, not far from Independence Hall in Philadelphia (Fig. 1). The fast-growing city had, by then, outgrown the bounds of William Penn's original square grid plan, and also outgrown Independence Hall, which served as the seat of city government. It was

Figure 1. John Nolen. *Nolen Papers, Cornell University Library.*

the second most populous city in the United States, much
larger in physical area than Boston or New York, and
much less densely built than the island of Manhattan or
the Shawmut peninsula. The unconstrained geography
of Philadelphia, combined with its widespread system of
building and loan societies, made home ownership more
widely available there than in other cities.[4] Nolen's family
lived in modest circumstances, north of the original city
boundaries. His mother, Matilda Nolen, was the youngest
child of Phillip and Margaret Thomas, who had arrived
from Würtemberg in the 1830s. His father, John Christopher Nolen, whose origins are uncertain, ran a hotel and
tavern at 733 Sansom Street; his name is listed in *Gopsill's
City Directory* followed by the word "liquors." John C.
Nolen was known as Shay, and in addition to his business he was evidently active in the era's rough-and-tumble
party politics.

Looking back to the time when Nolen was born, Lincoln Steffens wrote: "Having passed through all the typical stages of corruption, Philadelphia reached the period of
miscellaneous loot with a boss for chief thief, under James
McManus and the Gas Ring."[5] The Gas Works was a key
to the McManus Republican Party machine, which used
its continuous revenue stream and peculiar lending provisions as a source of patronage and a bank for graft.[6] The
fraudulence of the city's politics was widely recognized,
and elections were often an occasion for violence. Efforts to
reform the degraded democracy of Philadelphia met with
entrenched resistance, as they did in other cities and in the
federal and state governments as well. The Gas Works, an
important battleground of governmental reform in Philadelphia, would later engage Nolen's attention as a student,
but while he was still an infant, the city's ugly politics dra-
matically changed his life.

The historian Harry Silcox sets the scene: "Proclaiming their intention to clean up Philadelphia's political system, the Republicans, under [Attorney General] Colonel William B. Mann, enacted Philadelphia's Registry Act that took effect with the election of October 1870. Under the act . . . voters were required to register before the election."[7] But registration was controlled by the Republican majority, so it was used to insure Republican victories, not fair elections. (The 1870 election was the first where African Americans were enfranchised; the same year, in a remarkable example of democratic city planning, the voters chose between two locations for the new city hall.)

Anticipating the violence that might accompany African American enfranchisement, the federal government had dispatched troops, and Election Day proceeded without incident. Still, alert to the possibility of irregularities subsequent to the vote, Shay Nolen and other Democrats gathered the next day outside the courtroom where the election return judges met to read and certify the vote. When time came to hear the returns for the 26th ward, there was a controversy, and a motion was made to call William B. Mann to advise on the resolution of a legal question. One of the judges asked that they also summon Lewis Cassidy, leader of the Irish-Catholic faction of the Democratic Party, so that both sides of the question would be represented by counsel.

When Mann arrived and tried to enter the courtroom, he was challenged by a man in the crowd named John Ahern, who insisted that Mann wait for Cassidy. A scuffle ensued, and Mann gained entry to the courtroom. Shay Nolen slipped in behind him, and Ahern tried to get in too, but was caught in the closing door. The guards inside, armed with blackjacks, beat the trapped Ahern while the crowd outside struggled to free him by forcing the doors open. Eventually they succeeded and flooded into the courtroom. Chaos ensued, and while newspaper reporters looked on, Nolen and a bloodied Ahern chased William Crawford, a Republican judge, and Mann into a corner of the jury box. Nolen picked up a spittoon and hurled it at Crawford, who ducked as it smashed to pieces against the wall. Crawford was armed with a pistol and he stood his ground as Mann urged him on by shouting, "Defend yourself! Shoot, shoot!" Crawford, a war veteran, coolly took aim at Nolen, who crouched down, but not low enough to avoid the bullet that entered his neck and lodged next to his spine.

Shay Nolen was taken to his home at 937 Buttonwood Street, where he lay for two days drifting in and out of consciousness. He was able to make a statement identifying Crawford as his assailant and Mann as an accessory. One paper reported that the renowned surgeon Samuel D. Gross was called in to consult, but apparently to no avail. Nolen died three days after he was shot, leaving his widow, Matilda, to raise two daughters and a one-year-old son, John Nolen.[8] Crawford was immediately arrested and charged with murder, though allowed to finish his work as an election return judge before he was imprisoned to await trial. He pled self-defense and was acquitted by a coroner's jury. Charges against Mann were dropped.[9]

The years that followed must have been difficult for Matilda Nolen. The economic depression that hit Philadelphia particularly hard in the winter of 1873–74 took a toll, and during this period the two Nolen girls died, leaving her alone to care for her only remaining child, John.[10] In 1878, when John was nine, she was remarried to Caleb F. Aaronson, and the young boy, evidently not welcome in his stepfather's home in Trenton, New Jersey, was admitted to an orphanage called Girard College.

Stephen Girard had left the bulk of his vast shipping and banking fortune to found Girard College, a nonsectarian boarding school for orphaned white boys. After some legal wrangling over the estate, the trustees proceeded with the construction of an enormously expensive Greek Revival campus designed by Thomas U. Walter, which was completed in 1848 (Fig. 2). The terms of Girard's bequest put control of the college in the hands of Philadelphia's elected officials, but irregularities led to the amendment of the charter, and in 1869 the Office of City Trusts, directed by twelve lifetime trustees (appointed by the city judiciary), was established to oversee the college and its endowment. Girard was prosperous and growing when Nolen entered in 1878. There were 871 boys who followed a curriculum that changed frequently, reflecting uncertainty about whether

Figure 2. The main building at Girard College, the school for orphans where Nolen lived and studied from 1878 until 1887. *Nolen Papers, Cornell University Library.*

impoverished orphans should be given a liberal education or one that would prepare them for a practical trade. Nolen excelled at Girard, finishing at the head of his class and staying on after his graduation at fifteen, in 1884, to study drawing. During that time he went to work as an office-boy for the president of Girard, Adam Fetterholf. Then, in 1887, he was "bound out" to his mother and went to work as a clerk for John Smiley, a wholesale grocer. But after a few unpleasant months, another place was found for him within the Girard fold.[11]

Nolen had impressed his teachers and ingratiated himself with the leaders of Girard, several of whom made special efforts to nurture the bright young man. George E. Kirkpatrick, a childless man who ran the Girard Trust, hired Nolen and trained him in the financial management of the endowment as he had been trained by his father, who preceded him in the job.[12] He became a friend and advised the young man as he helped ease his transition from ward to employee. (Curiously, during the entire time Nolen was associated with Girard College and the Girard Trust, William B. Mann, the person his father had identified as an accessory to his murder, served on its board of trustees.) After four years in the Girard Trust office, Nolen's ambitions exceeded its confines and he applied to the newly formed Wharton School of Finance and Economy at the University of Pennsylvania.

WHARTON, ONTEORA, AND THE WHITE CITY

Nolen entered Wharton just as German universities were beginning to have a major impact in the United States. Their open, public character, their willingness to grapple with current political and social problems, and their innovative teaching methods provided a striking contrast to English models, which had long dominated American pedagogy.[13] Wharton was intended as an alternative to the University of Pennsylvania's classical curriculum, and it quickly joined Johns Hopkins as a major port of entry for German pedagogy and German ideas. As the school evolved under its first head, Albert Bolles, the curriculum focused broadly on administration and political economy. Subsequent additions to the faculty gave it a decidedly Germanic cast. In Edmund James, a new professor of public administration and finance, Bolles had found a German-educated scholar, writes Wharton historian Steven Sass, "with a commitment to reproduce in the United States the vaunted German system of generating civil servants and public policies." James, who would become Nolen's early mentor, "was true to the [German] *verein* idea and hoped to influence events as an academic, through research and command of the scholarly literature."[14]

The *verein* idea was derived from German associations that studied and developed policy initiatives, and in the process dissolved barriers between scholars, political activists, and government—something like a late-twentieth-century American think tank. This model of academic activism had crossed the Atlantic with the increasing number of German-trained American students, including James's Halle University classmate Simon Patten, who joined the Wharton faculty in 1885. Others, most notably Richard T. Ely and Herbert Baxter Adams, alumni of the same German universities, promoted similar methods and ideas at Johns Hopkins. Adams founded the American Historical Association, an offshoot of the American Social Science Association, and with James, Patten, and Ely he helped establish the American Economic Association (AEA). Through these organizations, publication of journals, and various connections with universities, the men sought to establish the *verein* idea in the United States.[15] Wharton was an important nexus of their activities, and there, Edmund James established the first American society for university extension teaching, where Nolen eventually began his career.

Along with the German pedagogy came an awareness of German communal traditions and advocacy of German-style socialism. The AEA, in its early days, worked to counter the prevailing laissez-faire economics, advocating state intervention in the "natural" workings of the economy. (Henry C. Carey and his circle in the Philadelphia Social Science Association had been thinking along similar lines, challenging laissez-faire orthodoxy by advocating protectionist tariffs as the linchpin of nationalistic economic policy since the end of the Civil War.) German ideas and administrative methods provided useful models for Americans who were reacting to the corruption and inefficiency of government and intent on its reform. It was an example that led the AEA to assert the principle that all levels of American government should take responsibility for the social and economic well-being of its citizens.[16]

Invigorating German ideas and techniques were being grafted onto American traditions of journalistic and clerical activism when Nolen entered Wharton in autumn of 1891. The curriculum had evolved to encompass the last two years of a college education, and Nolen was able to qualify, by examination, for entry as a junior. It was a small school then (fifty-nine students in 1892), and under the sway of Patten, whose powerful, imaginative mind came to dominate the school, and the socially active Edmund James, Nolen was introduced to important new currents in social, economic, and political thought.

Patten's books and exploration of the consequences of a surplus economy had wide influence in the academic world, but James's activism directly engaged social and political issues; he plunged headlong into the political controversy surrounding the management of the Philadelphia Gas Works in the 1880s, which presented a perfect case study of the political ideas and administrative methods he was teaching at Wharton. His documentation of the negative consequences inflicted upon the people of Philadelphia by the corrupt administration of the Gas Works provided a stark contrast to the beneficial municipal ownership and efficient operation of similar utilities in Germany.[17]

In the spring of 1893, at the end of his two years at Wharton, Nolen's class produced a book of essays on municipal government in Philadelphia, each student taking a different aspect of the city as a subject for his essay. Nolen chose the Philadelphia Gas Works. He described the successful "good government" effort led by James, which put the Gas Works under direct city control, and he explained how it had slipped back into inefficient private operation after only a few years under the reformed regime. Nolen's essay not only provides a coda to his teacher's efforts, it reveals his awareness of the political machine his father had recklessly opposed. It was his first published work.[18]

During the three summers of 1892–94, Nolen was employed at Onteora Park, Candace Wheeler's summer colony in the Catskill Mountains. Wheeler had founded Onteora near her native Delhi just two years after New York State had established the 34,000-acre Catskill Park in 1885. She was a multifaceted designer and gardener who, after a short-lived but fruitful partnership with the artist and designer Louis Comfort Tiffany (they collaborated on design work for the White House), had established Associated Artists, an all-woman enterprise devoted to textile making and interior design. Nolen was employed as superintendent of the thousand-acre resort, where he was involved with all aspects of the care and feeding of the three hundred cottagers and guests from New York City, Philadelphia, and elsewhere. At Onteora he was exposed to the advanced artistic tastes of Wheeler, Albert Herter, J. Carrol Beckwith, and other authors, illustrators, and artists.[19] Far from the torrid city heat, 2,500 feet above sea level in the cool mountain air, there was a very different kind of society from that at Wharton, one preoccupied with nature, art and visual design, literature, domestic comfort, and beauty. It was during this period that Wheeler was involved in the World's Columbian Exposition in Chicago. (The interior decoration of the Women's Building there was under her supervision.) She rhapsodized about the fair: "The whole thing seems to have sprung into being fully conceived and perfectly planned . . . a vision and foretaste of how the world will one day build in earnest."[20]

At the end of his second summer at Onteora, Nolen visited the Columbian Exposition. The fair was *the* attraction of the summer of 1893, proving to be an epiphany for some and an inspiration for all who visited the streets and lagoons of the shimmering White City. Not since the Spanish conquest had destroyed the urban complex in the valley of Mexico had there been such a magnificent integration of land, water, and architecture on the American continent. Indeed, such coherent (if ephemeral) planning was impressive even to Europeans. Moreover, it was public art, not a secluded idyll for private enjoyment of a few but a demonstration of stylistically and spatially unified architecture and landscape design open to all. It was the embodiment of a new civic ideal. Nolen was apparently overcome with admiration and excitement; after visiting its diverse exhibits he wrote of "a deep desire to do *something* in this great universe."[21]

EARLY CAREER, MARRIAGE, AND TRAVEL

Returning from his visit to the fair, Nolen began work as the assistant secretary of the American Society for the Extension of University Teaching (ASEUT), a position that had been offered to him by his Wharton professor Edmund James, who was president of the society. ASEUT was a realization of the *verein* idea described by Herbert Baxter Adams—an institution meant to broaden the availability of university-level instruction to include those who were unable to matriculate on a full-time basis. Nolen's work at ASEUT involved the administration of its lecture courses around Philadelphia, and it included travel, too, as he was sent out to help establish university extension programs in other cities and towns throughout Pennsylvania. He was able to further his own education by meeting the professors, overseeing the production of syllabi and reading lists, and often attending the lectures. He developed a wide acquaintance among the society's lecturers and participants, which included figures such as Woodrow Wilson and Samuel Gompers, and close, lifelong friendships with others, in particular the author Edward Griggs, who helped broaden Nolen's exposure to literature and art history. The diverse course offerings included philosophy, literature, history, art, science, and horticulture, and many of the courses focused on the reform of American civic life and municipal government. Paging through the monthly issues of the *Citizen*, the ASEUT magazine that Nolen edited, one finds articles on streets, water supply, transportation, and good government, all topics that became central to his later professional life.[22]

At the end of his first academic year at ASEUT, Nolen returned to Onteora for a final summer. From there he carried on a correspondence with Barbara Schatte, whom he had met in 1891. (His Girard friend Frank Zesinger had married Barbara's older sister, Emma, in 1892.) In a situation reminiscent of Nolen's own experience, Barbara and her sister had been orphaned in the 1870s and were consigned to the Episcopal Church Home for Children until they were eventually taken in by Mr. and Mrs. Effingham Perot, a well-to-do couple with no children of their own. The Perots kept a house in Philadelphia and in 1889 had built a country place in Ardmore called the Beeches. They became kindly parental figures for the close-knit sisters, unstintingly seeing to their education, chaperoning their courtships, and nurturing them well into adulthood. After finishing her education Barbara taught at James Forten Elementary Manual Training School, a public school for African American children in Philadelphia.[23]

In the fall of 1894 Nolen returned to his job at ASEUT with a 50-percent increase in salary—a strong vote of confidence given the difficult economy of the mid-1890s. The following year Edmund James resigned from ASEUT and went to the University of Chicago, where the extension university was more closely integrated with the regular curriculum. Nolen continued his work as assistant secretary until 1896, when the secretary, Edward T. Devine, left to become the general secretary of the Charity Organization of New York City. Nolen became acting secretary of ASEUT in 1897.

With the financial stability that accompanied his new position, Nolen married Barbara Schatte in spring 1896. The event was attended by friends and family, including Nolen's mother, who had returned to Philadelphia after the death of her second husband in 1894 and reestablished close ties with her only surviving child. The newlyweds went off on a trip that took them around England and to Paris, Brussels, and Cologne. Nolen had been abroad once before, when he went to Oxford for the annual Extension University Summer School, but the wedding trip was his first opportunity to follow his own European itinerary.[24]

Before leaving, John and Barbara Nolen arranged for the construction of a new house in Ardmore, not far from the Perots. Years later Nolen would explain that he was able to travel to Europe and build his house because of his participation in one of Philadelphia's building and loan societies, an economic model he repeatedly advocated as a method of encouraging and enabling home ownership.[25] The house, which the couple called Blytheham, introduced Nolen to commuting and other novel aspects of suburban living, and perhaps inspired by Candace Wheeler's gardens at Onteora, Nolen made his first foray into gardening and landscape design. From 1897 until 1902 he planted, nurtured, and tended the one-third-acre property (Fig. 3).

Domestic comfort and his position at ASEUT did not forestall Nolen's restlessness. He was curious to see the German municipal system firsthand and eager to study in a German university. So after seven years of administrative work he took a year, from 1900 to 1901, to travel in Europe with his family and attend the University of Munich.[26] There he enrolled in classes in Renaissance cultural history, Italian painting, and German architecture and sculpture, taught by Arthur Weese, author of a book on the architecture and urbanism of Munich.

At the turn of the twentieth century German city planning and administration were far in advance of other countries, and Munich was at the forefront. The long tradition of municipal home rule and the Bismarck era's administrative and legal reforms combined with rapid urban growth

Figure 3. The garden at Blytheham, John and Barbara Nolen's first house in Ardmore, Pennsylvania. *Country Life in America, Aug. 1905.*

to spur the development of detailed modern city planning techniques, which included hygienic innovations, zoning, and novel land development techniques, as well as new artistic approaches to urban design.[27] These were known in the United States through *Municipal Government in Continental Europe*, by Albert Shaw (writer of the introduction to the present volume), through lectures such as one given by the German architect Josef Stübben at the Chicago Exposition, and by way of British interpreters such as Thomas C. Horsfal. Many other transatlantic connections provided a growing awareness of German design technique, which continued to develop and change in the last decades of the nineteenth century. Much of the change was owing to the Viennese architect Camillo Sitte's critique of contemporary Beaux-Arts technique and its influence on the planning of the Vienna Ringstrasse, which appeared in his 1889 book, *Der Städtebau*. Sitte advocated a more intimately scaled, picturesque, and topographically responsive method of urban composition, which emulated the balanced asymmetry of medieval urbanism and eschewed the grandiose axial compositions and rigidity that had characterized European city planning of the nineteenth century.[28]

In 1900 Munich was being transformed by rapid growth and by the results of an influential design competition held seven years before. Sitte was on the competition jury, and his ideas could be recognized in winning schemes by Karl Henrici and others. The new plans attempted the coherent integration of city extension plans at the urban periphery (by then a well-rehearsed German specialty) with sympathetic changes made to the historic center. Implementation was under the supervision of Theodor Fischer, who wrote of Sitte,

> He sharply chastised the intellectually desolate schematicism of the times and demand[ed] freedom and artistic treatment. Practical attempts in these directions were entered upon amidst violent opposition. Among them Henrici's project for the extension of Munich is the most valuable. This gave Munich the advantage of being the first to adopt the new point of view.[29]

Nolen, with his interest in art and civic affairs, must have attended carefully to the ongoing physical realization of these innovative planning ideas.

HARVARD AND BOSTON

That year abroad was a turning point in Nolen's life. Upon his return, he resolved to leave his ASEUT position and enter the new landscape architecture program at Harvard. ASEUT's ambitious journal, the *Citizen,* had ceased publication, and with Edmund James's departure the leadership in university extension education had passed to other institutions. Moreover, Nolen was eager to play an active role beyond the confines of an institution whose activities relied on private funding. His experience nurturing the garden in Ardmore, too, foreshadowed the career change, though he saw landscape architecture as more than garden design. Rather, it was a means of combining his "love to be outdoors," his desire for artistic expression, and a "large and constant opportunity for public good."[30]

Specialized programs and professional schools proliferated at Harvard during the presidency of Charles W. Eliot, and a program in landscape architecture led by his son Charles Eliot had been contemplated in the late 1890s. But the untimely death of the younger Eliot delayed the program's start until 1900. In his place Fredrick Law Olmsted Jr. took the lead; his classes and those taught by Arthur Asahel Shurtleff were at the core of the landscape curriculum. At first these classes were pieced together with offerings in the Bussey Institution (a precursor of the Arnold Arboretum) and the Lawrence Scientific School, which was home to the architecture department. But by the time Nolen arrived in 1903, J. S. Pray, who went on to develop Harvard's planning program, had joined the faculty, and in 1904 Henry Hubbard, Harvard's first graduate with a degree in landscape architecture (1901), was teaching there.[31] It was still a small operation with only eleven students, and Nolen was older, if only by a little, than each of his landscape architecture teachers.

Nolen was admitted as a regular student in the second-year undergraduate class, but not as a candidate for a degree; by January 1904 he applied to change his status to become a candidate for a Master of Arts degree. He was an

exemplary student, but he struggled with freehand drawing and he dropped a course in elementary architectural
design. Otherwise he earned As and Bs in horticulture, forestry, landscape architecture, and a special advanced study
course with Olmsted Jr.[32]

All of Nolen's Harvard landscape teachers were employed
at one time or another in the Olmsted office, where Charles
Eliot and then Olmsted Jr. had assumed leadership in the
late 1890s as the old master's health declined. Their professional experience spilled over from office to classroom, and
the pedagogy emerged from the practice. According to the
historian Susan Klaus,

> Olmsted [Jr.]'s notes for the [landscape] course indi-
> cate that he began with an historical review of the
> gardens and landscapes of the ancient world and the
> Renaissance, then moved on to English landscape
> history and its influence in the American colonies.
> Fifteen lectures were allocated to contemporary land-
> scape treatment of private estates in the United States
> and abroad; the first year of instruction culminated
> with fourteen lectures on streets, parks, and public
> spaces in Washington, New York, and Boston.[33]

All three of these cities had been transformed by the Olmsted office.

Olmsted Jr. may have been leading a course of study
in landscape architecture, but he and his firm were at the
forefront of planning practice in the United States, and
the line between landscape architecture and city planning
often was hard to discern. Olmsted Jr. had accompanied
his father to planning meetings for the Chicago Exposition,
and in 1901–2 he collaborated with D. H. Burnham and
Charles McKim in the U.S. Senate Park Commission, which

produced what is often referred to as the McMillan Plan
for Washington, D.C. There Olmsted Jr. demonstrated
the latitude in planning that could be entrusted to a landscape architect, integrating parks and natural features with
far-reaching transportation improvements to create a city
plan structured as much by the landscape as by the architecture.[34] The wide publicity given the McMillan Plan cannot have escaped Nolen's attention; surely he viewed his
entrance in the new Harvard program as a viable route to
professional training in the innovative approach to urban
problems inherent in the comprehensiveness of the commission's Washington plan.

Olmsted Jr. was an important innovator, and Washington was a significant advance, but both were part of a
complex process by which city planning ideas had emerged
from the geography, politics, and personalities of Massachusetts at the end of the nineteenth century. Boston's remarkable municipal parks and parkways were the local result of
this process, but the consequences of the ideas were more
far-reaching. The metropolitan park system came to exem-
plify a distinctly American approach to city planning. The
art historians George and Christiane Collins characterized
it as "the design of city parks and green spaces on a large
metropolitan scale for the reclamation of land, the insula-
tion of residential areas, [and] recreational purposes." They
went on to identify Olmsted Sr. and Sylvester Baxter as
"pioneers in this development."[35]

Boston's metropolitan park system, like the Washington
plan, was as much a political as a physical achievement. It
necessitated the cooperation of the commonwealth of Massachusetts, the city of Boston, and the surrounding towns,
and the political methods for accomplishing such a complex project had a long gestation. Over a ten-year period,
beginning in the 1830s, a series of metropolitan water com-

missions sought a clean, protected source of water for the city, and this search necessarily extended beyond the city's topographically arbitrary borders. The water commissions wrestled with questions such as ecological versus political boundaries, resource protection versus urban growth, and public versus private ownership of essential land and utilities, all issues that would be revisited in planning the parks.

The experiences of the water commission leaders early in the nineteenth century informed the activities of their sons and grandsons as they worked to advance the idea of a metropolitan park system. Samuel Eliot, father of the Harvard president, was deeply involved in the water issue; he served as mayor of Boston from 1837 until 1839, when he lost his bid for reelection in part because of his role in the lengthy political wrangling over water. Other figures were crucial to the eventual creation of the water commission too, such as Nathan Hale Sr., the publisher of the *Boston Daily Advertiser*, who served on every one of the commissions and used his newspaper to editorialize in their favor. Edward Everett Hale continued his father's advocacy of metropolitan planning, and so did the *Advertiser* under the editorship of Nathaniel Hale Jr.[36] Charles W. Eliot, the president of Harvard, who maintained a lifelong interest in city planning, made the connection between the metropolitan water and parks commissions explicit in a 1908 letter he wrote explaining the cooperative efforts and interconnected land acquisition of the state, the Trustees of Public Reservations,[37] the Metropolitan Park Commission, and the Water Board, which resulted in Boston's exemplary park system.[38]

Of course the younger Charles Eliot's role in the establishment of the Massachusetts Trustees of Public Reservations is well documented, and his involvement with the

Metropolitan Park Commission, where he served as the first landscape architect, is even exaggerated in the hagiographic biography written by his father.[39] He held that post concurrently with Sylvester Baxter, who was the commission's first secretary and who had worked for the Hales at the *Advertiser* in the 1870s. In fact, the idea for a metropolitan park system was suggested by Baxter as early as 1891; unfortunately his crucial role is overlooked too often.[40]

The Olmsteds, the Eliots, the Hales, and Baxter were at the center of this series of encounters between the city, the natural landscape, and the complex political realities that shaped the peculiarly American amalgamation of landscape design and city planning. Nolen's experience at Harvard and in Boston was permeated by the influence of these events and the ideas of these men. The school was imbued with the values of the Olmsteds and the Eliots, and, like the parks and water systems, the new landscape program was a product of the long-standing, consanguineous intellectual and civic leadership unique to Boston.[41]

Nolen was thirty-six when he graduated in 1905. He emerged from his formal education with great advantages over others whose educational paths might have been less circuitous or prolonged. Earnest enthusiasm and a knack for impressing his teachers had won him a far-flung network of mentors, colleagues, acquaintances, and friends. He was as well prepared for work in city planning as anyone emerging from an American educational institution. His Wharton experience had acquainted him with the political, economic, and social issues that both stimulated and constrained urban reform, and his Harvard years had introduced him to the most advanced American landscape ideas and planning techniques. He was an experienced and skilled administrator, a capable writer, and an effective public speaker. He had studied the history of Western art and the structure of European cities, and he had advanced training in forestry and horticulture. All of this experience made him an ideal person to weave together the warp of urban form with the weft of Progressive social policy.

Nolen's background in political science and economics made him particularly receptive to the notion that the landscape might be an active instrument of reform rather than just a passive respite from the otherwise dismal urban environment. He learned from the Olmsteds to see the landscape as something worthy of quiet contemplation. But to an even greater degree than Olmsted Jr., he developed a utilitarian attitude toward the landscape, treating it as an armature that could structure and accommodate the interrelated social, economic, and physical needs of the modern city.

EARLY WORK AND EMERGENT PLANNING

Nolen's professional career began even before he finished at Harvard. In November 1904, as he started his second year, he undertook a landscape design for the Philadelphia factory grounds owned by Joseph Fels, who used his soap manufacturing fortune to pursue social reform and philanthropy. Fels was a supporter of ASEUT, an advocate of Henry George's tax reforms, and the organizer of the Philadelphia Vacant Land Cultivation Society.[42] The same year, Nolen was commissioned to design the landscape of a private place in Ardmore for a relative of the Perots, and in June 1905 he designed another residential landscape on Bailey's Island, Maine. But the big break came when Nolen was contacted by George Stephens, secretary of the Park and Tree Commission of Charlotte, North Carolina. The commission was endeavoring to construct Charlotte's first public park, and Nolen had been recommended by Charles W. Eliot and Horace McFarland, of the American Civic Association.[43] Allowed to forego his final exams to pursue the project, Nolen took the train to Charlotte and went to work on Independence Park, his first public commission. This was followed by designs for Vance Square (Fig. 4), other park projects in Charlotte, and a series of residential landscape projects that Stephens persuaded his friends to commission, compensating for the very low fees Nolen was paid for the public work.

On the strength of his good start in Charlotte, Nolen opened an office in Harvard Square, an area where he would maintain offices for the rest of his life. He and Barbara moved from a house they had rented on Trowbridge Street to another on Avon Place, where they lived until 1914, when they built a house on Garden Terrace. They always lived within walking distance of the office, and in the

Figure 4. Vance Square, one of Nolen's first projects for the Charlotte Park and Tree Commission, North Carolina. *Nolen Papers, Cornell University Library.*

early years Barbara helped out from time to time while looking after the Nolen children, Jack, Barbara, Edward, and Humphrey. Her steadfastness and resourcefulness continued throughout his professional life. If there had been any question about Nolen's direction within the field of landscape architecture when he started at Harvard, it was quickly answered as the number and size of his planning commissions grew, while privately commissioned landscapes remained a sideline.

A tireless traveler, writer, and public speaker, Nolen kept a frantic pace in his early years. Just as he graduated, *Country Life in America* published an illustrated article he had written about Blytheham, the house and garden he and his family had left behind in Ardmore.[44] The following year he collaborated with Olmsted Jr. on an article analyzing public space requirements in American towns and cities for *Charities and the Commons*.[45] Two years later he wrote an introduction to a new edition of Humphrey Repton's *The Art of Landscape Gardening*, published with the sponsorship of the American Society of Landscape Architects (ASLA), which he had joined in 1905. In 1907 he traveled to San Diego to meet George Marston, an energetic civic leader to whom the city owes Balboa Park (designed in part by Samuel Parsons) as well as Nolen's city plans of 1908 and 1926. It was his first trip to the West; thereafter, he would cross the continent many times as his work took him to California, Florida, and many states in between.

By 1908 he was busy with work in Madison and ambitious plans for the Wisconsin state park system, and he was offered a position that would combine this work with teaching at the University of Wisconsin. Lincoln Steffens had glowingly described the interconnected activities of Wisconsin's government and its university in an essay called "Sending a State to College," and Richard T. Ely was, by then, chairman of economics there.[46] The interconnected activities of the state and the university were the fullest realization of the *verein* idea, but Nolen apparently was confident enough now to maintain his independent course rather than commit to an institutional attachment.[47]

Nolen's growing practice and list of publications were complemented by his active participation in the many organizations concerned with issues of planning and urban reform. He was made a fellow of the ASLA in 1910. He was a vice president (1923) and president (1926–28) of the National Conference on City Planning and the American City Planning Institute. He served as a director of the National Housing Association, the American Parks Association, the American Civic Association, and the National Municipal League. He was a participant in the Garden City Association of America and numerous European organizations including the International Federation for Housing and Town Planning, where he was made the first American president in 1931. He attended meetings and conferences of these organizations, debating current issues, delivering papers, contributing to publications, and striving to encompass social and economic reform, physical planning, housing, and many other issues bearing on the emerging planning profession.[48]

The organizations that developed to deal with industrialized America's many urban problems had geographical as well as thematic differences. Housing reformers, for example, focused on the elimination of the wood-framed triple-decker tenement in New England, while in Philadelphia it was the filthy, crowded rear-court houses that required remedial action. But it was the appalling intensity of Manhattan's squalid tenements, and the distinctive institutions that had emerged to deal with them, that galvanized many aspects of early-twentieth-century reform. Nolen and others had approached problems as they arose in individual cities, but they began to realize that efforts aimed at such local manifestations overlooked their national scope. As the many different interests began to coalesce, New Yorkers brought them to a national stage.[49]

In 1909 the first national forum for the discussion of planning and urban issues was held in Washington D.C.— the National Conference on City Planning and Congestion of the Population. This meeting, which drew together the leaders of disparate urban reform movements, bore the particular imprint of Wharton-trained Benjamin Marsh and the New York City housing, settlement house, and social reform organizations. The conference was followed by a Senate hearing, during which the conference addresses were entered into the record. In Nolen's address, "What Is Needed in American City Planning?" he answered his own question first by exclaiming "everything" and then by advocating extensive social services, greater government efficiency, and a reformed tax structure. This he leavened with advocacy of more topographically determined and individualistic physical planning of American cities. The echoes of Germanic Wharton and the Anglophile Olmsteds are unmistakable.

Social issues and physical planning were at odds at the Washington conference.[50] Marsh harped on economic reforms including Henry George's single-tax ideas, which sought to keep the value of appreciating land in the hands of the community and thereby deprive the land speculator of his unearned increment of profit. This emphasis aroused fears that city planning meant broad government intervention in traditionally unfettered property rights. Olmsted Jr., who shared his father's skepticism about applying European models to America's very different "climatic, economic, social and political conditions,"[51] sought to disengage planning practice from contentious social and economic reforms. He opposed the single-tax idea and advocated a close study of planning methods and technique.[52] Between the radical Marsh and the cautious Olmsted Jr. stood Nolen. He believed (as his mentors James and Patten did) that economic and social issues were unavoidably linked to government policy, and he advanced a mild, Americanized version of German socialism intertwined with the physical and political reform of cities; this is what he meant by "comprehensive planning." His pragmatism, though, led him to embed his goals in the rhetoric of paternalism, cooperation, and voluntary community action, which reflected the values of most of his clients and the realities of his era.

Marsh was right, a single land tax would have provided a tidy mechanism to bring private land use into conformance with the communal goals of a city plan, but such a radical reordering of property rights was a frightening prospect, especially to property owners.[53] Eventually Olmsted Jr.'s cooler head prevailed, and the second National Conference on City Planning and Congestion of the Population, held in Rochester, New York, the following year, set the organization on a path that marginalized Marsh and dodged thorny questions of social and economic reform.[54] Following Olmsted's lead, Nolen addressed the second conference on the important technical subject of land subdivision. Afterward he was asked to join the General Committee of the renamed National Conference on City Planning, which became the key professional organization where the range of American planning practice was explored and developed.[55]

THE AMERICAN CONTEXT

Nolen's admiration for the procedures and results of German socialism did not blind him to the need to adapt

European ideas to an American context. One particular idea he championed was the adoption of building and loan societies such as the one that had helped him construct his own house in Ardmore. His paper "A Good Home for Every Wage Earner," delivered in various forms in the pre–World War I period, illustrates both the course he was able to navigate between economics and city design and his prescient advocacy of financing innovations that would eventually transform housing in America. The pattern of such locally developed institutions crossed permeable state borders with relative ease, but when reformers advocated the wholesale importation of German or English practice that relied on direct government intervention, constitutional impediments often frustrated their efforts. Though European spatial composition and physical organization were readily adaptable to American needs, the social, legal, and economic ideas and methods that had given rise to them were harder to import. Planners in the United States would struggle for decades to develop the legal techniques needed to implement their plans within the American constitutional framework.[56]

The federal government was constitutionally unable to attend to most urban problems because the power to do so was vested in the states. Cities were forced to seek charter revisions from their state legislatures to take on many urban problems, especially those having to do with eminent domain, annexation, borrowing limits, and zoning—all crucial elements of any planning effort. Structural reform of city government faced similar obstacles. This left city governments relatively weak, and consequently it often fell to private organizations to develop proposals for the physical environment, just as they did in the fields of governmental and social reform. Many of Nolen's early projects were funded by boards of trade, chambers of commerce, and similar private civic organizations, rather than by governmental entities.

Though civic groups often could muster the funds for plans, it was another matter entirely to identify the legal mechanisms, develop the political will, and find the money to implement them. City Beautiful building ensembles, diagonal boulevards cutting through existing checkerboard street systems, and other widely advocated improvements—no matter how appealing or necessary—proved to be extraordinarily difficult to accomplish. In the absence of the imperial power of Napoleon III or the bureaucratic guile of Baron Hausmann, the physical structure of American cities proved nearly intractable. École des Beaux-Arts–trained architects of the era such as John Carrère and Charles McKim aspired to French grandeur in their city plans, and occasionally they achieved it (for example, in Cleveland and Washington, D.C.), but these were extraordinary examples where the government sponsored the plans and funded their implementation.

The fluid market for inexpensive empty land differentiated the development of American planning too. If the congestion of America's older cities defied solution, there was an underdeveloped hinterland, some of it just a trolley extension or railroad tunnel away from the heart of the problem. The need to deal with these vast lands contributed to the dominance of landscape architects such as Olmsted Jr., Warren Manning, and Nolen within the emerging planning profession. In Europe architects and engineers such as Raymond Unwin, Josef Stübben, and Eugène Hénard dominated planning discourse. But American architects, who concentrated on hard-to-implement axial plans, on grandiose civic centers, or on local housing reform, usually left planning of open land at the municipal or regional scale to landscape architects.[57] The low density of many American cities allowed the landscape architects to use empty space to obviate problems of abutment and proximity that required complex architectural solutions in denser European cities. Moreover, the American preference for detached housing loosened the tethers between architecture and planning, allowing the discourse in these professions to drift apart while strengthening the connection of landscape architects to planning in all but the most densely built cities.

Nolen's decision to concentrate on smaller cities reflects these American circumstances. He recognized that opportunities to solve urban problems with open space rather than architecture were more likely to be found there; that detached, individually owned houses were more feasible there; and that strong, voluntary civic institutions and smaller governments were more likely to act in concert there. Perhaps most important, the acquisition of property in advance of development was more economical there. Furthermore, the impulse toward decentralization was firmly embedded in American traditions where hostility to big cities ran as deep as the idealization of small-town life.

REPLANNING

The early plans and reports produced by Nolen's firm varied greatly in scope, in detail, and, most important, in the degree to which they were implemented. Many of them had no life beyond the documents themselves, though at least these were actively circulated within the planning community in the United States and abroad.[58] Some cities used his firm's plans to accomplish one piecemeal aspect of a larger project. Sometimes, though, Nolen achieved significant results. These were the projects he included in his books, which chronicle the variety and comprehensiveness of plans that were, at least in part, implemented. Nolen emphasized built accomplishments.

In 1912 he published *Replanning Small Cities,* which sums up the first busy phase of his career with chapters on Roanoke, Virginia; Reading, Pennsylvania; Madison, Wisconsin; San Diego, California; and Montclair and Glen Ridge, New Jersey. Each chapter explores a different set of problems and solutions. The chapter on the old colonial city of Reading, for example, presents Nolen's attempt to deal with a city hemmed in by difficult geography on all sides, where a rigid grid of narrow streets was clogged by traffic congestion and its inhabitants were suffocating in densely packed housing. This project went on for years, not with altogether happy results.[59] But later, across the narrow Schuylkill River valley in Wyomissing, a better process led to one of North America's most elegantly planned suburbs. In part the work of the opinionated, incandescent German planner Werner Hegemann (who ridiculed a few of Nolen's recommendations for Reading), it contains some of Nolen's most beautifully designed residential streets.[60]

Chapters on Madison and San Diego reveal the persistent influence of the Washington mall on Nolen's early planning vocabulary. Such elongated rectangular spaces, precisely defined by continuous rows of civic buildings, appear over and over in his plans of this period. The form is a virtual trope of the City Beautiful movement, and though Nolen and nearly everyone else replaced the rhetoric of the City Beautiful with the more utilitarian "city practical," the preoccupations with the aesthetics of civic grandeur persisted. The lack of architectural imagination in these civic centers is balanced, however, by the thoughtful integration of rail, vehicular, pedestrian, and park systems. Nolen was able to transform the future of Madison and San Diego by untangling these pressing early-twentieth-century problems; moreover, he successfully advocated the acquisition of land for parks and parkways that soon would have become unavailable or unaffordable. The advantage of dealing with such problems while these cities were still small is evident.

Careful, innovative thinking is equally apparent in his plans for the adjacent New Jersey towns of Glen Ridge and Montclair. Already these towns were following the pattern of diffuse suburban development that carpeted the North American landscape by the end of the twentieth century. Nolen proposed the construction of lower-priced houses to increase economic diversity; civic and commercial centers to provide a convenient focus for community life; and interconnected parks, parkways, and pedestrian ways to improve access to Essex County's extensive park system. These proposals were an early recognition of deficiencies in the emerging suburban pattern, and a partially successful attempt to remedy them. Roads and parks in these towns were altered without too much opposition, but efforts at greater economic diversity inherent in Nolen's housing recommendations were less welcome.

The emphasis in *Replanning Small Cities* is on practice rather than theory, though the case studies are combined with summary chapters that provide a more general view of Nolen's developing ideas. The appendices, full of model state legislation, indicate his increasing awareness of the importance of legal issues to comprehensive planning. As the title indicated, these projects involved *re*planning existing towns and cities, where prosperity and growth had outrun the physical constraints imposed by history or geography. Each provided a distinctive plan of action for Nolen's civic-minded clients who wanted to reform their governments and their societies as well as the landscapes and cities that contained them. Able to see the needs for replanned streets, parks, and zoned districts in their political and economic contexts, Nolen applied theoretical principles, using his administrative skill and statistical training to collect, organize, and synthesize the many bits of disparate information into coherent planning proposals.

Nolen was confronting, on a small scale, age-old urban problems of decay, congestion, and change. New building types and transportation technologies had disrupted the traditional spatial, physical, and social matrix of the city, resulting in overcrowding, real estate speculation, and wide swings in property values. Smoke-billowing factories of unprecedented scale grew up beside residential neighborhoods, creating awkward and unhealthy adjacent functions that constrained industrial efficiency and added dismal living conditions to the other ills. City Beautiful malls and boulevards addressed only some of these problems, and Nolen worked hard to develop additional ideas and techniques, such as zoning to control the use of land and the density of buildings, housing for wage earners, and parks with recreation facilities for everyone.

Big plans were hard to implement, even in small cities, and the sensible, relatively modest proposals in *Replanning Small Cities* met with stiff resistance, which took legal, political, and economic forms. American municipalities were hamstrung by their governmental structures, so Nolen and his colleagues had to persuade, cajole, and persist to accomplish every small part of what they proposed. In circumstances where one street widening or the acquisition of private land to protect a watershed or create a public park might stir sufficient controversy to derail the whole city plan, comprehensive replanning was an elusive goal.[61]

Despite the difficulties, Nolen made important contributions to the evolving practice of planning, which included the integration of social and economic concerns within the framework of physical planning techniques. This was especially true in his 1914 plans for Bridgeport, Connecticut,

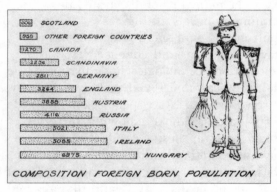

COMPOSITION FOREIGN BORN POPULATION

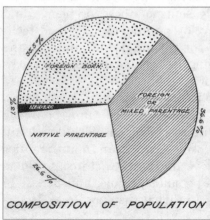

COMPOSITION OF POPULATION

Figures 5 and 6. Nolen used charts to show the foreign-born population of Bridgeport, Connecticut. This and other information was synthesized to produce surveys and planning reports. *Nolen Papers, Cornell University Library.*

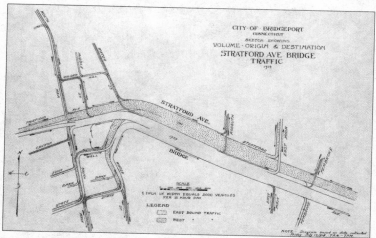

Figure 7. An analytical diagram recording traffic flows in Bridgeport. Nolen supported his planning proposals with diagrams that interpreted the statistics and other information he collected. *Nolen Papers, Cornell University Library.*

where elaborate social and physical survey information was used to produce a city plan of unprecedented comprehensiveness and scope (Figs. 5–7). He continued to refine and elaborate techniques developed there into clearer and better-organized maps and reports such as one for Akron, Ohio, in 1917.[62] In these projects Nolen was able to truly synthesize the two parts of his background: the Olmsteds' landscape art and the social science of his Wharton years. The expression of this synthesis was the city plans themselves, richly drawn, laden with information, and suggestive of otherwise invisible relationships of part to whole (Fig. 8). For these cities and some others such as Flint, Michigan, and Asheville, North Carolina, where Nolen produced plans in the 1920s, the art of landscape design is subsumed in the larger project of the city with all its cultural, economic, and physical complexity.

Figure 8. City maps such as this were used to show the overall scope of Nolen's replanning proposals; they were often accompanied by separate maps to show parks, roads, or zoning. *Nolen Papers, Cornell University Library.*

THE GARDEN CITY

New building on open land met much less resistance than rebuilding. It fit easily into established patterns of urban growth where landowners routinely platted new streets on private property at the urban edge. In America these plans often just extended the street grid, but under the influence of Olmsted Sr. and to some degree the Germans, picturesquely composed and topographically responsive urban extension plans entered the repertoire of American planners. Knowledge of German technique was often filtered through English interpreters such as Raymond Unwin. His 1909 book *Town Planning in Practice* shows the influence of Camillo Sitte's medievalizing, picturesque urban composition technique integrated into a broader English proposal for a new urban beginning known as the garden city.

Nolen used Charles B. Purdom's definition of the garden city: "a small town organized for modern industry and healthy living; of a size that makes possible a full measure of social life; but not larger; surrounded by a permanent belt of rural land; the whole of the land being in public ownership or held in trust for the community."[63] Such a mix of physical planning and social reform avoided the problems of existing cities, and it seemed ideally suited to American circumstances, where agrarian beginnings and Jeffersonian notions of democracy had evolved into an artistic cultivation of the rural ideal. The idea was first proposed in 1898 by Ebenezer Howard in *Tomorrow: A Peaceful Path to Real Reform*. Howard had been struck by the American Edward Bellamy's 1888 utopian socialist novel *Looking Backward* (he persuaded a London publisher to bring out an edition by agreeing to compile an index and buy a hundred copies). Though he eventually decided that Bellamy's conception of the all-encompassing state as one gigantic trust was the antithesis of true socialism, the idealized harmony of communal ownership and the tidy urban order that the novel described had a lasting effect.[64]

Howard's garden city diagram was taken up in England with great enthusiasm and grafted onto an earlier tradition of paternalistic company towns such as Bourneville and Port Sunlight, and by 1904 Letchworth, the first garden city, designed by Raymond Unwin and Barry Parker, was under construction in Hertfordshire. Not just a housing scheme, it was intended as a self-sustaining civic entity, complete with commercial center, low-density housing, and an enclosing agricultural perimeter—a growth-limiting device developed in imitation of the German tradition of municipally owned peripheral lands. Social and economic reforms also were integral to the plan; all the land and many of the improvements were communally owned.

In the United States the garden city model was adjusted to reflect local needs and realities. Co-ownership schemes, intended to capture the unearned increment of profit for the community rather than for the developer, proved a hard sell in the freewheeling, speculative real estate market of North America. Many of the other communitarian components of the scheme also failed to cross the Atlantic intact. But what did take hold was the low-density garden city *form*: a geometrically ordered town center devoted to civic and commercial activities; with radial connections to curving residential streets; surrounded by controlled undeveloped land; and with occasional provision for industry on the periphery. It proved to be a resilient and persistent model. By taking advantage of new transportation systems and less expensive outlying land, it offered a physical development pattern as a neat solution to overpopulation of the cities and depopulation of the countryside. Furthermore, it appealed to the peculiar American penchant for the fresh start.

American examples were especially deficient in cooperative or public ownership of the land, as Nolen was uncomfortably aware. He wrote that this was more English in character than American, and explained that Purdom's definition of the garden *suburb* was more applicable in America:

1. The area must be town-planned.
2. There must be a limitation of houses to not more than twelve per gross acre.
3. Provision must be made for social amenities, including open spaces.
4. As far as possible the good natural features of the site must be preserved.
5. An element of cooperative or public ownership of the site must exist.
6. The return on capital must be limited.[65]

He concluded that Purdom's conditions of land ownership found only a faint echo in American industrial villages where land was sold at low prices without speculative profit, or where return on invested capital was voluntarily limited by investors.[66] And even these conditions were only occasionally met. Although to Nolen and American social reformers the grass looked greener on the other side of the Atlantic, many financial aspects of the garden city that they admired ultimately proved untenable in England. (In 1928 Purdom was forced to resign his position at Welwyn, the second garden city [*NTFO*, p. 140], and shortly thereafter, "the garden city and its inhabitants were excluded from any interest in the company or its profits.")[67]

The social circumstances of the Americans were as different from those of the English as their economic and physical situations were. The English were dealing with population movement from the countryside to the crowded cities; the Americans faced the same problem, in addition to the greater challenge of assimilating the huge influx of immigrants, with their foreign languages and unfamiliar customs. The English needed mainly to house their population; the United States had to Americanize them. Though many immigrants readily acquiesced, native-born citizens, alarmed by the accelerating social and physical heterogeneity of their cities, constructed social machinery to aid such transformation. To some degree planners accepted their role in this, especially when making housing and neighborhood arrangements for the foreign-born, the rural poor, the wage earners, and others whose assimilation they sought.

The garden city evolved quickly in America, mixing with locally developed planning ideas about City Beautiful civic centers, extension suburbs, utopian settlements, and industrial housing. Mariemont, Ohio, is Nolen's purest realization of the garden city, but like most of his new towns and suburbs it fuses American ideas with English garden city prototypes. It is a sharp contrast with the *farm city*, a distinctively American hybrid, illustrated by Nolen's Penderlea, North Carolina, plan (*NTFO*, p. 12). This project was intended to mitigate the social isolation of the American farm by bringing cooperative management and urban social life into its midst. Its leaders included Albert Shaw and Elwood Mead, who had thought long and hard about solving the twin ills of urban congestion and rural depopulation with a combination of modern agricultural methods, communal cooperation, and education. Nolen did the land planning, and the project also included soil experts, agronomists, and others to teach the new farmers advanced techniques and cooperative economics. Penderlea was the confluence of scientific agriculture, social work, and the utopian tradition.[68] But "farm city" was an oxymoron; the challenge of combining urban density with farm plots of sufficient size for economical cultivation was too much for even the best planners. And there were good reasons, after all, why people had moved to the cities in the first place, and why immigrants stayed there.

After *Replanning Small Cities*, Nolen produced two books of a more theoretical nature. He edited *City Planning* (1916), which was an important collective effort of the American planning profession. An essay by Olmsted Jr. provided an overview and introduced chapters by leaders of the profession, each devoted to different aspects of planning technique ranging from sewers and transportation to condemnation laws and zoning. One of Nolen's two contributions was an essay on land subdivision and its bearing on housing configurations, but this was as close as anyone got to the subject of housing. The book, sponsored by the National Municipal League, proved sufficiently popular and useful to be reprinted in a second edition in 1929 with additional chapters, including one on regional planning by Nolen, who was always looking to expand the scope of American planning.

Just after the Great War, in 1919, the American City Bureau published *New Ideas in the Planning of Cities, Towns and Villages*, a little book Nolen had produced as a series of lectures to fill the idle hours of the Doughboys, whom General Pershing was determined to keep occupied with more than the customary activities of a victorious army.[69] This government-sponsored pedagogical effort, structured very much like the ASEUT courses Nolen had once administered, never really got going before the troops were hastened home, so Nolen recast the abandoned textbook as a citizens' manual on city planning.[70] It provides a concise, if rather rudimentary, summary of Nolen's theory.

During the war Nolen's office kept busy with work for the United States Emergency Fleet Corporation and the United States Housing Corporation, two unprecedented federal planning initiatives intended to alleviate the severe shortages in the housing markets near crucial matériel production centers. Nolen and other planners, eager for the opportunity to wield federal power and the federal purse, set out to demonstrate the effectiveness of ideas so often frustrated by local intransigence and parsimony. But the quick end to the war stopped most of these projects before they were built, and Congress hurried to dismantle them—wanting to allay concern that they had used the war emergency to tread on state and private-sector prerogatives.

NEW TOWNS FOR OLD

After the war Nolen entered the most active and productive phase of his career, in the midst of which the present volume, *New Towns for Old (NTFO)*, was conceived. After six years of intermittent effort, an edition of two thousand finally was published in 1927, just as Nolen's career reached flood tide during the building boom of the 1920s. Like *Replanning Small Cities*, the book was a careful selection of a few planning projects meant to represent the range of Nolen's work. It includes case studies adapted from planning reports, an introduction by Albert Shaw, and several sections devoted to a discussion of the history and the future of town planning.

One of the most interesting aspects of the book's history is that Nolen submitted the first *NTFO* manuscript for publication with Sylvester Baxter identified as its author. Baxter (Fig. 9) had begun his journalistic career at the *Boston Daily Advertiser* in the 1860s. He spent 1875–77 studying in

Figure 9. Sylvester Baxter. *New England Magazine, Aug. 1898.*

Leipzig and Berlin, where he worked as a foreign correspondent. Baxter also was influenced by Edward Bellamy's *Looking Backward,* for which he wrote an introduction. They were close friends, and Baxter participated in the short-lived political party spawned by Bellamy's socialist ideas. Eventually he retreated from this extreme and worked tirelessly to promote the idea of municipal planning along the lines of the much-admired German model.[71] He wrote on a range of subjects from the treatment of tuberculosis to Spanish colonial architecture, but the chief focus of his civic activism and journalistic enterprise was city and park planning in Boston. His writing on city planning and his translations of essays by the German architects Theodor Fischer and Cornelius Gurlett appeared in *Architectural Record,* the *Century, Atlantic Monthly,* and elsewhere. Baxter had a wide acquaintance in civic reform and literary and artistic circles including figures such as Olmsted Sr., whose work he championed, the novelist William Dean Howells, and the painter Frederic Church. He was married to Lucia Millet, sister of the painter Francis D. Millet. His wide network intersected Nolen's at many points, but how long they had known each other is not clear. Certainly they were acquainted: Baxter had supported the Wisconsin park plan in 1909, and they both had delivered papers at the second National Conference on City Planning and Congestion of the Population in Rochester.

Baxter was seventy-one years old in 1921 when he agreed to take the project on, during his annual winter sojourn in Puerto Rico. Nolen provided material including an article written by his employee Guy Wilfred Hayler, which had appeared in the December 1920 issue of Albert Shaw's American *Review of Reviews*. With the exception of Mariemont, Hayler's article had covered each of the projects in *NTFO* and formed the kernel of the book. After writing new sections and polishing old ones, Baxter sent the finished manuscript to Nolen in February, titling it *New Towns for Old* and listing himself as the author. Nolen then submitted it to Charles Scribner with a letter describing it as a book about his work written by Baxter. Scribner rejected the manuscript, and Nolen repeated the process with Houghton Mifflin. After they rejected it too, he sent it to Matilda Weil, an agent, editor, and book doctor, who suggested that Nolen would have more success finding a publisher if the book were both about him and by him. So he wrote Baxter that he had chosen "to rewrite and remake the book under my own authorship, as originally contemplated."[72]

Comparison of the Baxter manuscript[73] with Nolen's planning reports, on which it is based, makes clear that Baxter's original work focused on the morphology of American towns and is concentrated in the first two chapters. There he synthesizes the ideas of Camillo Sitte and Olmsted Sr. and uses New England examples to illustrate their applicability to modern circumstance. He emphasizes the advantages of irregular and diagonal streets over the "indolent rectangularity" of gridiron plans and advocates the continuation of local building traditions, to assure each locality the opportunity for its "finest self-expression." Baxter provides explanation and background, putting the development of New England towns and cities in the context of contemporary planning ideas.

Throughout the book Baxter's deft editorial hand lends grace and color to the technical prose of Nolen's planning reports. Once Nolen reasserted his claim to authorship he added a few paragraphs to the beginning and end of some sections, and revised Mariemont and the final chapters to cover developments in the long interval between Baxter's manuscript and the publication of the book. The joint authorship of the book ought to be plainly recognized.

Why Nolen hired Baxter to work on the book is a bit of a mystery; he had produced books before, and he wrote and lectured with a fluid if not inspired style. Maybe the abundance of work in the 1920s provided both the need and the resources to delegate this job, or perhaps he thought Baxter's name would appeal to a wider audience. Certainly Nolen recognized Baxter's eloquence and zeal, writing in his initial proposal of Baxter's "facility for describing works of landscape architecture and town planning."[74]

At Weil's suggestion, Nolen sent the manuscript to the Boston publisher Marshall Jones, who had brought out a number of books by the architect Ralph Adams Cram. Jones replied that it was a project he could "enthusiastically get behind"[75] and suggested that Nolen find a well-known figure to write an introduction. Nolen asked Albert Shaw, the editor of the *Review of Reviews*, who had a lifelong interest in urban affairs and eventually published the Kingsport chapter along with an admiring editorial. He and Nolen were not well acquainted, though they must have had some contact in connection with the farm city project in North Carolina. Shaw readily agreed to write the introduction.[76]

Like Baxter, whom he knew fairly well, Shaw had spent his life as a journalist.[77] After an early career in Iowa, where he attended Iowa College (later Grinnell) and edited the *Grinnell Herald,* he went to Johns Hopkins and studied under Henry Baxter Adams and Richard T. Ely. There he befriended Woodrow Wilson (a fellow glee club member), whose presidential papers he later edited. Shaw wrote his PhD dissertation on Icaria, the utopian socialist community in Iowa—a subject that was suggested to him by Ely.[78] After graduation he went to Europe to explore the intricacies of its city governments, and in 1895 he published his research in two volumes: *Municipal Government in Great Britain* and *Municipal Government in Continental Europe.* These books are dense with useful information on all aspects of urban affairs including planning, parks, streets, sewers, administration, and taxation. They are remarkable for the thorough comparative analysis they bring to varied techniques of European states and municipalities, which are catalogued for Shaw's American readers in glaring contrast to the dishevelment of their own urban situations. During a visit to England, Shaw met W. T. Stead, the crusading editor of the English magazine *Review of Reviews,* and with Stead's support he started an American magazine of the same name. Shaw continued to edit the American *Review of Reviews* from 1890 until 1937, advancing a broad reform agenda and championing the policies of Theodore Roosevelt. The magazine chronicles the development of Progressive-era causes and opinion.

Throughout Shaw's introductory essay he emphasizes the revival of the communitarian impulse and the distinctiveness of American circumstances. The essay displays a

confidence that civic groups, with expert advice, can implement needed and far-reaching change. As Nolen did throughout his career, Shaw emphasizes the role of new technologies
such as the telephone, the radio, and the automobile in the
movement toward more decentralized living arrangements.
Both men imagined a rejuvenation of small-town life as the
benefits of modern conveniences spread beyond the cities.
Neither, apparently, was able to foresee how these technologies might also lead to further urban concentration, suburban sprawl, and the erosion of small-town life.

Shaw provided a perceptive and enthusiastic assessment
of Nolen's achievements, placing them in the Progressive-
era context that Shaw himself had helped develop:

> Mr. Nolen has for years seen with undimmed eyes
> this vision of a restored, harmonized, and beautified
> country. Happily there are many people also who
> can share the vision; but there are not many men or
> women who are so capable as Mr. Nolen of turning
> from the pictures that his imagination conjures up, to
> the very difficult but essential task of working out the
> picture in the concrete—'on the ground,' so to speak.
> (*NTFO*, p. xxii)

The participation of Baxter and Shaw in *New Towns
for Old* makes it a document that spans a long and crucial phase of American urban history, connecting the
early-nineteenth-century utopian ideas that Shaw explored
in Icaria with Baxter's involvement in Bellamy's utopian
vision of industrial-age Boston. The idealism of these initiatives forms a backdrop for their pragmatic development and transformation in the Progressive era. Both men
shared with John Nolen a recognition of the need for the
reform of the American urban situation, and the desire to

make use of the German social, economic, and physical examples they had studied firsthand. Many of the ideas that the two journalists had spent their lifetimes studying and promoting were being realized in Nolen's work: he was not just fixing old towns, he was building new ones— logical, efficient, convenient, and expansive—a fulfillment of the Great Civic Awakening.

THE PROJECTS

With its individual case studies, *NTFO* is a practical companion to the more theoretical *New Ideals in the Planning of Cities, Towns and Villages.* Each project is framed as a set of specific local planning problems—new towns, satellite towns, new industrial cities, new residential suburbs, replanned colonial towns, new company towns, and a government-sponsored housing project. Each illuminates a different aspect of Nolen's remarkably diversified practice.

Walpole

In November 1912 an invitation to lecture in Walpole, Massachusetts, on either civic awakening or German city planning signaled the beginning of Nolen's relationship with the remarkable Bird family, who sponsored nearly all of his work in the town.[79] From 1913 until 1930 Nolen worked on Walpole park and town planning, on the Bird family's estate, and on other projects including Neponset Garden Village, which the Birds commissioned but never built. The progress made in Walpole was due, in large measure, to the wealth and political power of the Bird family, who owned Bird & Son, a paper company founded in the eighteenth century and at the time the town's largest employer. Charles Sumner Bird Jr. was heir not only to this thriving industrial concern but to a political dynasty as well—a tradition carried forward by his brother Francis William Bird, who was Elihu Root's law partner and a leader of the Progressive Party in New York State.[80] In the Bird family Nolen had found clients who embraced new planning ideas as well as social and economic reform. Bird Jr. became an enthusiastic city planning activist, and Nolen provided guidance, instruction, and advice for his many efforts including passage of city planning legislation in Massachusetts.

Bird & Son had a history as a paternalistic employer. In 1903 the company had cut the workday from twelve to eight hours without commensurately reducing wages. The family and the company took other steps to improve living conditions for employees, including making contributions to the town's schools and libraries and establishing loan and insurance operations that enabled employees to buy and build houses for themselves on advantageous terms. Some of these efforts arose from the influx of foreign-born workers, who accounted for a large part of the town's increasing population. In neighboring towns these workers were often housed in wood-frame triple-decker tenements, a building type that subverted the traditional physical and social matrix of the New England town. The Bird family sought housing alternatives closer to familiar village patterns.

Neponset Garden Village, planned for East Walpole near the Bird & Son factory and the rail station, was the most ambitious of Nolen's several Walpole plans. It was envisioned to satisfy both the physical and economic definitions of a true *garden village*, and it would be the first one in America if they could build it before a similar scheme being planned by Arthur Comey and Warren Manning at Billerica, Massachusetts. In an effort to devise the legal structure for the novel cooperative ownership arrangement Nolen and the Birds sought, they consulted widely with English and Canadian experts. Plans advanced through several stages, and Bird went as far as consulting Mann and McNeille, a New York firm with industrial housing expertise, about the architecture of the individual houses. Unfortunately economic changes in the prewar years and then the untimely death of Francis William Bird in 1918 led the family to alter their plans.[81] After the war they used most of the land for Francis William Park, a memorial to their eldest son. Thereafter, new housing was built on single lots or in small groups on land along the margins of the new park and interspersed through the town.

In *NTFO* Nolen never mentions the bitter disappointment of Neponset Garden Village (Fig. 10); rather, he characteristically emphasizes the many other aspects of the Walpole plans that *were* completed. These included street realignments, parks, playgrounds, and many related efforts to solve physical problems large and small. New

Figure 10. An aerial perspective of Neponset Garden Village in East Walpole, Massachusetts. *Nolen Papers, Cornell University Library.*

schools were designed by R. Clipston Sturgis (the Boston architect who would later interact with Nolen in the war housing endeavor) and a good deal of effort was expended to insure that their grounds harmonized with the town plan. Other accomplishments included establishing a town forest on land donated by George Plimpton, and the construction of Memorial Park in Walpole Center, which was led and in part financed by Phillip Allen, a Bird & Son partner.[82]

Francis William Park is Nolen's most richly conceived and fully realized public park (Figs. 11, 12). It reflects his desire to integrate a variety of accommodations for sport and leisure activities within the general aesthetic framework of an Olmsted-style park; for him the spiritual uplift of nature was complemented by the social benefit of organized physical activities. The long meadow in Nolen's park recalls Olmsted Sr.'s Prospect Park masterpiece of the same

Figure 11. Francis William Park, in Walpole, Massachusetts, included ponds, lawns, and wooded glades, as well as gates at various entry points such as the main one shown here. *Nolen Papers, Cornell University Library.*

Figure 12. Another entry to Francis William Park. This one connects a residential neighborhood to a corner of the park set off with coniferous trees and planned for tennis courts; it is now outfitted with playground equipment. *Photograph by Charles D. Warren.*

name, and the park's bridges, streams, and ponds evoke a similar feel in a slightly miniaturized form. But Nolen flanked his tree-fringed lawn with tennis courts and an outdoor theater, facilities that undermine its purely pastoral qualities. Similarly the stream, which gently wends its way through the park, was retained by a combined bridge and dam to create a concrete-bottomed pool for swimmers. Nolen allowed the passive pastoralism of Olmsted Sr. to yield to more active recreational pursuits, but it went only so far—playgrounds and other active sports were accommodated on separate land elsewhere. The Birds provided an endowment for the upkeep of the park, and in 2003 it was given to the Trustees of Reservations.

Some other efforts were only a partial or temporary success. Walpole Center was the location of a second Nolen park, Memorial Park, which was designed to integrate active and passive uses even more closely. Again a bridge and dam were combined to form a pond surrounded by woods and winding paths (Fig. 13). Playing fields were aligned with carefully located civic buildings in an attempt to integrate these diverse uses into the scenic structure of the landscape. But encroachments by parking lots, new buildings, and swimming pools have nearly obliterated the careful balance Nolen sought to achieve. Though the bridge/dam and the pond it forms still suggest what might have been, the lack of clear park boundaries combined with thoughtlessly placed new buildings and limited maintenance have whittled down the park to half its original size, and the pond and woods are just a beautiful vestige of the original design. The streams in these parks are tributaries to the

Figure 13. Memorial Bridge, intended to be a centerpiece of Memorial Park in East Walpole. It overlooks a pond formed by the small dam below it. *Photograph by Charles D. Warren.*

Neponset River, an upland part of the watershed of the Boston metropolitan parks system. Some of Nolen's other efforts to protect and enhance this watercourse also met with mixed success. It was still a vital industrial asset in those years, and Nolen was never able to bring all the land he thought necessary under town ownership or control.

The Birds became advocates for many of Nolen's ideas. Charles Sumner Bird Jr.'s mother, Anna, supported an effort to make planning a part of the curriculum in local schools, and both she and her son sponsored lectures to help convert their neighbors to the idea of planning.[83] Nolen was always eager to publicize his work, and in Bird Jr. he found an active collaborator. Determined to advertise Walpole as an exemplary small progressive city, Bird hired John A. Murphy to work with Nolen in the production of a book recording their efforts.[84] Nolen provided drawings, ideas, and text, and Murphy organized the material and did most of the writing of *Town Planning for Small Communities*. Published in 1917 as part of the National Municipal League series, it is a virtual manual, laying out the example of Walpole as a template for the physical, social, governmental, and economic reform of small towns.

Kingsport

In mid-October of 1915 Nolen received a note from J. H. Sears of D. Appleton, the publisher of *City Planning*. Sears mentioned "a friend" who was interested in building two or three small towns along a rail line. Other correspondence followed, and a meeting in New York was arranged for New Year's Eve between the friend, John B. Dennis, and Nolen. Dennis was chairman of the Securities Company and one of three partners in Blair and Co., a Wall Street firm dominated by Clinton Ledyard Blair, the grandson of the railroad baron John Insley Blair.[85] The meeting must have gone well because they immediately made plans for Nolen to visit the town site in eastern Tennessee.

In 1915 Kingsport was just an unpaved street grid dotted with tents and utilitarian frame buildings along the tracks of the Carolina, Clinchfield and Ohio (CC&O) railroad, which crossed the Blue Ridge Mountains and linked Spartanburg, South Carolina, to Elkhorn City, Kentucky. The CC&O rail project had been started by George Carter, a local man who, having assembled the land and started construction, had encountered financial difficulties before he could complete it. In 1905 he turned to an investment syndicate including Dennis, Blair, Thomas Fortune Ryan, and others, who acquired control of the unfinished railroad and much of its land.[86] In 1914 Dennis, Blair, and Mark W. Potter purchased an additional ten thousand acres of Holston River valley land from Carter and formed Kingsport Farms, announcing their intention to create one of the finest farms in the South.[87] Publicity for this agrarian project may have been meant to conceal their greater ambitions to build a town; eventually Kingsport Farms joined Kingsport Improvement Corporation in the complex corporate web that included the railroad, Cumberland Corporation (coal mines), the Securities Company, Blair and Co., and the individual interests of the capitalists who controlled them.

Blair's family had generations of experience in railroads and real estate, and Ryan, a flamboyant Wall Street capitalist, had made a fortune in street railways and then an even larger one through the acquisition of the Equitable Life Assurance Society. Later, using Blair and Co. as a front, he had gained control of the Seaboard Air Line Railroad after a bitter eight-year struggle. Dennis, Ryan, and the other investors were practiced in manipulation of the complex corporate structures and huge concentrations of capital that

Wall Street banking interests had developed by the beginning of the twentieth century.[88] These newly developed financial and management techniques played an important part in the planning of Kingsport.

Planned new towns had followed the railroads west, and by 1916 the real estate speculation that accompanied new rail lines was a well-established American practice.[89] The CC&O rail line tunneled through mountains and spanned deep river valleys, and the huge sums needed to build it spurred the investors to implement a scheme of resource exploitation, industrial integration, and real estate development that was a far more ambitious conception of a railroad town than the simply platted grid of streets, which had sufficed in earlier times.

At the start John B. Dennis took the lead in the Kingsport project, as he had in the railroad, but as things progressed Nolen also worked closely with John's brother Henry and with J. Fred Johnson, a native of Tennessee who served as a local point man, land sales agent, and general manager of various Kingsport interests.[90] Johnson was the brother-in-law of George Carter, and though his financial stake in the project was minor he had a proprietary attitude toward the town, which its people have acknowledged by naming many of its facilities for him. His repeated interventions, together with directives from the strong-willed Dennis brothers, tended to erode Nolen's control over the planning of the town.[91]

Nolen came late to this project, following in the trail of William Dunlap, a civil engineer who had first laid out the town for the railroad in 1906 (Fig. 14).[92] Various other civil engineers who had provided designs for water and sewer systems also preceded Nolen, and perhaps the architect Clinton Mackenzie did too. Mackenzie was Commissioner of Tenements in New Jersey and a board member of the

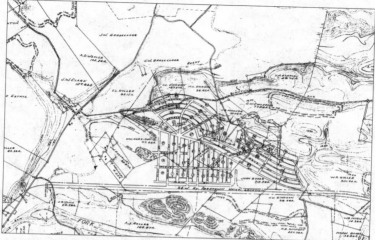

Figure 14. Portion of the plan of Kingsport, Tennessee, showing the streets as planned by the railroad's civil engineers. It was Nolen's starting point. The map "Lands Purchased by the Unaka Corporation" is a 1941 copy of the 1906 original. *Kingsport Library and Archive.*

National Housing Association; his office was just up Broad Street from Blair and Co., and he moved in the same social circles as Dennis. That Mackenzie may have wanted to do the town planning himself is indicated by an idealized plan bearing a striking resemblance to Kingsport, which he illustrated in his book *Industrial Housing* (Fig. 15); but he and Nolen became friends and collaborated effectively on Kingsport and again in Mariemont, Ohio.

Nolen did his best to correct the many errors in street arrangement and land subdivision created by Dunlap's awkward plans, but certain changes were impossible because some lots had already been platted and sold. The superiority of his new street plan can be seen in the resolution of problematic street intersections, but more vividly in development areas 2, 3, and 4 (*NTFO*, p. 53). Nolen

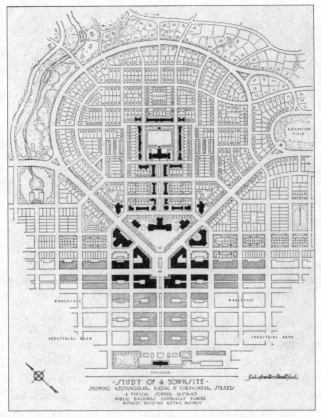

·STUDY OF A TOWNSITE·
SHOWING RECTANGULAR, RADIAL & CURVILINEAL STREETS
A TYPICAL SCHOOL DISTRICT
PUBLIC BUILDINGS CENTRALLY PLACED
WITHOUT DIVIDING RETAIL BUSINESS

Figure 15. An idealized plan published by Clinton Mackenzie in *Industrial Housing* (1920), which coincides closely with the circumstances at Kingsport. Nolen and Mackenzie exchanged sketches to work out building locations and street intersections.

ingeniously exploited the topography to arrange two of these housing developments around small hilltop parks, and the third on level ground southeast of the town center. The houses in development 2, known as the Fifties, were designed by Mackenzie, whose tentative command of the English Tudor style was defeated by the difficult terrain. Mackenzie was the architect for many other buildings in town including the train station and the Kingsport Inn; these and his attached houses along Shelby Street were more successfully composed. Nolen was called on to collaborate with others too. Grosvenor Atterbury, another wellborn New York housing expert, produced the finest ensemble in the city. Called White City because of the color of its clapboard houses, it surrounded Nolen's lozenge-shaped hilltop park adjacent to the high school (development 3). Both the planner and the architect exploited the topography to produce a group of handsome, deceptively simple houses with intricate multilevel plans. On the ridge above this group were more elaborate individual houses along Wautauga Street, and farther down the hill, in the area known as Little White City, were smaller, lower-cost houses by Mackenzie and Evarts Tracy, built to complete the neighborhood.[93] The coincidence of social and topographical hierarchy is striking—the workers' neighborhood was near the factories in the valley bottom, and each higher tier of land was occupied by a more prosperous group of residents. Isolated from the rest was development 4, which was eventually planned as Armstrong Village, a neighborhood designed for the ideal accommodation of the prevailing indecency of racial segregation.[94]

Other public buildings were designed by Atterbury, Tracy, and Electus Litchfield, a veteran of the architectural firm Carrère and Hastings. Thomas Hastings himself (whom Dennis referred to familiarly as Tommy) designed a civic center plan that was only partially executed; he ignored Nolen's civic center scheme, which had included a two-block park (*NTFO*, p. 63). Hastings's firm had designed the Blair and Co. building in Manhattan, two magnificent houses for C. Ledyard Blair, and several projects for Ryan, and evidently the investors preferred his plan, which did not require them to forego the profits on the sale of two valuable city blocks as Nolen's would have.

Nolen shuttled his talented young associate, Earle S. Draper, between Kingsport and Myers Park in Charlotte, trying to keep a foot on the ground as both projects moved swiftly ahead. Draper, recognizing the opportunity presented by Nolen's preoccupation, cultivated Johnson in Kingsport and George Stephens in Charlotte, and in 1917 he left the Nolen office to start his own practice in Charlotte. (Later he returned to Kingsport to design the Fairacres section.) When tree planting at Kingsport became a repeated problem (there were no nurseries in the remote hollows of eastern Tennessee), John B. Dennis on his own hired Lola Anderson, an experienced landscape architect who had studied at Cornell and had worked in Draper's Charlotte office for a time. She stayed on in Kingsport and eventually rescued Dennis from the bachelor's life he had led for sixty-two years. Nolen befriended Anderson, but his tenuous control over so many aspects of Kingsport's design frustrated several of his efforts.

The design of Kingsport involved many actors with different and, at times, incompatible goals. For Dennis the point of Kingsport was the unique integration of efficient resource exploitation and interlocking ownership. In pursuit of these ends, he, Ryan, and others added to their interests in coal, real estate, and the railroad with investments in a local brick company, a cement company, a textile mill, a vast printing company, and other industries.[95] Ultimately Dennis was successful in attracting established outside corporations such as Mead and Eastman Kodak, a paternalistic company that eventually came to dominate his new industrial city. For him, city building was a management problem. He sought expert advice to create the most up-to-date government structure, school system, and insurance program. Nolen's work was just one aspect of the project where the business plan, not the city plan, was of overriding importance. Kingsport was the "city practical" at its most utilitarian level; the local labor force was merely another resource to be efficiently managed, and results could be quantified on a profit-and-loss statement.

During Nolen's involvement in the project, a savings and loan society was established, modeled on a similar institution in Charlotte;[96] both cities took a lesson from his essay "A Good Home for Every Wage Earner." His broad view of the planner's role encompassed Kingsport's social and economic innovations, many of the kind he had long championed, but the physical aspects of the plan were less successful. Land set aside for parks proved too tempting and valuable, and most of it was eventually platted and sold, undermining Nolen's efforts to use park land to structure the city.[97] Still, confident that everything was better with planning, forethought, and cooperation, Nolen, always the enthusiastic collaborator, emphasized the advantages of this experiment in industrial efficiency. But his goals of social cooperation, civic order, and physical integration of city and landscape were not always compatible with Johnson's zeal for real estate sales or Dennis's drive to maximize railroad traffic and resource exploitation. The unearned increment of profit stayed in the hands of the investors.

Kistler

Kistler was an employer-sponsored town built by the Mount Union Refractory Company to provide housing for its workers just across the Juniata River from its factory on the outskirts of Mount Union, Pennsylvania (Fig. 16). The region was a center for the production of fireproof refractory ceramic materials, which were used in steel manufacturing and other industrial processes where resistance to high temperatures was required. The necessary raw materials, ganister rock and silica clay, were plentiful in the region, as was coal, which was brought to Mount Union on narrow-gauge railroads for local use or transferred to the Pennsylvania Railroad for shipment elsewhere. The combination of rail transportation and natural resources made Mount Union an ideal location for this specialized industry. The plant was opened in 1912 and run by R. P. M. Davis and Clinton V. Hackman, a veteran of Harbison-Walker, one of the town's older refractory producers.[98]

As steel production accelerated around the turn of the century, so did the demand for refractory brick, which was

Figure 16. The Mount Union Refractory plant, in Pennsylvania, viewed from the site of Kistler. *Nolen Papers, Cornell University Library.*

often made in special shapes to fit particular applications. It was a labor-intensive industry that required skilled workers. Some plants relied on local labor, but the thinly settled valleys could not provide enough men for the growing industries of Mount Union, so workers, some recent immigrants from Europe, were recruited from elsewhere to fill the gap. Most of the region's refractory producers provided some form of housing for their workers, which varied in quality and arrangement depending on whether the factories were near existing neighborhoods or open land.[99]

Mills and mines were often the sites of town-planning experiments in the nineteenth century as remote mineral deposits or hydraulic power necessitated concentrated workforces in undeveloped locations. Workers in these industries were usually paid very little, making it impossible for them to afford decent houses, and employers found it necessary to provide housing to attract them to remote locations, or to keep them there.[100] Labor shortages and labor unrest eventually persuaded industrialists of the advantages of improved conditions for workers, and by 1920 there was a well-developed literature dealing with the techniques of industrial housing. These books and articles outlined practices of particular regions and industries and dealt with such issues as costs, construction methods, and engineering techniques. Housing of workingmen was presented as a "problem" with a scientific "solution."[101]

Whatever the motivation, industrial housing projects provided planners with the opportunity—and the control—to demonstrate the efficiency of the planning methods they advocated, an efficiency that could be measured by retention of workers, increased company profits, and sometimes by the newly developed yardsticks of sociology. Nolen worked repeatedly on company-sponsored town plans and housing for workers, but Kistler is especially notable for its lovely riverside site (Fig. 17) and for

Figure 17. Kistler's riverbank site viewed from the railroad above it. This photograph was taken before construction work began. *Nolen Papers, Cornell University Library.*

the striking contrast it presents to the region's grim coal mining towns.

Mining towns often had the appearance of utilitarian military encampments—simple rows of wooden barracks and boxlike houses deployed across the complex topography in a senseless grid. They were self-contained settlements with the most minimal provision for anything beyond the basic needs of the workers. At Kistler, Nolen aspired to a higher standard, incorporating many of the features of the best industrial housing practices of the region and combining them with ideas from English company towns such as Saltaire and Port Sunlight and American ones such as Pullman, outside Chicago. He provided numerous sites for civic buildings and shared activities, emphasizing Kistler's intended character as a community rather than an encampment. An unusually large area was given over to parks, in part to deal with the floodplain of the river, and the overly dispersed spatial organization that resulted was exacerbated by the company's failure to complete many aspects of the plan. A community hall—really just a remodeled barn—was brilliantly integrated into the plan; it commanded the bluff above the river on one side and the elliptical town green on the other (*NTFO*, facing p. 70). Another public building, which served as both a company store and a school, was built in the location proposed by Nolen, but it did not follow the semicircular configuration on his plan. Rental housing was designed by Mann and McNeille of New York, with whom Nolen had worked in Walpole. There were some attached houses, but most were built for single families, and they included porches and indoor plumbing.[102] These were arranged along small street grids, which were carefully adjusted to the complex topography of the riverbank site.

Nolen's description of the town is notable for the paternalistic attitude he ascribes to his client, the Mount Union Refractory Company, whose role was to provide not only an attractive physical setting but one that engendered social life and good citizenship. His explicit concern was that "the population being so largely foreign in its make-up, there is a distinct necessity for a lead to be given in the direction of Americanism" (*NTFO*, p. 73). (The houses were labeled "Double Capri Villa," "Vermont Farm House," "Norman Cottage," in an unintentional allegory of assimilation.) Concern with foreign workers also comes up in discussions of Walpole, Mariemont, and Kingsport, indicating how troubling the domestic habits of impoverished newcomers were to third-generation Americans such as Nolen, or old Yankees such as Baxter. They hoped that an improved physical environment would lead to the development of good American citizens, but they also recognized the need to supplement the positive effects of decent housing and town planning with social work.[103]

As the growth of the steel industry slowed, the demand for refractory materials eased and the urgency of the housing problem eased with it. The diminished need for company involvement in worker housing led to the sale of the individual houses in the 1940s, and after a series of industry consolidations the Mount Union Refractory plant was closed and demolished in the early 1990s. Nolen's town had outlived its reason for being. Along the way the Works Progress Administration had built a small school where the barn had been, but it was destroyed by fire. The stores were demolished in 1990. All that is left of Kistler are its houses and some of its carefully arranged streets. It is no longer connected to the industry that spawned it, and it is no longer really a village.

Cohasset

On December 21, 1911, John Nolen delivered an illustrated address to the Cohasset Men's Club on the subject of town planning. The club's stated object was "to add to the pleasure of its members and join their individual interest into active co-operation for the good of the town. It is not political or partisan or prejudiced. It aims to lend its assistance to good town government and to progressive ideas."[104] This organization and hundreds like it were the embodiment of the village improvement movement that took root in the last third of the nineteenth century, and as these voluntary civic revivals advanced beyond tree planting and cosmetic improvements, some sought professional guidance from experts such as Nolen. But Cohasset was different from many Nolen projects; it was a small prosperous

village in Massachusetts, relatively untroubled by industrialization, immigration, and other forces that were causing
tumultuous changes in the cities. It already had a magnificent coastal landscape, a good government, and one of New
England's most beautiful town greens, yet the enthusiasms
of the era led citizens to seek progress toward a still better
and more beautiful place to live. To that end they engaged
Nolen to produce a planning report, which he submitted in
October 1912.[105] This was followed up with other studies in
1919 and 1920.

Nolen, as much as any of the American planners of his
generation, came to his career with a desire to improve the
conditions of workingmen, but his emphasis on the "city
practical" did not exclude a concern for civic beauty. Cohasset is a case in point. A charming seaport founded in 1670, it
had evolved into a summer colony and distant Boston suburb. It is just the sort of place that Baxter wrote about in the
first section of the book,[106] and Nolen's interventions demonstrate how much he was able to do when presented with
an opportunity rich in architectural and natural resources.
This was purely a replanning project, with no housing com-
ponent and no attempt to uplift the poor or Americanize
the foreign-born—rather a careful adjustment of parks,
beaches, and streets to the new realities of trains, automobiles, and seasonal residents.

Though the dredging of the harbor was funded in part
by the state, the other improvements were largely accomplished through voluntary subscription or contributions of
land by individuals. The town was lucky to have residents
with sufficient wealth and public spirit to accomplish many
of Nolen's suggestions, and he comments on the remarkable
voluntary civic culture that characterized such stable homogeneous American towns of his era.

Dr. Oliver Howe was the moving force behind the work

at Cohasset. His long, thorough letters to Nolen, with their small, craggy script, reveal his active interest in the morphology of New England towns and his keen attention to the civic life of Cohasset. By 1920 he was so thoroughly converted to the gospel of city planning that he tried some preaching of his own in two articles for *American Architect*, and in 1926 he wrote "Stumbling Blocks to Civic Planning" for the *Modern City*.[107] He contributed to the local newspaper too, describing the activities of the Cohasset Improvement Association, which had grown out of the encounter between Nolen and the Men's Club: "It will . . . strive to cultivate the community spirit—that constant desire of the individual for the welfare of the whole community. Thus and thus only, can we have a town worthy of our best living; and thus only can we so live as to be worthy of our town."[108] Howe lived in Cohasset, but seasonal residents such as the Bostonian Charles W. Gammons were active in the town's civic affairs too, and they were aided by other wealthy summer colonists including Mrs. Hugh Bancroft, heir to the fortune her stepfather Clarence Barron had made at the *Wall Street Journal*. She donated land for a bird sanctuary and a carillon for the beautiful if stylistically incongruous Gothic-style church that Ralph Adams Cram had designed to grow from a rock outcropping at the periphery of the town green.

Nolen consulted on everything from curb details, street widening, and park planning to the acquisition of English bells for the carillon. By the spring of 1917 Howe was able to describe three major achievements: acquisition of Sandy Beach, acquisition of Whitney Woods, and the removal of the St. John stores from the edge of the town common. Nolen uses before-and-after photographs (*NTFO*, facing p. 81) to illustrate the improved connection between the colonial village green and the Cram church, which resulted from the St. John stores' demolition. This improvement required good timing and a consensus that included the citizens, who paid for the demolished buildings, and also the owner of the buildings, who, though he was retiring, could have obstructed the project by simply refusing to sell the prime commercial location. Similar good results were achieved in the vicinity of the rail station, where stable barns were removed to present a better view of the church tower to arriving visitors (Figs. 18–20).[109]

Nolen chided the town in his planning report for its failure to heed the 1892 Trustees of Public Reservations call for the preservation of open spaces, and he recommended specific locations for acquisition as parkland. Sandy Beach was one of them, and though he would have preferred to have it acquired by a public authority rather than a private association, he was happy that it was preserved for communal use, hoping it would eventually be made into a public park. He proudly illustrates the bath house, neatly tucked

Figure 18. The train station was a primary gateway to Cohasset, Massachusetts, and the Tilden stables pictured here were just across the street. Once they were acquired and demolished Nolen designed a small park for the site. *Cohasset Historical Society.*

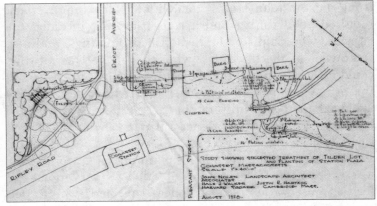

Figure 19. The park plan Nolen developed for the site of the Tilden stables. Removal of the stables opened an oblique view to the Gothic-style tower of St. Stephen's Church. *Nolen Papers, Cornell University Library.*

Figure 20. Nolen's plan for the area around the Cohasset Station. The trees structure the space and conceal the barns and the backs of buildings. His plan was not adopted, and this area remains as a poorly arranged parking lot. *Nolen Papers, Cornell University Library.*

in below a bluff, which replaced the ad hoc chaos of impro-
vised cabanas that had proliferated when the land was in
private hands (*NTFO*, facing p. 83).

Nolen had not specifically recommended the acquisition
of the Whitney Woods near Turkey Hill, the high ground
that separated Cohasset from Hingham. But in the wake
of his report, this land was purchased by Whitney Woods
Associates, another public-spirited private association,
which turned some of the land into a golf course and used
the remainder for riding and wilderness paths. These six
hundred acres of land were donated to the Trustees of Public Reservations in 1933, and perhaps some part of the idea
may be traced to Nolen's urgent pleas for preservation of
"rockbound hills," and his reiteration of similar Trust recommendations for hilltop preservation.

A more complex proposal for public land involved the
acquisition of the verdant salt marsh around which the
town had grown. Nolen wanted to fill the marsh and use
it for active recreation while channeling the tidal stream
that drained it—and evidently some of the town's sewage
too. Nolen thought the town needed playing fields and playgrounds, and he lived in an era when wetlands were seen
as something to be drained rather than preserved. He illustrates his proposal (*NTFO*, p. 84), but the need to acquire
the backyards of so many different properties insured the
failure of this idea. It is one instance where his ideas were
better left on paper.

The relative ease with which some of these crucial
beautification and land preservation projects were accomplished served to reinforce Nolen's notion that more could
be accomplished in the planning of small towns than in
large ones, but it also demonstrated what was possible with
wealth, social cohesion, and voluntary civic spirit. Government-sponsored planning was a tougher thing to achieve in

the self-reliant civic culture of Cohasset. Building codes and planning ordinances were repeatedly defeated in the town meetings, and the town went without a zoning ordinance until 1955.[110] Even today nothing has been done to place ugly power lines underground, a measure recommended in Nolen's 1912 report. Still, the forward-looking actions of Cohasset's civic leaders and its early planner helped renew its center and protect its edges, a restructuring that allowed it to gracefully adapt to the changes of the twentieth century.

Union Park Gardens

When the United States entered the Great War, ideas about the role of the state in local planning efforts that had preoccupied Nolen and his Wharton mentors took on a new urgency. Constitutional niceties were, at least temporarily, overlooked as the nation mobilized for war. Two ambiguously public corporate entities were formed: the Emergency Fleet Corporation, which dealt with the needs of the shipbuilding industry, and the United States Housing Corporation, which dealt specifically with housing the influx of workers needed to produce matériel for the war. The housing program of the Fleet Corporation got started earlier than the larger, more deliberately organized work of the Housing Corporation, whose planning department was headed by Olmsted Jr. The projects of both corporations were concentrated around shipyards and factories essential to the war effort. Nolen's long study of housing and planning prepared him as well as anyone for these unprecedented government programs, and he worked for both corporations, which drew together the talent and expertise in planning and housing that had been developing in the United States for decades. The German war suddenly freed planners of the ponderous constraints ordinarily imposed by the layered sovereignty of the American governmental system, enabling them finally to experiment with the German planning methods they had studied so carefully.[111] Nolen worked on sites in Niagara Falls, New York, and in Eddystone and Ridley Park, Pennsylvania, for the Housing Corporation and in Wilmington, Delaware, for the Fleet Corporation.

Nolen was familiar with Wilmington from his work on Overlook Colony for the General Chemical Corporation on the other side of town near the Pennsylvania state line (*NTFO,* p. 5). He had played a central role there on prewar housing for workingmen, as he did in Bridgeport, Connecticut. For Union Park Gardens, leaders in the chamber of commerce formed the Wilmington Housing Company through a sale of stock, and the money raised was then used to buy land that was given to the federal government. Loans and financial arrangements between Liberty Land Company (the operating company) and the government resulted in a complex partnership between the U.S. Fleet Corporation and the Wilmington business community, whose shared goal was the construction of housing. Liberty Land Company was to manage the project once it was finished, opting out of a briefly contemplated cooperative ownership arrangement modeled on the English garden city and renting the houses at market rates.[112]

Union Park Gardens was located just beyond Wilmington's street grid and partially beyond the city limits, but the trolley extended there, making the industrial area around the river easily accessible. Nolen was particularly pleased that the adjacent property, across Union Street and Lancaster Avenue, was made part of the project, enabling him to control the planning of both sides of the surrounding major streets. The architecture was designed by Ballinger and Perot, a Philadelphia firm that had also worked in nearby

Marcus Hook, Pennsylvania; they designed an apartment building, individual houses, and groups of attached houses, all combined in the manner of earlier English garden cities and arranged on varied, irregularly shaped blocks. Land on the interior of several blocks was planned for allotment gardens, with the proviso that they be used for garages, if the need arose (and it did). Land was reserved for a community building and a school, but these were never built; the neighborhood stores on Union and Lancaster are the only nonresidential part of the project that was completed.

The landscape was the principal organizing element, and Nolen used the course of a small creek to determine the street arrangement. The plan (*NTFO,* p. 92) also shows the creek forming a variety of water features as it ran along the gently sloping terrain, but this aspect of the project was not realized; the creek bed was filled in and covered with lawn. Still, the departure from both the rigid street pattern and the relentless mid-Atlantic row houses of the adjacent area sets Union Park Gardens apart. Nolen's design allowed the taut geometry of the city to relax into the easier, naturalistic contours of the park. This subtle shift from straight to curved streets formed a graceful transition from the geometric, urban grid to the irregular forms of the woodland park beyond; it was a clever bit of composition that allowed Union Park Gardens to stand alone as a neighborhood enclave, while integrating the surrounding area into an artful urban sequence. Housing density also becomes sparser and more irregularly planned as the parkway blends into the park, enhancing, quite explicitly, the transition from the city to the country.

Once the American troops were trained, transported, and deployed on the European front, the war was brought to a speedy conclusion, and Congress hastened to dismantle the corporations that had sponsored the war housing effort.[113] Many projects were sold off in a partially completed state. Union Park Gardens is one of the few that were brought nearly to completion, lacking only the civic buildings, and its houses, too, were sold to willing tenants or other buyers. For the most part Union Park Gardens remains as it was designed, disrupted only by subsequent construction in the park, which has subverted the larger aims of Nolen's urban aesthetics. The neighborhood's well-defined center and edges, combined with its distinctive architecture, continue to demonstrate the long-lasting benefits of careful collaboration among planners, architects, civic groups, and government.

Myers Park

The Charlotte Park and Tree Commission had been one of Nolen's first clients, and its secretary, George Stephens, proved to be one of his most steadfast supporters. Nolen had designed the grounds of Stephens's residence, and Stephens had persuaded many of his friends to commission Nolen to design theirs as well. As textile mills and other forms of industrialization proliferated in the "New South," Charlotte prospered. The energetic Stephens, a University of North Carolina football star who invented the forward pass, was also an innovator in the sale of real estate. He subdivided land for sale as residential lots around the Nolen-designed Independence Park, and as the city kept growing and property farther out became accessible by trolley, he hatched a larger development scheme called Myers Park.[114]

The land for Myers Park belonged to John S. Myers. During the time that he and Stephens were planning to turn it to more profitable use, Stephens married Myers's daughter Sophie. Consequently, Stephens was able to arrange to pay his father-in-law after the land was subdivided and sold. Undoubtedly this made it easier to finance the high-quality roads, sewers, and other improvements that were needed to turn the old farm fields into Charlotte's premier residential suburb. Nolen first worked on the plan in 1911, and construction began in 1912. The project's one-acre lots were each within two blocks of a broad boulevard loop and the trolley, which ran down a center esplanade as it wound through the property. Though the trolley loop was never fully completed, it was viewed as essential and service was, at least at the start, subsidized by Stephens. A site for Queens College was planned at the center of the project, and sites were also designated for churches and civic buildings, as well as a small commercial center along Providence Road, which was planned but never built. The plan was arranged to allow for the protection of Sugar Creek lying west of the property, which Nolen later proposed as part of a city park system, and other small parks were interspersed to preserve ravines and other features such as the site of the old Myers house.[115]

George Stephens had a clear understanding of the importance of social position as a determining factor in real estate values, so he exulted when the tobacco and electric power tycoon James B. Duke bought a house and nearly an entire block to accommodate his garden.[116] Stephens built his own house near the topographical high point of the site a few years later. Nolen's office designed the grounds for many of the early houses, and to handle this business Nolen sent his young associate Earle S. Draper to Charlotte to provide on-site services. Trees were an important element, both of the individual properties and as a means to define the arboreal urbanism of the broad trolley boulevard. Extraordinary efforts were made to transplant large ones to quickly overcome the rawness of the empty cotton fields. They played a crucial role in the design of street sections, where Nolen carefully integrated trees, planting margins, and sidewalks, calibrating them to different street widths to reinforce a spatial hierarchy among principal and secondary thoroughfares.

As the Myers Park work went along, the Charlotte Chamber of Commerce contemplated commissioning a city plan. After Nolen resisted requests for unpaid visits to discuss the matter, they invited him to speak at their annual dinner in February 1916, evidently hoping his evangelizing rhetoric would inspire interest in the planning project. Shortly after Nolen agreed to the date, John B. Dennis contacted him about the Kingsport project. Nolen tried to convince Dennis to adjust the scheduled Kingsport trip to accommodate the previously arranged Charlotte speaking engagement, but to no avail. Nolen had to cancel the Charlotte appearance (after the invitations had been made) so that he could visit the Kingsport site with Dennis and get back to his office to meet the tight deadlines of the very promising client. All of this got him off to a bad start with the Charlotte Chamber of Commerce. Eventually Nolen rescheduled his speech, and after more delay the chamber hired him to do a plan; the contract was finally signed in February 1917. In the midst of these complications, Draper, who later in his life emphasized his own importance by diminishing the role played by Nolen in almost everything, had established a relationship with Stephens that led him to leave Nolen's employ.[117] When Stephens subsequently hired Draper to complete the work on Myers Park, he handled the situation gently and with great tact; both he and Nolen recognized that a public, professional separation would allow Nolen (in appearance and in fact) to assume a more even-handed role in his planning effort for the Charlotte Chamber of Commerce.[118]

The city plan committee made the awkward choice of

Earle Draper as its secretary, and then Nolen foolishly hired him on an independent basis to produce the city survey that was to form the basis of his planning effort. This tense arrangement came to grief when Nolen found Draper's survey work completely unsatisfactory, and after telling Draper so in a letter listing its deficiencies, he lost no time in telling the committee too. Ugly correspondence flew back and forth, the committee backed Draper, and Nolen was forced to make do with a survey he found unacceptable. As work progressed, the chamber was slow to pay Nolen, leading to further friction and more unpleasant correspondence, and requiring the intercession of Stephens. A plan was finally submitted in March 1918, but by then the leadership of the chamber was changing and everyone's attention was on the European war.[119] Nolen's Charlotte plan went no further.

All through this process Stephens was Nolen's steadfast friend, and evidently also he grew frustrated with Charlotte and its leaders. After buying a half interest in the Asheville, North Carolina, newspaper, he redirected his energy there (in October 1919 he wrote to Nolen about doing a plan for Asheville).[120] Draper, who was later head planner for the TVA, continued with work at Myers Park and opened an office in Charlotte. He made significant modifications to the parts of Nolen's plan that had not been implemented, smoothing out the street curves and redividing some blocks to provide more lots (Fig. 21). These changes reflect the fact that the trolley loop was being superseded by the automobile; Draper's smooth curves accommodate the car's greater speed, but his design lacks the finer-scale topographic sensitivity of Nolen's original plan (*NTFO,* p. 102).

The difference between Nolen and Draper is evident in the earlier and later plans, and other instructive planning comparisons abound in Charlotte. Draper's preference for

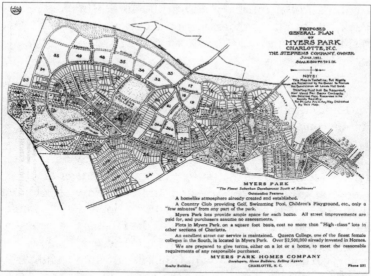

Figure 21. Myers Park, Charlotte, North Carolina, sales map from June 1921. Comparison with Nolen's map of the same property on p. 102 of *NTFO* shows the smaller lots and smoother curves made by Earle S. Draper after he took over planning there. *Myers Park Foundation.*

wide streets and sweeping curves can be seen at Eastover, a land subdivision across Providence Road that he designed on his own. Several blocks away in Dilworth, the Olmsted office produced another planned suburb. That project was hastily proposed just as Olmsted Jr. was leaving on his wedding trip, and the work was largely handled by Percival Gallagher.[121] A simple, well-designed plan, it lacks the idiosyncratic topographical accommodation of Myers Park and seems a bit formulaic, though plainly informed by the long experience of the Olmsteds in street design and salable lot standards. In this case Nolen had found the better client, and he produced a project whose distinctive combination of intricacy and grandeur still makes Myers Park, in its intact older sections, one of America's great residential suburbs.

Mariemont

Philanthropy was one response to the degraded urban living conditions in crowded, newly industrialized cities. Unfortunately the magnitude of the problem was such that subsidizing the construction of housing or paying directly for it quickly found the bottom of even very deep pockets. Consequently, projects large and small were often attempted as models of what might or should be done. For example, Jacob Schmidlapp's Cincinnati Model Homes Corporation, a limited-dividend corporation, built decent housing for wage earners in downtown Cincinnati while voluntarily limiting its profits (an approach that had many precursors in England and larger East Coast cities). If the speculator's unearned increment of profit was a cause of the housing problem, limiting profits from rent and real estate sales was one logical solution.

Mariemont, Ohio, was a demonstration project on a much grander scale, comparable to examples farther afield such as Forest Hills Gardens in New York and Hampstead Garden Suburb in London. Funded with the immense fortune that Mary Emery had inherited from her husband, Thomas, a Cincinnati candle manufacturer and real estate investor, Mariemont was named for the couple's summer estate in Newport. Nearly all aspects of the project were under the control of Mrs. Emery's adviser, Charles J. Livingood, a Harvard classmate of the Emerys' late son. With her authorization, Livingood had traveled widely to study city planning examples in the United States and abroad,[122] and he began quietly assembling land for the project outside Cincinnati before the Great War. Acting as agent for

Mrs. Emery, he remained deeply involved in the process throughout and worked directly with Nolen's office to create a remarkable garden suburb, perhaps Nolen's greatest built project.

Writing in 1927, Livingood explained to Nolen that he had chosen him for Mariemont because of "the good impression you made at various conventions where I watched you closely. I selected you because of your sanity and strong character."[123] Nolen was absent when Livingood first came by his office in 1920 to discuss the project, so his associate Philip Foster handled the initial contact. Concerned that word of the project would complicate and add expense to land acquisitions, Livingood insisted that it remain secret for two years, until 1922, when Nolen made a carefully orchestrated presentation to the Cincinnati Commercial Club. Ground was broken in spring of 1923.[124]

Located on the outskirts of Cincinnati, Mariemont occupies a high bluff overlooking the Little Miami River valley. Originally the tentacles of the municipal street rail system stretched out along its northern side and connected rental housing in the Dale Park section, intended for "wage earners," to nearby industrial areas. This quadrant of the plan was separated from the others by Dogwood Park, Dale Park, and the schoolyards (*NTFO,* facing pp. 119 and 125), which were strung along a ravine that deepens as it traverses southwest across the site. The other three quadrants of the plan accommodate individual houses on larger lots, more oriented to the automobile access of Wooster Pike and the main train line in the valley along the town's southern edge. This geographical separation of economic strata was reinforced by the Dale Park section's separate neighborhood commercial center (*NTFO,* facing p. 120) and only partially overcome by the unifying matrix of streets radiating from the octagonal town center. Such integration of social and geographical structure is characteristic of Nolen's plans, as is the preservation of watersheds and ravines in parkland (*NTFO,* p. 122).

The north-to-south axis of this central street pattern connects the town center through a series of progressively narrower streets to a dramatic termination at an exedra with commanding views across the verdant river valley (Fig. 22). (This crucial connection has been weakened by subsequent construction.) Similarly, the perpendicular west-to-east axis, along the Wooster Pike, widens by small increments in its transit across the site until the planted esplanade separating its traffic lanes becomes a forested park. Both axial sequences rely more on tree trunks and canopies than on architecture to establish spatial order. Both also express quite literally the notion of the American garden city as a mediation between city and country. These interconnected

Figure 22. The Concourse, designed by Nolen's associate Philip Foster, is an exedra that overlooks the Little Miami River valley. It terminates the central north-south axis of Mariemont, Ohio. *Photograph by Charles D. Warren.*

social ideas and spatial sequences, even compromised as they are by incomplete or disruptive architecture, suggest the possibility that the landscape and the city might share the artistic structure of the garden, and that, in Nolen's words, "art is used for life's sake, and life is recognized as art."[125]

The plan shares many elements with other garden city plans of the period, such as those at Letchworth and Welwyn (*NTFO*, pp. 3 and 140). It has the usual geometric center, well defined by roads if not always by buildings; streets radiating in orthogonal and diagonal directions and gradually becoming more curvilinear to signal the transition to residential sections; and one axis that is given emphasis with a long park or esplanade on which prominent civic or commercial buildings are located. In Mariemont these features are adapted to accommodate the particular transportation circumstances and to enhance the dramatic river bluff site.

The garden city social program was also adapted to local circumstances. Though Livingood was a knowledgeable and sympathetic client who understood the social and economic ideas behind the garden city, he viewed Mariemont as a voluntary philanthropic enterprise, not a manifestation of fundamental social reform. He and Mrs. Emery did not waver from the generous implementation of their plans, but they controlled the unsold land and rental property, and so it continued as philanthropy only as long as they chose. (In 1931 Mariemont's assets were turned over to the Thomas J. Emery Memorial Trust, and the Dale Park apartments were sold in the 1950s.)[126] Communal or cooperative ownership, one of the defining characteristics of the garden city, was only vaguely contemplated and never instituted, though rents were kept affordable and profits were limited or never realized. But all of this was done without the social redefinition that a restructured system of ownership would have entailed.

Though Nolen suggested a list of architects to work on the buildings, Livingood had some ideas of his own, and evidently he enjoyed dispensing commissions to distinguished practitioners. Selections were carefully made so that each architect had control of a coherent group, and so that jarring juxtapositions of style would be avoided. Wanting the architecture to grow out of his designs, Nolen provided a color-coded plan to show Livingood how to group the commissions, emphasizing building pairs at street intersections and careful placement of buildings at vista terminations.[127] Existing architectural features are treated sympathetically; for example, a Georgian-style brick farmhouse on the property is flanked on one side by stylistically similar, if oddly horizontal, buildings by Richard H. Dana Jr. (*NTFO,* facing p. 121), and on the other by beautifully proportioned and ingeniously planned brick townhouses designed by Edmund B. Gilchrist (*NTFO,* facing p. 113). All three harmonize with Colonial-revival schools nearby (*NTFO,* facing p. 124) to form a stylistically coherent district. Many other groups are designed in English cottage styles, or Arts and Crafts adaptations of them, reflecting the English sources of the garden city. Among these, three ensembles designed by Grosvenor Atterbury, Robert R. McGoodwin, and the partners Lois Howe and Eleanor Manning (*NTFO,* facing p. 118) make particularly beautiful residential closes. The quality and variety of the architecture are key to the success of the northwest quadrant of the plan, which relies on enclosed allotment gardens to mitigate its dense building pattern. Even the less successful examples, such as an ungainly corner apartment building by Clinton Mackenzie, are well enough integrated with the whole that they are more idiosyncrasies than glaring flaws.

Nolen's chapter on Mariemont is based on a paper he

presented at the International Cities and Town Planning Conference held at Göteborg, Sweden, in summer of 1923. The conference was accompanied by an exhibition of planning projects including a huge collection of Nolen's, which was by far the largest in the show. The paper he delivered there and the Mariemont chapter in *NTFO* both focus on the early understanding by the management theorist Roger Babson (a client of Nolen's) of the planning and real estate implications of widespread automobile use in the United States, but the differences between the two pieces are telling. Well-intentioned though he was, Charles Livingood might not have wanted to read such sentences in the Göteborg paper as "We think it is necessary that Garden city enterprises should be under the control of bodies which have some connection to public authorities." Nolen tactfully revised the paper for publication, deemphasizing the necessity for state participation and highlighting the positive planning achievements in the United States.

Mariemont was one of the most elaborate and well-designed new towns of the era, but that was not sufficient for Nolen, who wanted the physical plan to be accompanied by economic reform. Years later he asserted that because of the lack of cooperative or public ownership "the United States has no 'garden city.'"[128] Nolen was willing to work within constraints that excluded restructured ownership, but he never could ignore his preferred, cooperative ideal.

FINAL CHAPTER

The bright future of Florida, where Nolen had a branch office in the late 1920s, weaves in and out of the optimistic text of his final chapter. To illustrate his busy practice there, he features Venice, Florida (*NTFO,* facing p. 154), one of his most ambitious plans. His original client, the renowned orthopedic surgeon Dr. Fred Albee, had bought Nokomis and Bay Point in 1917. After he acquired the land for Venice, across Roberts Bay, in 1924, he wrote to Nolen for advice on planning the property. Nolen made plans for all three sites, and Albee used his Bay Point plan to sell individual lots, but in 1925 he sold the Venice property to the already shaky investment arm of the Brotherhood of Locomotive Engineers (BLE). The union wanted to solve its financial problems by making a quick profit in Florida real estate, and it piled one land deal upon another, acquiring a vast property of 30,000 acres stretching inland from the original coastal site.[129] At Albee's urging, the BLE continued to work with Nolen, who extended his plans to encompass agricultural lands devoted to dairies and five-to-ten-acre cooperative farmsteads as well as a separate village called Little Harlem, whose odious intent is evident from its name. (Nolen encouraged at least decent housing for African Americans, but he did not resist the shameful norms of the era that resulted in separate civic improvements conceived unequally, along with everything else.) The result of Nolen's effort was a plan of regional scope to fulfill the promise of leisure and prosperity in the sunny climate of the booming state (Fig. 23).

The end of *NTFO* is a forward-looking pendant to the previous chapters' discussion of New England planning traditions. The optimism of Roger Babson's prescient understanding of the complex changes brought on by automobiles, radio, and the increase in leisure time pervades the text. Not surprisingly, Nolen advocates planning by national and state governments, by industry and railroads, and by limited-dividend companies. His belief in the capacity of his profession to meet the challenges of the future was stronger than ever, and his zeal to expand its scope of action energizes his conclusion.

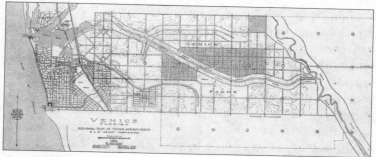

Figure 23. Nolen's regional plan for Venice, Florida, stretching to the Myaka River and including Nokomis, Bay Point, Little Harlem, and Venice Farms. *Nolen Papers, Cornell University Library.*

Five appendices were intended for the first edition of *NTFO*, but three were omitted.[130] Only the list of published American planning reports and a bibliography were included in the original edition. These provoked a scolding letter from Theodora Kimball Hubbard, the Harvard librarian and wife of Nolen's teacher Henry, who chided Nolen for including too many references to his own publications and found "the bibliography far below the standard of the text and illustrations of the book itself."[131] Others greeted the book more warmly. Ebenezer Howard wrote that it was a "Prophet of what is to come,"[132] and the *New York Times* noticed it positively as a "valuable little book . . . aimed at the general reader."[133] Thanks came from friends at home and abroad, most of whom had received the volume as a gift from Nolen (he bought five hundred copies and used them to promote his work, his ideas, and himself). Sylvester Baxter was given a vague acknowledgment at the front of the book, but he died in 1927 and may never have seen the finished volume.

New Towns for Old marks a high point in Nolen's eventful career. Shortly before it was finished, Nolen's long-time associate Philip Foster, intoxicated by the

Florida boom, set out on his own. His departure threw the Jacksonville office into turmoil, but it was a small problem compared to what was to follow.[134] As the Florida real estate bubble burst and the national economy came crashing down, so did Nolen's practice. By 1931 his office consisted of himself, his associate Justin Hartzog, and a secretary. Nolen kept busy, but not with work that paid anything. Once the federal government began spending on public works, he was able to participate as state planner for New Hampshire, and he served as special planning consultant at-large under the National Resources Planning Board and as a consultant on several National Park Service projects. He also served in various capacities at other agencies including the departments of Interior and Agriculture.[135] These were fitting roles for an elder statesman who had spent his career encouraging active government involvement in planning.

His practice, his writing, and his participation in planning organizations had made him one of the profession's international leaders, a status that took on new importance as the crisis of the Great Depression made policy makers more open to foreign planning ideas.[136] In 1931 he received a grant from the Oberlander Trust to study European waterfront improvements, and at the International Federation of Housing and Town Planning (IFHTP) that year he was elected president, making him the organization's third leader after Ebenezer Howard and Raymond Unwin. Nolen's broad background, combined with his interest in housing, land planning, and the garden city idea, gave him a kinship with the Europeans, and he was active in many European organizations and conferences, though IFHTP was his chief focus abroad.[137]

When Unwin visited the United States in October 1922, Nolen went to great lengths organizing the visit, and the two men's cordiality soon grew into friendship. The Nolens befriended Unwin's daughter, who lived in the United States, and in 1923 their own daughter Barbara spent part of the summer living with the Unwins in Hampstead. Nolen returned the favor when Unwin's son Edward came to work in Nolen's office for a time in 1926. Nolen went to Europe, in 1932, his twelfth trip, and again in 1935 for his IFHTP work, and Unwin came to the United States on a lecture tour in 1937. He was in New York when Barbara Nolen called to tell him that John was gravely ill. Immediately he wrote to his friend:

> You may at least have this consolation—beyond what is true for most—that you have lived your life to some purpose; that the value of your work in the pioneer period of planning over here is recognised and is most highly appreciated by those best qualified to assess it, not only in this country but in England and in many other lands where your leadership in the field is known, and where your genial and helpful personality have endeared you to a very wide circle. From that circle you will be greatly missed: the gap which your absence from it will create will be a sad one. For myself I cannot tell you how much I have valued your help, your experience, and above all your personal friendship . . . I wish to you . . . with all my heart as great a measure of courage as you may need, and of faith to believe that in some way beyond what we can realise all is part of a greater plan than we can yet see.[138]

John Nolen lived long enough to receive this tribute, and even managed to send a reply, but on February 18, 1937, he died at his home in Cambridge. Much was left unfinished, including half-implemented plans for a second edition of *New Towns for Old*. In the end, only thirty-one copies of the second edition were produced, and these were cobbled together by rebinding new material with old.[139]

It is in the nature of town planning to start more than can be finished, but by the centenary of Nolen's Harvard graduation many of his goals had been achieved. The planning process had been institutionalized in most American cities with zoning and a professional planning bureaucracy, the states had adopted planning as a tool, and even the federal government had become involved, directly and indirectly, in housing, slum clearance, and transportation infrastructure, including the sprawling interstate highway system. The densely intertwined functions of the city had been decentralized and teased apart into discrete residential, commercial, and industrial sectors, and home ownership had reached historic highs through financing methods Nolen had long championed. But solutions to early-twentieth-century problems have created other, new problems, which now confront citizens and planners. The planning bureaucracy has a life of its own, and it sometimes mistakes clear process for clear goals. Many seek to reform the entrenched preoccupation with roads and parking and the bias against the density and mixtures of activities that make urban living enjoyable and convenient. Some act to mitigate the negative effects of the metastasizing highway system, which has replaced congestion of the population with congestion of the cars, and still others struggle to regain the civic culture that was lost in the dispersion of urban activities. Nolen recognized the need for constant revision of the city plan to cope with changing circumstances, and this was never more necessary than it is today.

It may be that the way forward can be found through study of the places he created rather than in the processes he advocated. These towns and cities are his living legacy, where individuality has been established, distinctiveness preserved, and physical situation accented. The best of them are documented in *New Towns for Old,* and they illustrate the social and artistic balance John Nolen tried to negotiate between American culture and the American landscape.

NOTES

Research for this essay was funded in part by a grant from the John Nolen Research Fund, Cornell University Library. Elaine Engst and the staff of the Division of Rare and Manuscript Collections at Cornell made working there a pleasure, and I gratefully acknowledge their assistance. Tom Hanchett of the Levine Museum of the New South, Brian Wilson of the Kingsport Public Library, and David Smith of the New York Public Library each have provided indispensable guidance and help. Illustrations for the introduction and the cover were made possible by Evelyn and Michael Jefcoat, whose enthusiasm and support have added greatly to the project. I also wish to thank the Viburnum Foundation, whose forward-looking commitment to thoughtful land stewardship has made the new edition of this book possible.

NP = Nolen Papers, Cornell University Library
NYPL = New York Public Library

1. Sylvester Baxter, "A Great Civic Awakening in America: The Organized Instruments for the Creation and Preservation of Beauty in Public Places," *The Century* 64 (June 1902): 255–65; Jon A. Petersen, *The Birth of City Planning in the United States, 1841–1917* (Baltimore: Johns Hopkins University Press, 2003).

2. John Nolen, *Replanning Small Cities* (New York: Huebsch, 1912), 5.

3. John Loretz Hancock, "John Nolen and the American City Planning Movement: A History of Culture Change and Community Response, 1900–1940" (PhD diss., University of Pennsylvania, Philadelphia, 1964), 18. Hancock's dissertation is the indispensable guide to Nolen's career and its relation to the emergence of the American planning profession.

4. H. Morton Bodfish, ed., *History of Building and Loan in the United States* (Chicago: Building and Loan League, 1931), chaps. 3, 4; Joseph Sundheim, "Pennsylvania," in *History of Building and Loan*, ed. Bodfish, 547–58.

5. Lincoln Steffens, *The Shame of the Cities* (New York: McClure, Phillips and Co., 1907), 196.

6. Dorothy Gondos Beers, "The Centennial City: 1865–1876," in *Philadelphia: A Three-Hundred-Year History*, ed. Russel F. Weigley (New York: Norton, 1984), 438–39.

7. Harry C. Silcox, *Philadelphia Politics from the Ground Up: The Life of Irishman William McMullin, 1824–1901* (Philadelphia: Balch Institute Press, 1989), 72–73.

8. U.S. Bureau of the Census, 1870, Series M593, Roll 1407, p. 607, indicates that John Nolen lived in the 20th Ward, 68th District, but newspaper accounts repeatedly refer to the Buttonwood Street address. The Census also records the daughters, Stella, eleven years old, and Nettie, six years old, which makes it doubtful that the elder girl was the child of Matilda Nolen, who was only twenty-five.

9. See the following articles in the *Philadelphia Inquirer* of 1870: "Riot and Bloodshed," Oct. 14; "The Police Again," Oct. 14; "His Condition," Oct. 15; "The Law Against Carrying Concealed Weapons," Oct. 17; "The Arrest of William B. Mann," Oct. 18; "The Nolen Homicide," Oct. 18; "City Intelligence," Oct. 20; "City Intelligence," Oct. 24.

10. John Nolen Jr. and Barbara Nolen Strong, *The Nolen Family Album: A Record of Five Generations*, NP, 5.

11. Ibid.

12. Cheesman O. Herrick, *History of Girard College* (Philadelphia: Girard College, 1927), 81. Herrick worked with Nolen at the American Society

for the Extension of University Teaching prior to his appointment as president of Girard.

13. Steven A. Sass, *The Pragmatic Imagination: A History of the Wharton School, 1881–1981* (Philadelphia: University of Pennsylvania Press, 1982); Daniel T. Rodgers, *Atlantic Crossings: Social Politics in a Progressive Age* (Cambridge, Mass.: Harvard University Press, 1998), chap. 3.

14. Sass, *Pragmatic Imagination*, 57.

15. Ibid., 73.

16. For a thorough exploration of the relationship between German-trained economists and the development of American social reform, see Rodgers, *Atlantic Crossings*.

17. Sass, *Pragmatic Imagination*, 73–75.

18. John Nolen, "The Philadelphia Gas Works," in *The City Government of Philadelphia*, ed. Edmund J. James (Philadelphia: Wharton School, 1893).

19. "Catskill Cottage Life," *New York Times*, June 4, 1893; see also *NYT*, Sept. 1, 1893, July 15, 1894, and July 22, 1894.

20. Candace Wheeler, "Dream City," *Harper's Monthly* (May 1893): 830–47.

21. Nolen Jr. and Strong, *Nolen Family Album*, NP, 10.

22. Hancock, "John Nolen and the American City Planning Movement," 18.

23. Nolen Jr. and Strong, *Nolen Family Album*, NP, 11.

24. John Nolen, "Oxford Summer Meeting," *The Citizen* 5 (1895): 195.

25. John Nolen, *A Good Home for Every Wage Earner* (Washington, D.C.: American City Pamphlets, 1917); Bodfish, ed., *Building and Loan*. Building and loan societies in the United States started outside Philadelphia, and the city remained the center of this movement. The financial arrangements of these voluntary societies exemplified Nolen's notion of cooperation.

26. Hancock, "John Nolen and the American City Planning Movement," 24.

27. Under the direction of Max von Pettenkofer, "who made the science of public health a German one[,] Munich . . . became a model of salubrity." George R. Collins and Christiane Craseman Collins, *Camillo Sitte: The Birth of Modern City Planning* (New York: Rizzoli, 1986), 38.

28. Camillo Sitte, *City Planning According to Artistic Principles: A Con-*

tribution to the Solution of Modern Problems of Architecture and Monumental Sculpture Especially with Regard to the City of Vienna, trans. George R. Collins and Christiane Craseman Collins (New York: Random House, 1965). This is the best translation of Sitte's book, which was first published in 1889 as *Der Städtebau nach seinen künstlerischen Grundsätzen.* The Collinses' translation is reprinted in their *Camillo Sitte,* 129–332.

29. Theodor Fischer, "City Building," trans. Sylvester Baxter, 1908, typescript in U.S. Library of Congress. According to Collins and Collins there is another copy at Harvard. For the significance of Fischer, Henrici, Sitte, and this phase of German planning, see Collins and Collins, *Camillo Sitte.*

30. Hancock, "John Nolen and the American City Planning Movement," 36, quoting a passage in a letter from Nolen to Barbara Nolen.

31. J. S. Pray, "The Department of Landscape Architecture at Harvard," *Landscape Architecture* 1 (Jan. 1911): 53.

32. Student records, Harvard University archives.

33. Susan L. Klaus, *A Modern Arcadia: Frederick Law Olmsted Jr. and the Plan for Forest Hills Gardens* (Amherst: Library of American Landscape History/University of Massachusetts Press, 2002), 170–71, n. 17.

34. Petersen, *Birth of City Planning,* 77–97.

35. Collins and Collins, *Camillo Sitte,* 114.

36. For the water supply as a precursor to the development of American city planning, see Petersen, *Birth of City Planning,* chap. 2. Nathan Hale Sr. (nephew of the martyred patriot) was a member of all water commissions from 1837 to 1846. He and his sons Nathan Jr. and Edward Everett, along with Charles Dunbar, Robert Morris Copeland, and Sylvester Baxter, were active advocates of metropolitan parks and planning. For Hale Sr. and the water commissions, see Nelson Manfred Blake, *Water for the Cities: A History of the Urban Water Supply in the U.S.* (Syracuse, N.Y.: Syracuse University Press, 1956). For Copeland's connection to the *Boston Daily Advertiser,* see Daniel J. Nadenicek and Lance M. Neckar, Introduction to H. W. S. Cleveland, *Landscape Architecture, as Applied to the Wants of the West* (1873; reprint, Amherst: Library

of American Landscape History/University of Massachusetts Press, 2002), xxxiii, n. 47. For E. E. Hale and metropolitan parks, see Cynthia Zaitzevsky, *Frederick Law Olmsted and the Boston Park System* (Cambridge, Mass.: Harvard University Press, 1982).

37. The Trustees of Public Reservations changed its name to The Trustees of Reservations in 1954.

38. "Massachusetts is acquiring public reservations . . . through the actions of state appointed commissions, like the Metropolitan Water Board and the Metropolitan Park Commission. . . . In this way the Metropolitan Parks and Parkways around Boston have been created and large reservations have been secured on the watershed of the Metropolitan Water Supply." Letter supporting state parks in John Nolen, *State Parks for Wisconsin* (Madison: State Park Board, 1909), 45–46.

39. Keith Morgan, "The Man Behind the Monograph," Introduction to Charles W. Eliot, *Charles Eliot: Landscape Architect* (1902; reprint, Amherst: Library of American Landscape History/University of Massachusetts Press, 1999), xi.

40. William de las Casas, one of the first Metropolitan Park commissioners and a Malden neighbor of Baxter's, identifies the genesis of the idea for the metropolitan parks system in Baxter's 1891 *Boston Herald* article "Greater Boston." See William B. de las Casas, "The Middlesex Fels," *New England Magazine* 24, no. 6 (Aug. 1898): 717. Baxter makes a similar, subtler claim in his *Boston Park Guide* (Boston: Pinkham Press, n.d.), 39. Keith Morgan also credits Baxter in "Man Behind the Monograph," xi.

41. For a thorough discussion of Boston's interconnected elite, see E. Digby Baltzell, *Puritan Boston and Quaker Philadelphia* (New Brunswick, N.J.: Transaction, 1996), chap. 14.

42. *National Cyclopaedia of American Biography* (New York: J. T. White and Co., 1893–1975), 419–20.

43. Mary Norton Kratt and Thomas W. Hanchett, *Legacy: The Myers Park Story* (Charlotte: Myers Park Foundation, 1986), 24.

44. John Nolen, "A Suburban Home for Six Thousand Dollars," *Country Life in America* (Aug. 1905): 425–26.

45. Frederick Law Olmsted Jr. and John Nolen, "The Normal Requirements of American Towns and Cities in Respect to Public Open Spaces," *Charities and the Commons* (Aug. 1906): 411–26. This magazine was edited by Edward T. Devine, Nolen's predecessor as secretary of ASEUT.

46. Lincoln Steffens, "Sending a State to College: What the University of Wisconsin Is Doing for Its People," *American Magazine* 67 (Feb. 1909): 349–64.

47. Hancock, "John Nolen and the American City Planning Movement," 231.

48. See John L. Hancock, *John Nolen, Landscape Architect, Town, City and Regional Planner: A Bibliographic Record of Achievement* (Ithaca, N.Y.: Program in Urban and Regional Studies, Cornell University, 1976), and Appendix in the present volume. See also Hancock, "John Nolen and the American Planning Movement," 157–230; Petersen, *Birth of City Planning*, 236–47.

49. Petersen, *Birth of City Planning*, chaps. 10, 11; Gregory Gilmartin, *Shaping the City* (New York: Clarkson Potter, 1999), 150–82.

50. Frederick Law Olmsted Jr., "Is an Increment Tax Feasible?" *Colliers*, Sept. 13, 1913, 6.

51. Frederick Law Olmsted Jr., "The Scope and Results of City Planning in Europe" (address to the National Conference on City Planning and Congestion of the Population, 61st Cong., 2nd sess., May 1990, Senate Doc. 442), 70.

52. For a complete account of Marsh and the Washington conference, see Peterson, *Birth of City Planning*, 236–42, 246–55.

53. Gilmartin, *Shaping the City*, 165, 168–70, 182.

54. Petersen, *Birth of City Planning*, chap. 11.

55. *Proceedings of the Second National Conference on City Planning and the Problem of Congestion, Rochester, New York, May 2–4, 1910* (Boston: The University Press, 1910), 11.

56. For the growth of building and loan societies, see Bodfish, ed., *Building and Loan*, chap. 4. For the difficulties of importing European social policy, see Rodgers, *Atlantic Crossings*, 200–2.

57. Anthony Sutcliffe, *Towards the Planned City: Germany, Britain, the United States and France, 1780–1914* (New York: St. Martin's Press, 1981), 94.

58. Nolen to John C. Olmsted, Sept. 16, 1915, NP, box 97.

59. Nolen ends the Reading chapter with an exhortation to the forces of good in the city. Funding to implement his plan, opposed by the powerful Reading Railroad, was defeated at the polls in 1910; evidently the city's growing Socialist Party also opposed it. For a thorough analysis, see Hancock, "John Nolen and the American City Planning Movement," chap. 6.

60. Werner Hegemann and Elbert Peets, *American Vitruvius: An Architects' Handbook of Civic Art* (New York: Architectural Book Publishing, 1922), 259.

61. Hancock, "John Nolen and the American City Planning Movement," chap. 4.

62. Petersen, *Birth of City Planning*, 314–15.

63. Nolen includes this definition in a footnote on p. 133, and he quotes it in slightly abridged form in John Nolen, "Garden Cities—United States," unpublished typescript, NP, box 30. It is the definition adopted by the Garden Cities and Town Planning Association in 1919, which appears in C. B. Purdom, "An Introductory Chapter," in *Town Theory and Practice*, ed. C. B. Purdom (London: Benn Brothers, 1926).

64. Robert Beevers, *The Garden City Utopia: A Critical Biography of Ebenezer Howard* (New York: St. Martin's Press, 1988), 28.

65. John Nolen, "Garden Cities—United States," NP, box 30.

66. Ibid.

67. Beevers, *Garden City Utopia*, 175.

68. Hancock, "John Nolen and the American City Planning Movement," 363–67; Rodgers, *Atlantic Crossings*, 352.

69. John Nolen, *The Planning of Cities, Towns and Villages, Outline of Lectures* (Washington, D.C.: Army Educational Commission, 1919); Frank E. Vandiver, *Black Jack: The Life and Times of John J. Pershing* (College Station: Texas A&M University Press, 1977), 1013.

70. The American City Bureau was founded by Edgar and Harold Butten-

heim, the publisher and editor of *American City Magazine*, respectively. It was started to organize the City Planning Exhibition at the New York Public Library in 1913, which traveled extensively to chambers of commerce and civic groups across the United States.

71. For the Baxter-Bellamy connection and the Nationalist Party, see Arthur Ernest Morgan, *Edward Bellamy* (New York: Columbia University Press, 1944), 94, 249, 291.

72. Baxter to Nolen, Feb. 8, 1922; Nolen to Baxter, Dec. 3, 1921, Mar. 19, 1923, and Dec. 24, 1926, NP, box 1.

73. Baxter material in NP, boxes 1, 101.

74. Nolen to Baxter, Oct. 27, 1921, NP, box 1.

75. Jones to Nolen, Aug. 17, 1926, NP, box 1.

76. Nolen to Shaw, Dec. 2, 1926, Shaw papers, NYPL, box 116. For background on the farm city projects, Elwood Mead's farm towns, and Shaw's connection to them, see Rodgers, *Atlantic Crossings*, 343–52.

77. See Shaw papers, NYPL, box 47. Baxter wrote a number of articles for Shaw's *Review of Reviews,* and the two corresponded on matters of mutual interest. They were on sufficiently intimate terms that Baxter sent Shaw a wedding announcement when he married Lucia Allen Millet.

78. Lloyd J. Graybar, *Albert Shaw of the Review of Reviews* (Lexington: University Press of Kentucky, 1974), 26.

79. Bird & Son to Nolen, Nov. 1, 1912, NP, box 37.

80. His grandfather, Francis William Bird, was a well-known abolitionist and the 1872 Republican gubernatorial candidate in Massachusetts. His mother, Anna Child Bird, was a Republican Party activist and a suffragette.

81. George Gore (a Bird & Son employee involved in planning projects) to Nolen, Nov. 6, 1914, NP, box 37. After the collapse of the Progressive Party in 1914, Francis William Bird moved back to Massachusetts and bought the *Boston Daily Advertiser* and the *Boston Evening Record.* The papers were sold in 1918, and he died shortly thereafter.

82. Various correspondence, NP, box 37; Walpole Town Planning Committee, *Town Planning for Small Communities* (New York: D. Appleton, 1917).

INTRODUCTION *cxi*

83. Anna C. Bird, "Game Plan," Feb. 1934, NP, box 37.

84. Various correspondence among Murphy, Bird, and Nolen, NP, box 37.

85. At the dissolution of Blair and Co. in 1920, the partners' ownership stakes were Blair, 48 percent, Dennis, 30 percent, and Edgar L. Marston, 22 percent. Upon dissolution the records were destroyed. See "Partner in Blair & Co., Dissolved in 1920, Sued for Accounting by Member's Estate," *New York Times,* Feb. 10, 1937, 33.

86. Margaret Ripley Wolfe, *Kingsport, Tennessee: A Planned American City* (Lexington: University Press of Kentucky, 1987), 17. According to Wolfe the other investors included Isaac T. Mann, W. M. Ritter, Norman B. Ream, and James A. Blair.

87. "New Yorkers Buy Big Farm," *New York Times,* June 3, 1914, 1.

88. "How Ryan Rose in Wall Street," *New York Times,* Nov. 24, 1928, 8.

89. John Reps, *The Making of Urban America: A History of City Planning in the United States* (Princeton: Princeton University Press, 1965), 382–412.

90. Dennis and his brother Henry had more than a business connection to the Blairs. James A. Blair, who was C. Ledyard Blair's bachelor cousin (and who appears in the photograph of railroad investors in the Kingsport archive), left nearly his entire estate to John Dennis with the exception of his personal effects, which he left to Henry Dennis and his wife. "Col. Blair left $955,030," *New York Times,* Jan. 30, 1936, 20.

91. See Wolfe, *Kingsport,* 16–17. Useful details can be culled from Wolfe's book, though some facts are inaccurate (Nolen's doctorate from Hamilton was honorary, not earned; J. B. Duke was not the client for Myers Park, though he lived there). Her conclusions about the importance of Johnson relative to the large capitalist interests who, for all practical purposes, controlled the project overlook the larger context, and such misplaced emphasis is a repeated flaw.

92. Ibid., 36, 43.

93. Ibid., 55.

94. The village was named for Samuel Chapman Armstrong, a brevet general in the Civil War and founder of Hampton Institute, a school in Virginia intended to educate freedmen. The village was platted and

built, but it was used to house the employees of the nearby Borden Mills, rather than as a racially segregated neighborhood.

95. T. F. Ryan had large holdings of CC&O Railroad, Clinchfield Coal Corp., Holliston Mills, Inc., the printing company J. J. Little, the Securities Company, and Pennsylvania-Dixie Cement Corp., all local Kingsport industries or corporations with subsidiaries there. For a listing, see "Stock Holdings in the Ryan Estate," *New York Times,* Feb. 16, 1932, 14. According to Wolfe (*Kingsport,* 34) the Securities Company owned more than half of the Kingsport Brick Co.

96. Wolfe, *Kingsport,* 25.

97. Draper thought the park area was too large to be supported by the size of the community. See James Arthur Glass, "John Nolen and the Planning of New Towns: Three Case Studies" (Master's thesis, Cornell University, Ithaca, N.Y., 1984), 67, 107 n. 60.

98. *Refractories Company Towns,* Historic American Building Survey no. PA-5976, National Park Service, Dept. of Interior, Washington, D.C.; Kim E. Wallace, *Brickyard Towns: A History of the Refractories Industry Communities in South-Central Pennsylvania* (Washington, D.C.: America's Industrial Heritage Project and Historic American Buildings Survey/Historic American Engineering Record, 1993).

99. Margaret Crawford, *Building Workingman's Paradise: The Design of American Company Towns* (New York: Verso, 1995), 160; Wallace, *Brickyard Towns.*

100. Reps, *Making of Urban America,* 414–38.

101. See, for example, Clinton Mackenzie, *Industrial Housing* (New York: Knickerbocker Press, 1920); Morris Knowles, *Industrial Housing: With a Discussion of Accompanying Activities* (New York: McGraw-Hill, 1920); and Leifur Magnusson, *Housing by Employers in the U.S.,* Bulletin of the U.S. Bureau of Labor Statistics, no. 263 (Washington, D.C.: Government Printing Office, 1920). The Plan of Ojibway, Ontario (*NTFO,* p. 72), is a steel industry example that appears in Knowles's book; it was designed by the firm of Carrère and Hastings, but was never completed beyond street layout.

102. "Model Factory Town Is Planned in Pennsylvania," *Christian Science Monitor,* May 24, 1916, 13.

103. Charles C. May, "Some Aspects of Industrial Housing III: The Need for Maintenance Measures," *Architectural Forum* (Mar. 1918): 75–80. This article, referred to on page 60, was one of three proposed for inclusion in the book as appendices. It describes the misuse of industrial housing by tenants and the need to teach them how to properly live in and maintain the houses built for them. It refers specifically to Kingsport, and demonstrates the impulse to Americanize foreign workers, or change the domestic habits of those recently relocated to a more urban setting. See notes 106 and 130 herein on other omitted appendices.

104. Meeting announcement for Cohasset Men's Club, Dec. 21, 1911, NP, box 72.

105. John Nolen, "Town of Cohasset: Recommendations and Report," unpublished typescript, 1912, NP, box 72.

106. See F. L. Olmsted, "Village Improvement," *Atlantic Monthly* (June 1905): 798–803. This article, referred to on pages 16–17, was one of three proposed for inclusion in the book as appendices. It was found among the papers of Fredrick Law Olmsted Sr. by his son Fredrick Jr., who added material to the beginning and end. The elder Olmsted describes the simple charms of New England village life during his boyhood, and Olmsted Jr. discusses good and bad aspects of the New England village improvement movement. The article expresses Nolen's admiration and Baxter's evident love for New England village life. See notes 103 and 130 herein on other omitted appendices.

107. Oliver H. Howe, "Civic Centers of New England," *American Architect* (Feb. 1920): 173–76; "Early Town Planning in New England," *American Architect* (Oct. 1920): 464–69; "Stumbling Blocks to Civic Planning," *Modern City* (Mar./Apr. 1926): 42–45.

108. Oliver H. Howe, "Public Spirit in Cohasset," *Cohasset Citizen*, May 4, 1917.

109. "Beautifying Cohasset," Boston transcript, July 17, 1917; Oliver H. Howe, "Public Spirit in Cohasset," *Cohasset Citizen*, May 11, 1917.

110. Burtram J. Pratt, *A Narrative History of the Town of Cohasset, Massachusetts*, vol. 2 (Cohasset: Committee on Town History, 1956).

111. The irony of German methods being used in the war effort against the Germans was not lost on Sylvester Baxter; see his article "The Gov-

ernment's Housing Activities," *Architectural Record* 44 (Dec. 1918): 561–65.

112. William E. Groben, "Union Park Gardens: A Model Garden Suburb for Shipworkers at Wilmington, Delaware," *Architectural Record* 45 (Jan. 1919): 45–64.

113. *War Emergency Housing Report of the United States Housing Corporation* (Washington, D.C.: Government Printing Office, 1920).

114. For a thorough account of Myers Park and its relationship to Charlotte, see Thomas W. Hanchett, *Sorting Out the New South City: Race, Class, and Urban Development in Charlotte, 1875–1975* (Chapel Hill: University of North Carolina Press, 1998); see also Kratt and Hanchett, *Legacy.*

115. Hanchett, *New South City,* 170–81.

116. Stephens to Nolen, July, 21, 1919, NP, box 99. Duke planned to spend $150,000 on improvements.

117. Wolfe, *Kingsport,* 38. Draper is quoted as saying, "We are all very fond of Dr. Nolen, but when he comes to the office to look over the plans, the only comment he ever makes is 'Shall we have white prints or blueprints, and how many?'" Such a statement ought to be seen in light of the fact that Draper worked for Nolen rather briefly, spent most of his time in the field, and ended his association with some acrimony; see also Glass, "Nolen and New Towns," n. 100.

118. Various Charlotte correspondence, NP, box 98.

119. Ibid.

120. Stephens to Nolen, Oct. 28, 1919, NP, box 98. It is notable that Stephens did not turn to Draper for help with the Asheville plan.

121. Records of Olmsted Associates, microfilm reel 245, file 5109, Manuscript Division, U.S. Library of Congress.

122. Millard F. Rogers, *John Nolen and Mariemont: Building a New Town in Ohio* (Baltimore: Johns Hopkins University Press, 2001), 10–12.

123. Livingood to Nolen, Jan. 19, 1927, NP, box 29, file 24.

124. For a complete account of the development of Mariemont, see Rogers, *John Nolen and Mariemont.*

125. John Nolen, *John Edward Howard Griggs: His Personality and Work* (New York: Huebsch, n.d.), 8.

126. Rogers, *Nolen and Mariemont*, chap. 7.

127. Various drawings, Mariemont folder, NP.

128. John Nolen, "Garden Cities—United States," NP, box 30.

129. Gregg M. Turner, *Venice in the 1920s* (Charleston, S.C.: Arcadia, 2000).

130. Planning books of the period, and Nolen's in particular, have extensive bibliographies and appendices full of reference material. Each of the three appendices proposed in Baxter's manuscript but omitted from *NTFO* sheds light on the text and the period. See notes 103 and 106 herein on the first two omitted appendices; the third was an excerpt from a contemporary novel that described the conflict between the street layout of San Francisco and its hilly topography—an issue that preoccupied both Nolen and Baxter. A small part of it appears in the caption to the picture of San Francisco (*NTFO,* facing p. 14). See Gelett Burgess, *The Heart Line: A Drama of San Francisco* (Indianapolis: Bobbs and Merrill, 1907), 246–49.

131. T. K. Hubbard to Nolen, May 25, 1927, NP, box 1.

132. Howard to Nolen, June 21, 1927, NP, box 1.

133. "In City Planning a Vision of a New America," *New York Times*, Nov. 13, 1927, BR 2.

134. Foster to Nolen, June 6, 1926, NP, box 76.

135. Hancock, "John Nolen and the American City Planning Movement," 604.

136. Rodgers, *Atlantic Crossings*, 414–16.

137. Hancock, "John Nolen and the American City Planning Movement," 441–47.

138. Unwin to Nolen, Feb. 2, 1937, NP, box 8.

139. H. B. Doust to Nolen, Feb. 24, 1937, and note to Nolen Jr., Apr. 9, 1937, NP, box 1.

NEW TOWNS FOR OLD

BY JOHN NOLEN

MARIEMONT, OHIO

Airplane view of new town and surrounding country

NEW TOWNS
FOR OLD

ACHIEVEMENTS IN CIVIC IMPROVEMENT
IN SOME AMERICAN SMALL TOWNS
AND NEIGHBORHOODS

By JOHN NOLEN

INTRODUCTION
By ALBERT SHAW

MARSHALL JONES COMPANY
BOSTON · MASSACHUSETTS

Printed in the United States of America

THE MURRAY PRINTING COMPANY
CAMBRIDGE, MASS.

PREFACE

The primary purpose of this book is to describe a few representative examples of civic improvement actually carried out. It is not a treatise or outline or summary of town planning. The scope of the volume is intentionally limited. It deals with a few selected places only, and with them mainly for the purpose of showing results accomplished and the method employed. While not in any sense a textbook, it furnishes what textbooks so often lack, namely, concrete illustrations of fundamental principles.

Town planning is an indispensable art. Its value, however, depends upon the success with which it can be applied. City-planning commissions and the general public are often impatient for results, but in a subject as difficult and complex as town planning, results come slowly. Changes in existing towns cannot be made in a day, and new towns are usually of slow growth. The story of achievement here set forth in word and plan and picture is based upon a record of about a decade, and makes one optimistic for the future.

The book has also two secondary purposes. One is to draw attention to the economic and social advantages of towns or relatively small cities (especially if well connected as satellites of greater population centers), and to the ease with which they can be improved. Cohasset and Walpole are fair examples. The other purpose is to plead for more new towns, skillfully planned in favorable locations better to meet modern requirements and higher standards. It is believed that the account of the places here selected for description is convincing, especially the records and photographic illustrations of Myers Park, Kingsport and Mariemont.

Successful town planning cannot be the work of a narrow specialist, or of a single profession. The call is for versatility, special knowledge and coöperation. For town planning is engineering plus something; architecture plus something; or landscape architecture plus something; and that plus is as indispensable as the direct professional equipment in the more usual and better-recognized fields. So it has been with the execution of these projects. The town planner would have little to present if he had failed to secure in each place the help and coöperation of architects, landscape architects and engineers. Special mention should be made of the architectural work of Mr. Clinton Mackenzie and the landscape gardening work of Miss Lola Anderson at Kingsport, and the work of Messrs. Walker and Gillette as architects at Venice; and of the large and distinguished group of architects at Mariemont, working under the leadership of Mr. Charles J.

Livingood with Mr. George L. Mirick as general manager.

Grateful acknowledgments are likewise due to numerous individuals in Walpole, Kingsport, Kistler, Cohasset, Union Park Gardens, Myers Park, Mariemont and Venice, for coöperation in gathering information and photographs to show the actual results of plans and recommendations; to Messrs. Wurts Brothers, New York, for permission to use their unusual photographs of Kingsport; to Mr. Sylvester Baxter of Boston, for suggestions and help in preparing the manuscript, especially the chapters dealing with the early history of towns and villages in New England, and the contrast of random growth with stereotyped planning; to the professional associates in my office for invaluable aid; to Dr. Albert Shaw for repeated encouragement and his able introduction to the book; and to the national and local leaders of the American Civic Association and the National Conference on City Planning, without whose pioneering efforts much of the civic improvement here described would not have been possible.

JOHN NOLEN.

CAMBRIDGE, MASSACHUSETTS,
JANUARY, 1927.

CONTENTS

v

LIST OF PLATES

vii

LIST OF ILLUSTRATIONS IN THE TEXT

xi

INTRODUCTION

I

For many years I have studied the character and results of pioneering times in America, and the newer movements for the more permanent adjustment of community life. The settlements of the seventeenth century in New England and along the Atlantic seaboard east of the Alleghanies have left their indelible impress upon town and country. The movements of the eighteenth century previous to the Revolutionary War greatly extended the inhabited areas, pushing the frontiers westward and rapidly multiplying the numbers of an American-born population. Characteristics had begun to show themselves that signified a new race, keeping indeed some European habits and customs, but having no longer a European consciousness. The communities, whether villages and towns or more open farm country, and whether in the North or the South, were not transplanted, but indigenous. After the Revolution came the great sweep that had carried the Americans all the way to California by the middle of the nineteenth century. The remaining fifty years of the century may be said to have been occupied with the pioneering of the great region that lay between the Mississippi River and the Pacific Coast. Everywhere, these American beginnings were those of a people destined to evolve a stable and lasting life, in well-coördinated communities.

The methods of pioneering, as everybody now well understands, have been wasteful to an extent that is serious, though not beyond redemption. Forests could have been fully utilized, without impairing the natural processes of reforestation. Lands could have been farmed to advantage, without the ruinous consequences of soil exhaustion and erosion that followed the farm practices of the tobacco planters of Virginia. Devastation that had rendered their old homes no longer tenable had sent scores of thousands of pioneers from the seaboard states across the mountains to Kentucky and Ohio. This had happened while Washington and Jefferson were still alive; and in their last years they were bitterly deploring the wastefulness and lack of forethought that were resulting in the wholesale abandonment of Eastern farms and the breaking down of the established life of neighborhoods.

By the middle of the nineteenth century some of the same symptoms began to disclose themselves in Ohio and Kentucky. The waste of the forests resulted in freshets and floods that ruined many fertile valley farms along the tributaries of the Ohio and the other affluents of the Mississippi.

Not only were economic and social conditions in the original states affected by the shortsighted-ness of their own private exploiters, and the lack of public regulation, but the East also became the victim of an unsettling competition produced by successive Western booms. The craze for land speculation had almost as much to do with the Western pioneer movements as the genuine aspiration for the planting of new homes and the making of new communities in the Mississippi Valley and the states beyond.

The single-cropping for Europe of tobacco and other products that had so injured Virginia and the South began to be paralleled by the overproduction of wheat and corn in the new West; and not only was this undue cultivation of single crops harmful to the Western regions, but it reacted painfully upon the beginnings of a stabilized and permanent agriculture in Pennsylvania, New York and New England. Cheap foodstuffs from the West, flooding the Eastern states, resulted in a corresponding exodus of hundreds of thousands of the best and most vigorous people from the older to the newer parts of the country.

It requires very little study of these forces to see clearly that a profound disturbance of equilibrium, due to the geographical sweep of the westward movement, had resulted in a terrible depression that affected in particular the rural communities of the East. People were driven from villages and adjacent farms; and if they did not go west, they went to the manufacturing centers and the commercial cities of the East. The speculative agricultural West was too young to have developed manufactures to any great extent; while the Eastern states, which had adopted the factory system through sheer necessity, under the stimulus of Jefferson's Embargo Act during the War of 1812, expanded and intensified their industrial undertakings. They saw their opportunity to supply the growing West and the agricultural South with textiles, iron and steel products — everything, in short, from clothespins and clocks to locomotives. They gradually increased their protective tariffs from moderate rates to very high ones, and from a few listed articles to schedules enumerating hundreds of articles and products.

With the beginning of the twentieth century the great conservation movement made its appearance. The future historian of our civilization will perceive that we were pioneering for nearly three centuries, and that we then began to grasp the notion that our country, East as well as West, had permanent values that were to be cherished and sustained, and that wasteful exploitation was no longer to be permitted. I have no peculiar passion for dividing time into periods in order to simplify the discussion of problems. What I call the pioneering process embraces points of view as well as methods; and these will be found here and there working their heedless way far into the new century. Nevertheless, for purposes of understanding what has happened in the past, and what wise people are trying to do in the present, it is well enough to note these transitions in terms of centuries.

The present fact is that migration no longer sweeps westward. More farmers have been coming from beyond the Alleghanies to Virginia, New York, Pennsylvania, and even to New England in the last few years, than have been going out from these Eastern states to take up agriculture beyond the Mississippi. The more notable recent drift has been on diagonal lines. Taking Iowa as a starting-point, there has been an immense sweep into Northwest Canada and an almost equally impressive migration to Southern California. The difference, of course, is that the younger men have gone to Saskatchewan to raise wheat and speculate in rich new lands, while the older generation, selling high-priced farms in Iowa, have gone to California to seek mild climate and repose in the gardens and orchards of the Pacific Coast. By the scores of thousands, also, farm families have gone from the Middle West to Texas, Louisiana, Alabama and Mississippi. Above all, they have been joining in the eager rush to Florida, learning how to make homes under conditions no longer wasteful but at once permanent, scientific and æsthetic, in that reborn commonwealth of winter sunshine and outdoor pursuits.

II

But how much has all this recital of shifts and changes to do with a little volume that has been written by John Nolen and that bears the title, " New Towns for Old "? I answer at once that I am acquainted with no man in the United States who better understands the bearings of these epochal movements than does the eminent landscape architect and town planner who has brought patient study, and great knowledge in broad fields, not less than professional skill and constructive genius, to the service of what is nothing less than a permanent reshaping of the externals of American life.

There are out-of-door things that cannot be done successfully at certain seasons of the year. There are also things pertaining to epochs which have to recognize the spirit of the times. When all of our winds were blowing westward, when the emigrant trains were carrying myriads towards the sunset over a dozen parallel lines of new railroad, following the trails of the covered wagons of earlier decades, the American people obviously were in no mood for reshaping their Eastern villages. They were rushing to the cities, or else they were following relatives and neighbors to the new regions. Now, times have altered, and the best hopes for most people are in the opportunities near at hand.

Sometimes the prosperous Westerners came back — at intervals ever less frequent — to visit the scenes of their own childhood, or the homes of their parents east of the Alleghanies. They had an affection for the old neighborhoods; but they were rather apologetic because their families perchance had come from hill farms or rural villages, rather than from Boston or New York. Fifty years, or even twenty-five, have wrought a transformation, both in scenes and in sentiments.

Mr. Nolen's present volume is not pretentious, but it is highly significant. It describes the making of certain new communities on modern lines for convenience, permanence and beauty, in view of all the changed conditions that have been produced by good roads, the automobile, the telephone, the graded school, and a hundred other transforming circumstances. But besides the description and analysis of new communities, Mr. Nolen shows a delightful sympathy with the awakened interest in restoring and improving the old villages and towns. No longer do intelligent people apologize for the little neighborhoods where their American ancestors lived. They have come to realize that the best future of the United States lies not in the great industrial and metropolitan centers, nor in the volume of surplus crops of wheat and corn and cotton produced in the West and South, nor yet in the sheer number of automobiles manufactured, or the magnitude of annual output of iron and steel.

It is not that intelligent people decry the mass production of useful commodities. But what they are most interested in is the distribution of these commodities in such a way that people may live happily where they naturally belong, and may with confidence feel that individual, family, and social well-being in the future is to be widely diffused. Not only is it to be so distributed that, in the sense of wealth and culture, social classes are virtually to disappear; but also, through the electrical transmission of power and through all of the more modern facilities, life may be lived, not with disadvantage but even with some positive superiorities, in the smaller places.

Thus it is possible to have a theory of Uncle Sam's farm as being properly laid out, with restored forests on the mountain slopes and upland regions that protect the sources of rivers. In like manner, the conception brings us a map of the country that shows the benefits that may follow wise national and state policies, and that may be extended to the closer pattern of counties, townships, small cities, villages, and strictly rural or farm neighborhoods.

Mr. Nolen has for years seen with undimmed eyes this vision of a restored, harmonized, and beautified country. Happily there are many people also who can share in the vision; but there are not many men or women who are so capable as Mr. Nolen of turning from the pictures that his imagination conjures up, to the very difficult but essential task of working out the picture in the concrete — " on the ground," so to speak. Our author has been, and continues to be, a great demonstrator. It has been Mr. Nolen's mission to help cities and towns in adapting their facilities to the new opportunities of life. He has learned to diagnose a given community as regards those things which enable its people to live well and pleasantly while earning a livelihood. Having joined in making the requisite survey, he has through much experience and careful study been able to show the local town-planning committee what it is feasible to do at once, and what comprehensive plans ought to be adopted looking to future growth and change. This means parks and playgrounds, the suitable placing of public buildings, protective zoning so that factories and residential districts may be suitably adjusted to their environment, and appointments of all kinds for the education, recreation, and health of the inhabitants.

III

There was a time — and it is not yet ended — when municipal arrangements in our larger cities were so much more advanced and progressive than the corresponding facilities in the smaller places that urban growth was in no small measure due to a centrifugal attraction that deserved no censure. People crowded within municipal bounds for the sake of educational opportunities and other similar advantages. Together with this growth of population was the concentration of wealth, so that a million people living in a large city could levy taxes to maintain a uniform school system, for example, equally available for rich and poor. Clearly, this was far superior to the schools that a second million people, scattered in small neighborhoods, could possibly afford to provide. The remedy for such a condition obviously lies in a state policy that should pool revenues for school support, and then distribute them in such a way as to provide for rural schools as efficiently and suitably as for urban.

Gradually these ideas are taking firm hold. In the South, as in California, they are fully perceived. They are making their way in Pennsylvania, New York, and New England. The larger cities have become congested, and good roads and the automobile are helping in the new movement for decentralization. The prevalence of short hours of labor and of high wages is bringing industrial classes into harmony with the spirit of country life. It is no longer a reproach to know an elm from an oak, or a hemlock from a white pine. Schools may now be as advantageous in the smaller places as in the great centers. Bucolic lore is disseminated, and gladly received. The denominational competition that had almost destroyed church life in villages has passed through its worst phases, and the church sees its new mission more sanely and hopefully. The dramatic stage in large cities is now chiefly given over to the very same motion pictures that are seen to equal advantage in small villages. The radio brings music into the country home, where it can be heard often to better advantage than in the auditorium where the chorus sings, or the hotel dining-room of the city where the orchestra plays.

Mr. Nolen's little volume is inspiring in its enthusiasm for things that may be done. Our author is indeed visionary, but in the true sense of that word. He demonstrates, in the pages that follow, how visions and dreams can be realized. A movement is spreading through the fine villages and old " towns " of New England, the nature of which is charmingly set forth in Mr. Nolen's account of the revivifying of Walpole, Massachusetts.

Some years or decades ago it became fashionable for wealthy men living in large cities, notably in Boston, New York, Chicago and St. Louis, but often in places still farther west, to revisit the village of their ancestors, and to build a memorial library as a tribute to the past and also in token of a pardonable family pride. These benefactors as a rule had not much faith in the continuing life of what they regarded as down-at-the-heel communities. They found traditions broken in continuity, and frequently they encountered new populations speaking various European dialects.

But this is now changing. Men and women of knowledge and culture are using the libraries, and there is growing in hundreds of these neighborhoods a sentiment that is no longer apologetic or Philistine. This new feeling can be summed up in

the statement that people are now saying to one
another that after all there is no better place in
which to live and to bring up families than in the
" old home town."

When people arrive at that conviction, they are
quickly responsive to the leadership of an energetic
group that forms a town-planning committee, and
that proposes to save what is historic and beautiful,
and to insure the future by such public and private
building arrangements, and such landscape effects,
as are appropriate.

It begins to be seen that the beauty and charm
of a town and a neighborhood not only make for
local pride and satisfaction, but also are valuable in
the economic sense. New England in particular has
a vast resource of wealth in its summer climate
and its opportunities for automobile touring and
recreation; and to invest thought, money and professional experience in correcting and perfecting
the landscape and the local entourage is profitable
in material returns.

IV

A particularly impressive chapter in Mr.
Nolen's present volume tells us of the new community plan upon which the admirable Tennessee
manufacturing town of Kingsport has been projected. Here we have a group of industries utilizing
the raw material and resources of the vicinity,
coöperating with one another for business success,

and at the same time uniting to create a model city with a maximum of convenience, beauty and happiness on every acre.

For these purposes of rejuvenation, Ohio is also one of the older states, and the description of Mariemont, a projected industrial village adjacent to Cincinnati, is suggestive of the new things that are to be tried increasingly throughout the country. A grandfather and a great-grandfather of mine lived just there, on the Little Miami River, east of the Ohio-valley metropolis; and it is pleasant to read of the newer phases of life in that vicinity.

Mr. Nolen was one of the experts most authoritative in making plans for housing workers engaged in shipyards and munition mills during the emergency period of the World War. Some model villages were created as examples. Undoubtedly that impulse has had much to do with the emancipation of the minds of many men who control great industries. They desire so to provide homes for their workers as to impart a sense of permanence and contentment. This motive has become widespread under the new conditions, and it is producing brilliant results in numerous instances. Thus we have entered upon a hopeful stage in the business of rehousing the people of the United States, in ways to bring associated families up to a higher level of refinement, of neighborhood responsibility, and of good citizenship.

We still have millions of people who eke out

an existence in decaying log-houses, for the survival of which — as human abodes — there is no longer any excuse, or in frame shanties unfit for the decencies of American life. In England, in spite of the industrial and financial difficulties that have prevailed since the War, there are large projects, that are advancing in deadly earnest, for the better housing of all workers. There is no suspicion of iconoclasm, nor any thought of the destruction of things worth preserving for their historic associations, or their antiquarian interest. But these re-housing plans and enterprises do show how firm is the faith of the English people in their own future, and how devoted is their affection for every square mile of their storied land.

We are entitled to have the same feeling about our localities in the United States. Fortunately, also, the new prospects of an economic character justify what we may call a communal investment in the things that belong to the functioning of the neighborhood—parks, schools, roads, libraries, and so on, while also lifting all doubts regarding private investment in the maintenance of homes, removing anxiety as to reasonable opportunities for gaining a livelihood without abandonment of familiar haunts and neighborhoods.

People are learning to value more wisely the things that cannot be appraised in terms of money. In many a small neighborhood a relatively small income can be made to suffice for protection against poverty in old age, while associating itself from day to day with the kind of contentment and felicity that a much larger income could not procure for the same family as strangers in some overcrowded city.

The present volume is by no means the first permanent record Mr. Nolen has given us of his achievements as a town planner. For twenty years he has been editing classics in landscape architecture, and producing on his own account successive volumes on town and city planning that are themselves to remain as classics, while they are setting up milestones along the course of our community rebuilding. He has studied housing and town-planning movements in various parts of Europe, where he is widely recognized as a foremost authority. A large number of places in various states might well paraphrase the familiar epitaph of Sir Christopher Wren; for the visitor has only to look about him to find enduring monuments to the memory and to the artistic achievements of John Nolen.

ALBERT SHAW.

NEW YORK,
JANUARY, 1927.

NEW TOWNS FOR OLD

NEW TOWNS FOR OLD

I

PLANNING THE SMALL COMMUNITY

INDUSTRIAL AND SOCIAL TENDENCIES TOWARDS LESSER POPULATION CENTERS

THE steadily increasing attention shown to every influence affecting the improvement of civic life is a notable attitude of American interest, both public and personal. Newspapers devote entire pages to outlining a new plan for the city, commissions study transportation problems, the harbors and the highways, committees consider further development of recreational means, of better homes, of public health. A far-reaching interest in community living forces itself to the front, due partly to the vastly greater complexity of modern life, partly to the evils resulting from the lack of skill and experience in planning and constructing American communities, but especially to the new civic spirit. Throughout the United States, civic, commercial, neighborhood and other organizations, motivated by the feeling that what is everybody's business *is* everybody's business, have undertaken to cope vigorously with the problem of making the

1

most of the opportunities available in the life of the community.

This widespread civic awakening is no vague movement, with vague and indefinite aims. It seeks to provide convenience in streets and buildings, to meet the requirements of public health, to recognize the true function and place of art, to regard obligations to future generations, to supply the imperative needs of children, to satisfy the love of nature and the desire for outdoor life. The form of this civic awakening that is most significant and promising is the recognition of the need of comprehensive planning and replanning, especially of the smaller cities.

It now looks as if the industrial future would lie with the city or town of moderate size — of about fifty thousand inhabitants, or perhaps thirty thousand as an average — rather than with the huge, million-peopled aggregations that modernity has produced. A few gigantic cities have doubtless been necessary. It is quite possible that other and more flexible conditions of organization and transportation will change the present tendency towards concentration. The garden city and garden suburb movements in Great Britain have been significant indications, as was also the remarkable attention paid to the planning of minor industrial centers in Germany before the World War — doubtless already resumed as an element of the new day of a German democracy.

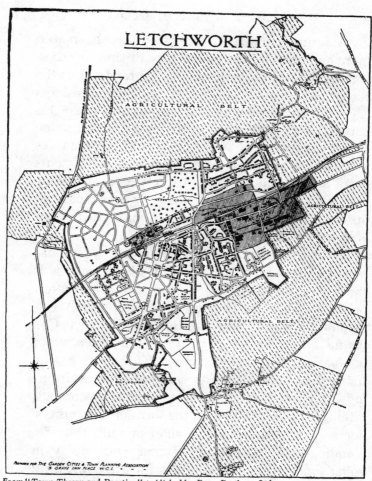

LETCHWORTH

From "Town Theory and Practice," published by Benn Brothers, Ltd.

LETCHWORTH

Map of Letchworth, England, first garden city. The original town plan
(1904) was prepared by Messrs. Parker and Unwin, Architects

3

American emphasis, also, seems to be placed more and more on the desirability of smaller cities. A most significant testimony to this tendency is the recent manifestation of Mr. Henry Ford's business sagacity, in his declared intention to diffuse his activities throughout the country by encouraging the development of minor industrial communities at favorable points, locating branch establishments there and promoting their attractions as dwelling-places for workers, and by financing municipal and other improvements necessary to make them suitable centers of production.

Another indication that in recent years has been pointing more and more in like directions is the policy of various great manufacturing enterprises—such as the General Electric Co., the Westinghouse Electric, and the General Chemical Co., for instance — to locate plants in minor centers of population all over the country. This is being done for various reasons: better social conditions, insuring a higher class of workers — more prosperous, intelligent and contented; the location of workers' homes more convenient to shop or mill, thus demanding less expenditure of time and energy in going to and fro; opportunities for the economical manufacture of various parts, for which the raw materials to be worked exist in, or are produced in, a given region, or to which special activity the class of skilled workers resident in given localities is best adapted; economies in transportation affected

OVERLOOK COLONY

Plan prepared for the General Chemical Company for a development
near Wilmington, Delaware

by manufacturing in the neighborhood of important markets.

It is therefore felt that this little volume will prove timely, devoted as it mainly is to concrete instances of, and certain recent results from, the planning of comparatively small communities. It has been written in response to an evident demand for information about what has been accomplished in these directions under intelligent consideration of the various problems involved.

Questions of this sort must, of course, be regarded in liberal perspective, so to speak. Modern circumstances are anything but rigid. We have but to look at transportation conditions to see this. An eminent authority in transportation once remarked that in planning for railroad development one could look ahead intelligently for not more than twenty-five years, so many unforeseen factors being almost certain to change the situation.

Transportation problems are basic considerations for all community planning. When modern conditions became dynamic and began to rebuild the world, the start was made in terms of transportation. First came the turnpikes (foreshadowed in an age long past by the road systems of the Roman Empire), and then the waterways, canals with animal traction, followed by a wide use of rivers, lakes and oceans in steam navigation. Next came the railways, successively developed under animal traction, steam locomotives, electric trac-

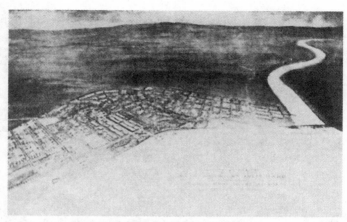

AMERICAN FALLS, IDAHO

Plan prepared by Russell V. Black. Ample space has been devoted to parks, playgrounds, and public-building sites. The streets are of economical widths and arrangement. The development is regulated by zoning and reinforced by land contract restrictions.

KINGSPORT, TENNESSEE
An industrial town founded to make business for a railroad

STREET SCENE IN AMHERST, MASSACHUSETTS

STREET SCENE IN COLORADO SPRINGS, COLORADO

tion. All these things have been of paramount influence in the location and growth of population centers.

In the development of these centers the most constant factor has been the necessity for planning their internal thoroughfares to meet the needs of local circulation. First the advent of electric traction by trolley lines, and later the marvelous development of the motor vehicle with the internal combustion engine, showed that highway planning must be changed to meet the new conditions, with correspondingly revolutionary changes in construction. Long-distance bus and truck lines are now extending in all directions, flexible and elastic, presenting ever-varying economic problems; and, in addition, the average American family owns its means for personal transportation. We are now in the early stages of transit by air routes, with the prospect of commensurate changes in community conditions. It looks as if this new form of traffic, with its demand for suitable landing-places and accommodations, would at no distant day bring new elements into play for town planners, who will be called upon to consider the shaping of communities to such needs.

Progress of this sort indicates the importance of maintaining a liberal-mindedness in regard to prospective demands. Yet it should be kept in mind that when a community has been well planned in the light of existing conditions there is little danger that the work done will be rendered obsolete by the advent of unforeseen factors, however revolutionary. A town that has been properly shaped for conditions as they are can be better adapted to new circumstances than one that has not.

The attractiveness of city life as against life in the country has long been an irresistible force in the building up of the huge urban populations of the present age. The fascination of feeling one's self a part of a vast whole, the incessant movement, the excitement, the spectacular aspects, have often determined the choice of residence. The balance is now turning in favor of the smaller urban unit. Even for rural regions, most of the modern conveniences and instruments for enjoyment, formerly peculiar to the city, have been made available. The telephone, for instance, has freed the country districts from their isolation; the central graded school, with free conveyance of distant pupils over good roads by motor traction, has supplanted the " little red schoolhouse." Electricity has brought power and convenience, until it seems as if life were everywhere being made almost alarmingly uniform and standardized. Good roads have made the automobile ubiquitous, changing a day's travel to one of an hour, bringing the city to the country, and the country to the city.

In the way of comfortable, orderly and pleasurable existence the smaller city community today enjoys almost all the advantages that were once to be had only under metropolitan conditions. The perfected phonograph and radio have made the best (and the worst) of music available to every household. The most artistic films can be seen in the small-town motion-picture houses. Like conditions hold true, or are being realized, in almost every field of art. In a great metropolis how minute a fraction of the entire public can ever enjoy the exclusive, high-class entertainments, such as the grand opera! The lesser the population of a community, the greater the proportion that can enjoy such things. As compared with such repugnant factors as the rush hours, the indecent crowding in subway jams and blockades, the congestion of street traffic, the slums, the vermin that invade even the better districts, the crime, how superior are living conditions in the small city or town, where the air is clean and the beautiful country lies near at hand!

Even with every effort made for improving the unsatisfactory aspects of great cities, the weight and permanence of their very size make it impossible to change them for the better as it is possible to change small towns. Comprehensive planning, especially with our restricted charters and the hampering laws of our states, can have only narrowly limited influence on larger places, relieving only the worst civic conditions, ameliorating merely the most acute forms of congestion. Wide, many-sided, imaginative planning, so far as very large American cities are concerned, must be confined for the present mainly to the extension of those cities, and to the betterment of what are really separate communities on the outskirts. Yet, even within rigid outlines, there are many large cities that are availing themselves of great opportunities in improving water frontage, in grouping public buildings, in widening main streets, providing for transportation in twentieth-century fashion, and making adequate and accessible areas for recreation.

With the smaller cities — cities with a population ranging from twenty-five hundred to one hundred thousand — the case is simpler. Comprehensive planning or replanning may be to them of far-reaching and permanent service. There is scarcely anything in the smaller places that cannot be changed. In these cities, for example, railroad approaches can be set right; grade crossings eliminated; waterfronts redeemed for commerce or recreation, or both; open spaces acquired even in partly built-up sections; a satisfactory street plan carried out and adequate main thoroughfares established, by cutting new streets if necessary, and regrouping public buildings; and a park system, composed of well-distributed and well-balanced public grounds, definitely outlined for gradual and systematic development. Residential districts can be helped to be attractive and delightful by the determination of housing standards and the prevention of undesirable building, and by street standardization in uses, widths and materials. No argument is necessary to convince the most skeptical that a community which offers the most comforts and conveniences, from a living and business standpoint, is the most naturally advertised by its inhabitants and consequently becomes magnetic to others.

It is to be seen, in the enumeration of these various ways for improvements, that city planning is not necessarily a method to make a "City Beautiful." It does not aim to beautify in a superficial sense. Its purposes are fundamental. It tries consciously to provide those facilities that are for the common good, that concern everybody; it seeks to save waste due to unskillful and planless procedure. By doing things at the right time and in the right way, comprehensive city planning saves far more than it costs. Any city planning that is worthy of the name is concerned primarily with use and secondarily with beauty. But if there is a reasonably high standard in providing the useful improvements of a town or city, it will invariably be found that utility and beauty go hand in hand and are virtually inseparable.

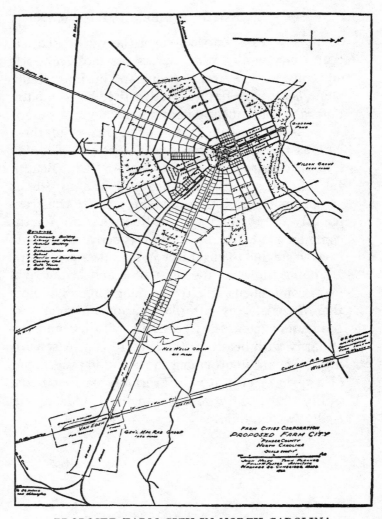

PROPOSED FARM CITY IN NORTH CAROLINA

Plan for a ten-thousand-acre tract. The purpose of the farm city is to provide means whereby owners of small farms may, by the practice of scientifically directed, intensified and diversified agriculture, supply themselves with good living and a profitable occupation. The community center and industrial section will bring the social and economic advantages that are usually associated only with life in the larger cities.

II
TOWN DEVELOPMENT
Historic and Modern Examples

Intelligent growth is the ideal for the community, as for the individual. It now seems possible to approach this ideal in a remarkable degree. A vital question of today is how to achieve its realization in yet greater fullness. There can be no one answer. It must vary according to the nature of the subject. It is not a new question, although in its present aspects it involves distinctively modern problems. From time immemorial, perhaps ever since civilization began, communities have been built according to plan and have also been developed at random. Yet the worst results have come from stereotyped planning, especially on uneven ground. Of the two, it is often preferable for a community to grow at random, provided such growth has the guidance of shore lines, topography or other natural features.

Inhabitants of our raw, mushroom towns and cities are inclined to hold that with all their faults of rectangularity they at least have the saving grace of modernity and up-to-dateness. Yet they are dead wrong. The ancient Chinese cities were rectangular. Nearly all of the old Latin-American

13

cities since the days of Columbus are of the same design. Philadelphia was laid out in that way, and the example infected all the westward country, being easy to do, requiring no brains.

The random growths, or apparently random, of the mediæval towns of Europe, as well as those of New England, are far better than the definitely intentional yet badly planned communities of nearly all the rest of this country. New York at first grew spontaneously under its Dutch founders and their early English successors. But when it began to spread it adopted a more formal plan, little more than that of an ineffectual gridiron. As soon as the great city reached into the more northerly sections, with their corrugated contours and rocky ledges, it was like squashing the gridiron through irregular masses of dough down to a stated level, requiring everything above to be dug or blasted off and carted away at enormous cost. The acme of absurdity came when this sort of plan was adopted for San Francisco, with its sand hills and steep slopes. Gelett Burgess, in a novel devoted to life in San Francisco, puts to good use his architectural training by a scathing account of what a splendid opportunity was thus lost in failing to take advantage of one of the most beautiful city sites in the world.

Proverbially, Boston was built along the tortuous lines of paths made by cows passing to and from their pastures. But careful investigations have

From "San Francisco" by Joseph Pennell

SACRAMENTO STREET, SAN FRANCISCO, CALIFORNIA

"O'Farrell bound the city that was to be forever to a gridiron of right-angled streets and blocks of parallelograms. He knew no compromise. His streets took their straight and narrow way, up hill and down dale, without regard to grade or expense. Unswerving was their rectitude. Their angles were exactly ninety degrees of his compass, north and south, east and west. Where might have been entrancingly beautiful terraces, rising avenue above avenue to the heights, preserving the master view of the continent, now the streets, committed to his plan, are hacked out of the earth and rock, precipitous, inaccessible, grotesque. So sprawls the fey, leaden-colored town over its dozen hills, its roads mounting to the sky or diving to the sea."—*Gelett Burgess.*

COHASSET, MASSACHUSETTS
Old New England common

LEXINGTON, MASSACHUSETTS
Old New England common

shown a development more deliberate; various rambling streets were built along the old waterfronts, remaining when the shore lines were gradually extended outward by the " made land " needed for expansion. Other streets followed natural contours along lines of least resistance, with correspondingly easy gradients; they are correspondingly easy to move around in. Then, as more new land was made, streets were well and definitely planned.

Down to the present, this sort of spontaneous development has characterized almost the entire metropolitan growth of the city, with generally good radial lines throughout, so that when the Metropolitan Improvements Commission came to study the problems of a metropolitan plan for Greater Boston, they found a strikingly desirable basis of natural growth to work upon. The obstacles to be overcome proved vastly less formidable than those presented in the great rectangular cities, where diagonal and radial lines must be cut through at enormous cost if modern traffic circulation is to be accommodated. It should be remembered that the straight streets of old Philadelphia are not only as narrow as the rambling streets of old Boston, but much less convenient in getting from point to point.

Like conditions hold true concerning the smaller communities of New England, which so largely grew bit by bit from beginnings of wayside settlements along winding roads, meeting here and there to form crossroads at points where a few country stores multiplied into business districts. At such points training-fields, village greens, or commons where the cows were pastured, often came into being, and meeting-houses or churches, town halls, perhaps courthouses, and later schools and public libraries, formed civic centers of an admirable sort. Mills were built at stream-sides, railroads and trolley lines came in on good gradients, and flourishing industries, frequently highly specialized and again manifold in kind, were established. Towns became large communities, often considerable cities. As they expanded their growth was planned for, too often without intelligent foresight, but not infrequently serving fairly well their practical purposes, and of good effect.

The tourist in New England encounters numerous examples of this type of growth, all with a sort of family resemblance but presenting a considerable diversity as well, and possessing a particularly individual charm. It is worth remembering that Metropolitan Boston is made up of a gradual expansion and reintegration of small old New England towns whose beginnings may be traced today in some centers once locally called " the village " — as in Old Cambridge about Harvard Square, in Roxbury, Chelsea, Dorchester, Watertown, and what is still known as Brookline Village. The unique quality of the New England village has been described in a little masterpiece of prose, a fragment found among the papers of the senior Frederick Law Olmsted by his son.

The diversity of the New England town, both in plan and aspect, appears significantly when we compare the typical examples common along the Atlantic coast on the one hand, and on the other those in the central sections along the Connecticut valley and in neighboring regions. The populations of the coast-belt are, as a rule, of random and spontaneous growth, with accretions that represent more or less deliberate, but fragmentary, planning, as the communities gradually expanded into the industrial towns that nearly all of them have become. In other instances we have the crossroads type, the roads intersecting irregularly and the village clustering about the neighborhood. Where the roads come together there is often a small, irregular open space. The central " squares " in the Greater Boston communities of Medford and Malden, and of Brookline and Cambridge, are typical instances. Such developments are frequently of quite picturesque effect, with civic centers — public or otherwise monumental buildings of various sorts — characterizing the neighborhood.

A beautiful example of such a center is offered by the old town of Reading, Massachusetts, where a common of the rural type is faced by a parish church, of good Colonial design, and other public buildings. Wakefield, an adjacent town, is notable for the admirable use made of its opportunity for

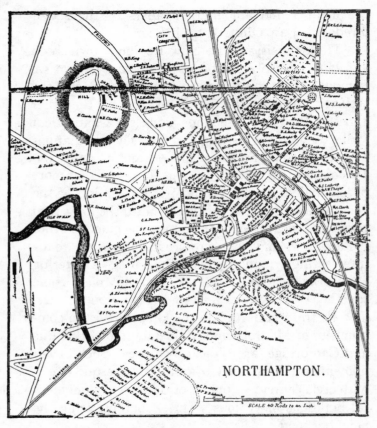

MAP OF NORTHAMPTON, MASSACHUSETTS
An example of random but often intelligent town development

18

development, in a fine central open space of formal
design, connecting with the picturesquely improved
shores of a large lake beyond.

The Boston neighborhood gives many other
comparatively recent examples of the felicitous use
of opportunities to develop beautiful features,
offered by such natural circumstances as rivers,
brooks, ponds, lakes and other elements of landscape, perhaps long and sadly neglected until some-
body became aware of their fine possibilities. Winchester has been particularly fortunate in the way
in which it has made a farsighted use of such
opportunities—the splendid results of property values enhanced through high-class residential attractiveness encouraging a scheme of planning for
intelligent growth. Arlington, Belmont and Lexington deserve specific mention in this category:
Arlington for its civic acquisitions, of a town hall
and a public library, generous gifts from a public-
spirited citizen; Belmont for its civic center — like
Winchester's, of informal type; and Lexington
for its historic common, featuring a monumental
"Minute-Man." There are, indeed, so many admirable instances of these informal developments from
random origins that it is hoped that these specific
examples may not seem invidious.

The type of old town that characterizes the
Connecticut valley and central New England in
general is distinctively formal. Just how it had
its origin is not clear. Perhaps it had an English

Drawn by J. W. Barber—Engraved by S. E. Brown, Boston.

NORTHAMPTON, MASSACHUSETTS

Old print of central part of Northampton, Massachusetts, showing courthouse,
First Congregational Church, and other buildings

20

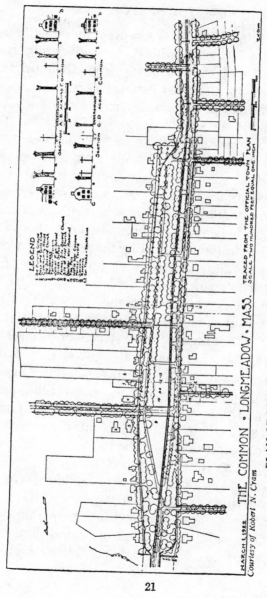

PLAN OF THE COMMON AT LONGMEADOW, MASSACHUSETTS

A fine example of a broad, open space, three hundred feet between buildings, with beautiful trees
A forerunner of the modern boulevard and parkway

prototype; possibly it represents a more deliberate intention, which came with the secondary migration of Pilgrim and Puritan, away from their primary settlements on the coast into the rich and even, or gently undulating, intervale lands along the Connecticut. At all events, it is significant that this type furnishes the first instances of conscious town planning, according to a definite idea, that we have in the British colonies of that day. Its fundamental element is an exceedingly broad main street, perhaps two hundred feet or more in width. Very sensibly the roadway itself occupies only the width needed for traffic; the rest of the space is devoted to turf, except the sidewalks. Quite commonly there is a quadruple row of the noble elms that are the pride and glory of New England. Along this street has been built the town as a long belt of population. In its growth, minor parallel streets or intersecting ways may have been laid out. Towns like Hadley and Longmeadow in Massachusetts, and Glastonbury in Connecticut, extend for long reaches parallel with the general course of the river. Such broad streets, with their beautiful plantations, may be considered forerunners of the modern boulevard or parkway in its American form.

This type is not infrequently combined with the crossroads idea in a formal regularity, the intersecting way being a thoroughfare of perhaps corresponding width, or at least of liberal dimension. Pittsfield, Massachusetts, is a notable example. In the main thoroughfare here, the central portion near the city center has been enclosed as a common, with roadways on either side. The other principal street, intersecting it at right angles, is of lesser but still generous width. Pittsfield has expanded into an important industrial city; and so far as they go its two great intersecting thoroughfares admirably meet modern traffic conditions. But circulation would be more conveniently served were the rectangular plan modified by diagonals from the center. Farther out, however, this need is in a measure met by roads running variously along the lines of least resistance into the country, in the indeterminate New England fashion that contrasts so pleasantly, as well as conveniently, with the rigid insistence upon " section line " courses which binds Western regions to extravagant wastefulness of time and energy.

The type exemplified by Pittsfield is clearly akin to that of the " county seat " plan common to the West—which, moreover, is somewhat related to the central plaza motive of Spanish America, except that, instead of occupying the square itself, as the courthouse almost invariably does (and if not the courthouse, the city hall), in the plaza scheme the square is left open, either smoothly paved as a sort of forum or formally treated in garden fashion. This unoccupied square motive is preferable. The civic or other monumental buildings frame the plaza, with immense economy in construction as well as

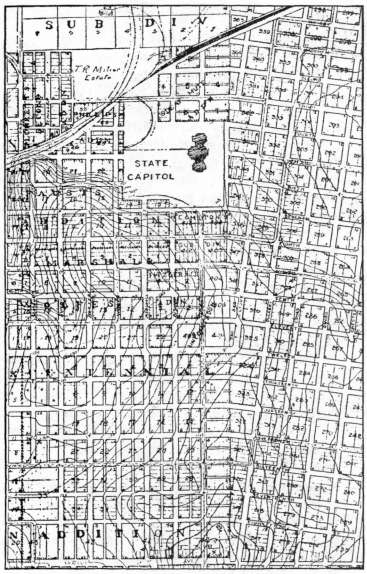

Typical gridiron plan of a section of an American city laid out
regardless of topography and other features

a correspondingly greater architectural effectiveness. In this connection it cannot be too strongly
reiterated that the radial-arteries method has vast
advantages over an indolent rectangularity.

It is of interest to note here the fact that the
central New England type of town is also a feature of the second-oldest community of the Massachusetts Bay Colony, the large industrial city of
Lynn — Lynn Common being a long central reserved space similar to that of Pittsfield, in a wide
street with two roadways. Had this been a feature
of the ancient town, it might have indicated a derivation from English examples. But since the neighborhood is of much later settlement, this feature
perhaps represents reflex influence from the Connecticut valley. Hingham in Massachusetts offers
a similar example at Hingham Center; Fall River,
also, in its Eight-Rod Way.

Well-considered town planning must bear in
mind not only the importance of local and regional
circumstance in the way of topography, climate
and other factors of environment, but the more
impalpable elements of tradition, historical character and social custom. While it can be eclectic and
borrow discreetly of the finest wherever found, it
should take regard of local character in its best and
most typical manifestations. A locality must be
studied primarily with reference to itself, so that
the plan may represent its best self-expression.
What might be well for New England might not

be at all in keeping with the Middle West, the trans-Missouri plains, the arid Southwest or the coast regions of the Pacific. Especially should this be heeded when it comes to what the plan underlies, the architectural expression of it and of its social character. California offers an admirable example in this respect. The Spanish traditions that so interestingly color its history have been respected and treasured; their expression and development in richer and more ample aspects have proved so admirably suited to climatic conditions and the surrounding floral beauty as to have immensely enriched the charm of that part of the country and correspondingly heightened its attractiveness. In general, the specific quality of Mediterranean cultures is so thoroughly in harmony with the regional character not only of California but of our entire Southwest from Texas on, derived from both climate and tradition, that we feel it manifestly in better keeping there than any derivation from the landscape and architectural attributes of our mother country, or of northern Europe, as transmitted to our Atlantic seaboard.

In the early years, the differences in regional architecture developed from definite foundations, not only as the expression of social life and traditions, but as the result of climate and the availability of certain building materials. The long roof of the shingled New England farmhouse was set low and sloping against the harsh north wind, and the outbuildings were attached protectingly to the main structure. The stucco tropical dwelling, with its inner patio for shade and privacy, is the natural evolution of a life whose consideration is with heat and not with cold.

Attempts to adjust extreme types to their opposite localities are valueless and shortsighted, and such foreign importations despoil a community of its opportunity for finest self-expression. Each of the United States still has the possibility of placing emphasis upon charms and inheritances peculiar to itself alone. Nature gave each an environment differentiated from the others not by artificial lines on the map, but by glorious innate differences. Their best attractions, their best advertisements, lie in intensifying these differences, whether expressed in food, habits, or architecture. In no other American setting can the candle-lighting on Christmas Eve be as quaint and picturesque as on Beacon Hill, can Easter service be as impressive as on Mt. Rubidoux, or can a Flower Fair be as vivacious and yet as aristocratic as in Mt. Vernon Square, Baltimore.

The several examples of planning for the improvement or the development of comparatively small communities considered in this volume, in their diversity of subject and local environment, are typical of the social and economic aspects involved. Kingsport, Tennessee, for instance, is a most notable example of what must go on in the

Southern states in ever-increasing degree to meet
the peculiar necessities of that section. Although
the South, up to within a generation, has been
socially and industrially the most backward section
of the Union, its more advanced public has to a
most remarkable extent become alive to the importance of intelligent community planning. This is
manifestly because the extraordinary richness of
that section in natural resources is leading to its
rapid development. Work like that done at Kingsport will be in demand in innumerable instances, if
the necessities of communities similarly destined to
spring *de novo* out of the new economic conditions
of the South are to be intelligently provided for —
as in Kingsport, a town built to order purely for the
sake of providing traffic for a new railroad. It
shows admirably the advantage of starting from a
clean slate.

Another Southern instance of extensive planning for a new community is that of Myers Park.
Although corporately a separate entity, Myers Park
was created to meet the demand for a high-class
residential suburb adjacent to the old city of Charlotte, North Carolina. Another newly created residential suburb, but of a different character, is Union
Park Gardens, adjacent to Wilmington, Delaware.
This undertaking is a capital example of the many
new communities, or new city quarters, created to
meet the imperative housing demand occasioned by
large industries, such as shipbuilding, or the manu-

facture of munitions and other supplies, under the emergencies of the World War. Fortunately, these large housing projects were intelligently planned and of substantial construction, so that for the greater part they have remained permanent assets in the regions where they were located. They were elements of no little consequence in meeting the needs of the widespread housing famine that became most acute after the war.

Yet another community built to order is the industrial residential village of Kistler, Pennsylvania, established to meet the needs of a large manufacturing plant by providing comfortable homes for its workmen, close at hand.

The foregoing illustrate the problems presented where new communities, or additions to old communities, are planned for. The remaining two instances are of a different order, involving problems of reconstruction and modification which, like remodelling an old house, are often more perplexing to meet. These are devoted to two old towns, or townships, in one of the oldest and most intensively developed sections of the Union — Walpole and Cohasset, both in Massachusetts. The two are of contrasting character. Walpole is territorially a large township containing three distinct villages. The region was at first agricultural, but has gradually developed industrially as the seat of large manufacturing enterprises growing primarily out of the water-power of a small river. Cohasset is an old New England seacoast town, originally maritime in its interests, but long in favor for high-class summer residence. As an outer suburb of Greater Boston it has a permanent population of commuters and their families. Yet other types are illustrated in the exceptionally important new Cincinnati suburb for industrial workers, the town of Mariemont; and in Venice, a new town in Florida.

It is notable that in all these instances there has been an individual initiative, appreciative of the benefits that come with intelligent planning for community development. This is particularly significant in the case of the two old communities, indicating that in hundreds of other such towns and cities throughout the country some one person, public-spirited and alive to opportunities for improvement and growth, often has but to take the first step in order to set the ball rolling. Under such an awakening out of lethargic indifference, many an old town and somnolent little city may step forward into new life and prosperity.

III

RESHAPING AN INDUSTRIAL TOWN

WALPOLE, MASSACHUSETTS

WALPOLE, nineteen miles from Boston, might be termed a satellite of that New England metropolis. It has a population of six thousand, five hundred and eight and has made an increase of nineteen and one-half per cent since 1920. It is therefore progressive in population tendencies. How far it has coupled this with a town-planning program will here be shown. It was in 1912 that an official committee of the town government took up the question of civic improvement. A body of five members, headed by Charles Sumner Bird, Jr., as chairman, was formed. From the first the committee took its duties seriously. In consequence it has become something even more than a Walpole body, for its methods and efforts have been studied and adopted in a score of communities throughout the land.[1] It began first with an expert survey of the town and district — an analysis of civic conditions and possibilities. Out of this work grew the official town plan, a schedule to be followed in future devel-

[1] For a detailed account of Walpole's planned development, see "Town Planning for Small Communities," by Charles Sumner Bird, Jr., 1917.

opment. The adoption of such a plan for future growth, as a permanent policy in directing all development, was far-reaching, altering not only the growth of this old Massachusetts town, but its organization and administration.

Walpole until recent years was primarily an agricultural community, its population scattered over a wide area devoted to farming, and attending to pastures and wood lots. But the Neponset River was in its midst, offering power to industries; because of this fact an industrial transformation has occurred. First came saw-mills and grist-mills, then factories; and, concurrently, local trading coincident with more residents.

The community which for many miles was formerly termed " Walpole " is now centralized at three points: Walpole Center, East Walpole, South Walpole. Walpole Center may be said to be the actual center of the neighborhood; it contains the town hall, the common, the principal stores and the best railroad service. East Walpole is the next in importance. This section is the focal point of the factories. It is also a terminal of trolley lines connecting with the elevated railroad of Boston. South Walpole, though small, is an important district to the south of Walpole Center. It is a good residential area, and contains the shops of the Bird Machine Company. This district is on a route which takes through traffic from Lowell, Fitchburg, Framingham and vicinity, to Foxboro, Mansfield, Attleboro, Taunton, New Bedford, Fall River and the Cape.

The change in the character of Walpole from agricultural to industrial is shown by the increase of two hundred and forty-nine per cent in the foreign-born population from 1900 to 1910, and the decrease of over thirty-two per cent in the native-born element. The industrial development is strikingly illustrated by the figures of the Massachusetts Bureau of Statistics, giving an increase of capital investment in industrial concerns from two million to seven million dollars. The biggest increase has been since 1910. The changes in the neighborhood have taken place without an adequate increase of housing. Many workers have therefore been obliged to seek homes elsewhere. The adoption of a comprehensive town plan has been an incentive to a broader town development, making provision for residential needs as well as other incidentals of commercial expansion — incidentals which are in reality indispensable for a continuous and efficient prosperity.

STEPS TOWARDS A BETTER TOWN

In the Walpole town plan the needs of the three divisions of the area were considered in detail, and an attempt made not only to unify their interests, but to take into account the regional requirements. At Walpole Center a new location for a proposed

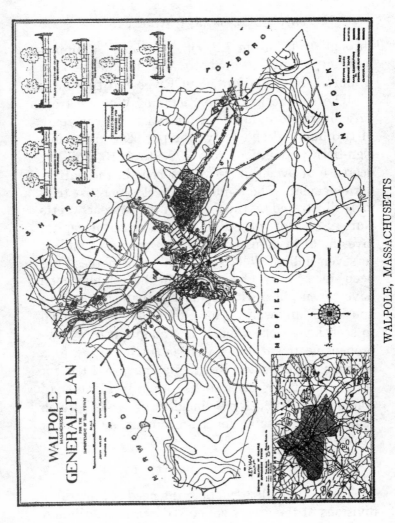

WALPOLE, MASSACHUSETTS

General plan for improvement of town, with a key map and typical street sections

town hall was made, at the junction of Main and Common streets — a most commanding site. The widening and straightening of Main Street, and also of Stone and West streets, are likewise part of this new scheme for a civic center. The common, as a community pivot, came into its own again and was redesigned with a view to a better relationship to the surrounding streets. A new post-office site and a new fire-station site were included in the better street planning. These changes opened up the possibilities of the Mill Pond, which was made the central feature of a park in connection with a chain system of river reservation. The railway station was given a new location with better accessibility to the town. Both the park and the railway station were brought into alignment with the plan for the civic center.

INDUSTRIAL LIFE HUMANIZED

While there are some factories at Walpole Center, East Walpole is even more distinctively an industrial section. The factories now located there, together with the highways leading to Norwood, Canton, Stoughton, Sharon and Medfield, make it an important focal point.

East Walpole is a good example of what can be done in a small community to make life pleasanter for the people, and to solve in practical ways the local town-planning problems. Definite mention should be made of the improvement in the layout,

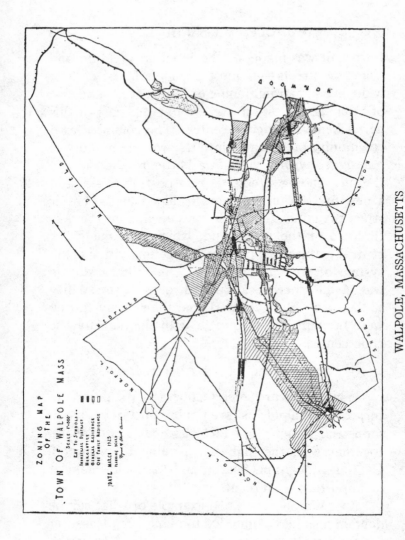

WALPOLE, MASSACHUSETTS

Zoning map of the town, showing industrial, mercantile, general residence and one-family residence districts

arrangement and construction of East Walpole Square. The traffic situation was carefully studied and plans were made for a safe and orderly construction of sidewalks, curbs and road pavements. Provision was made also for seats and planting.

Home building and home ownership are fundamental problems in every community and they are of special importance and difficulty in industrial centers. In East Walpole the importance of the home has been wisely recognized. The Walpole Home Building Company, Inc., was created with the single purpose of serving the communities surrounding the East Walpole and Norwood mills. Its principal function was to help the people to build and to own the right kind of homes. Specifically the company does the following things: it rents houses, insisting that its tenants maintain the standards of a worth-while community; it seeks to find lands on which owners may build; it offers every service to prospective home owners to build judiciously. As far as possible it provides community conveniences, such as coal at reasonable prices and clean photoplays, and interests itself in all movements for community betterment. The Walpole Home Building Company, Inc., is not a profit-making organization. It meets expenses but it is not a money-maker.

Specifically, the Walpole Home Building Company, Inc., provides the following: lots for sale at prices that are fair — one hundred and fifty dollars to five hundred dollars in good locations; convenient methods for making loans on first and second mortgages; time payments on principal arranged so that such payments can be easily met; a method for the disposition of the property in case of removal; and opportunity for securing good plans and in other ways facilitating home building.

The most notable achievement in East Walpole, however, is the creation of Francis William Park, and the adjacent athletic field. Francis William Park is a beautiful tract of seventy acres created and endowed for the people of Walpole by Mr. and Mrs. Charles Sumner Bird in memory of their son, Francis William Bird. This park is located between Washington and Pleasant streets in East Walpole. The main entrance, on Washington Street, is built with seam-faced granite. It has an inviting and restful appearance, suggesting the quiet and beauty that lie beyond. On the bronze tablets at the entrance are the following inscriptions:

FRANCIS WILLIAM PARK
CREATED AND ENDOWED BY
CHARLES SUMNER BIRD   ANNA CHILD BIRD
FOR THE
PEOPLE OF WALPOLE
A. D. 1925

FRANCIS WILLIAM PARK
DEDICATED TO THE MEMORY OF
FRANCIS WILLIAM BIRD
1881 – 1918

ENTRANCE GATES, FRANCIS WILLIAM PARK, EAST WALPOLE, MASSACHUSETTS

Courtesy of C. L. Smith & Company

VIEWS IN FRANCIS WILLIAM PARK, EAST WALPOLE

When the work of planning Francis William Park was begun, the following statement was drawn up by the landscape architect with the approval of Mr. Bird:

" The general character of the park landscape should be that of the New England meadows and hillsides at their best. The broad meadows and open spaces across which would be wide, uninterrupted views, would be contrasted with the border tree plantings and the groves of oak, maple and pine on the hillsides. These hilltop plantings will tend to increase the apparent height of the knolls and make the present attractive topography of the park even more pronounced. The stream valleys offer a wonderful opportunity for interesting features, the life and movement of the brook being again in contrast with the broad quiet of the fields: while in the course of the brook itself variety and interest can be had where the running stream changes to the stillness of the pools.

" The keynote in the development of the park should be dignity and simplicity, doing away with large formal areas of elaborate construction, but at the same time having the park full of charm and appeal. Specimen trees and collections of uncommon trees and shrubs, labeled for those unfamiliar with them, would be of educational value and general interest. A small, simple flower garden or perennial border would also be of value, and tend to develop a sentiment for similar planting on home lots. Interest in the park can further be increased by well-designed bridges, light standards, and other utilitarian objects and by the introduction of a

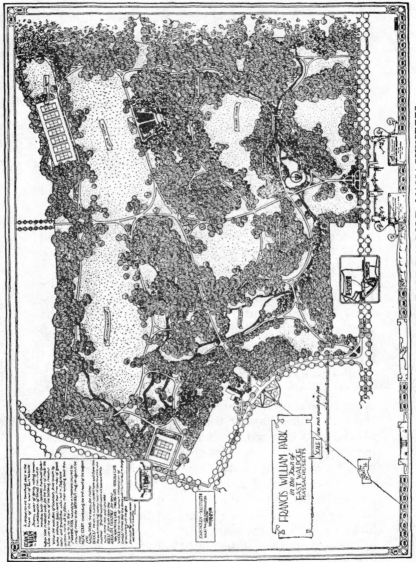

FRANCIS WILLIAM PARK, EAST WALPOLE, MASSACHUSETTS

40

number of special features or curios, such as a Japanese stone lantern, stone bench or similar object.

" A park should be made for use, and the measure of its success can be gauged by the number of people it serves. Recreation should be thought of in its broadest sense, and facilities provided for the entertainment and enjoyment of young and old, men, women and children. Broad fields have been planned for general games, pageants, drills and big gatherings."

Every feature of Francis William Park has been carefully studied and planned, and the scheme as a whole has been constantly in mind. One of the principal features is the swimming pool. An attractive concrete dam and spillway have been built across the small brook which flows through the grounds, resulting in a pool of irregular and natural outlines two hundred feet long and one hundred and eight feet wide, concrete-lined throughout and floored with a layer of sand. Large rocks and natural boulders with open beaches between are so arranged as to give the place a cool, pleasant, seaside appearance. In the center a spray of town water is sent up by a fountain, supplementing the waters of the brook and adding charm to the scene. A well-built bathhouse nearby furnishes accommodations for over two hundred bathers. The construction and layout are attractive and in some respects unique. Both above and below the bathhouse two seamfaced granite bridges cross the stream, and directly in front of the entrance to the bathhouse a causeway leads across the shallow water at the head of the pool. The bridges, ten in all, constitute a special feature. Seven types of architecture and construction have been used: seam-faced granite, rustic stone, modern wood, brick, iron, concrete, and Japanese wood.

The park is made convenient of access by eight entrances. There are also four service gates. At each entrance a granolithic walk of interesting color and design winds its way over mounds and meadow, crossing other walks and gravel pathways, and furnishing the park with a convenient system of circulation. The grading and planting have been given particular attention. Thirty large trees have been moved into the park and great numbers of young trees and shrubs have already been planted. The lawns, furnishing broad, restful, open spaces, have been worked out with great care. Other features in the final development and construction of Francis William Park are now under way.

In order that Francis William Park might be more perfect and more restful as a park, the donor has provided a tract of about seven acres nearby for use as a separate athletic field. This area has been carefully graded and laid out to meet the highest specifications of a first-class professional athletic field for major sports. It is located at the corner of East and June streets, East Walpole; it has been carefully fenced, and is equipped with a good grandstand for spectators. All of the grading nearby has been done in such a way as to afford additional convenient places for watching the games.

SOUTH WALPOLE: A FUTURE HOME TOWN

One's home town might mean a good deal more if it were actually a " home " town. With this idea as the objective, a redesign of the central portion of South Walpole has been undertaken. This section has easy connection by bus lines with Walpole Center and Foxboro, and is a pleasant and convenient residential district. Its highways also connect it with Mansfield, Attleboro and Plainville. The present town green is shown preserved, while the adjoining streets are harmoniously treated in connection therewith. An excellent position for a public building was given the new fire station, at the junction of Neponset and Summer streets. The railroad station has been moved to the south side of Summer Street, near the railroad crossing. The most striking feature of the plans is the conservation of the natural beauty of the locality. The Mill Pond, a piece of slack water in the Neponset River, becomes part of the River Valley Park System, so that at this point the adjacent land is laid out in a manner which brings the latent attractiveness of water into an agreeable relationship with the surrounding district.

NEW PARK RESERVATIONS

The wisdom of acquiring new park reservations was realized. The ponds, brooks and natural scen-

ery of the Walpole district, now owned by private
individuals and liable at any time to be diverted to
industrial use, have been thoroughly surveyed and
a program of conservation formulated. As the population increases, these open areas will become
more and more valuable for recreation and pleasure.
Industrial expansion should mean the progress and
prosperity of the people. Yet, at the same time, it
is likely to be a detriment, unless its development is
controlled and directed into proper channels.

With this point in view was laid out a definite
policy to acquire the valley of the Neponset River
for a park reservation. The river flows through
the town from end to end, passing through the three
centers of population. As the dominant landscape
feature, its contemplated acquisition by the public
authorities is in line with the best practice of modern town planning. It is proposed to acquire at
least one hundred feet on either bank of the stream
as a parkway; in addition, at all the three centers
of Walpole the plan makes ample provision for extensive park tracts. Morey's, Diamond and Clark's
ponds are all beautiful little sheets of water with
well-wooded shores. Stetson's Pond is also of particular beauty, with heavily wooded land to the
west; this extends to Morey's Pond and is almost
an unbroken forest. Treated as a forest reservation
this area would eventually be a financial asset as
well as valuable for public recreation purposes.
The brook valley above Clark's Pond is included

FRANCIS WILLIAM PARK, EAST WALPOLE
Swimming pool

SWIMMING POOL, EAST WALPOLE

Courtesy of C. L. Smith & Company

BRIDGE, FRANCIS WILLIAM PARK, EAST WALPOLE

in the park system, forming a link of extension into the systems of neighboring towns. In the plan proposed for Walpole Center the low-lying land between Stone, East and Diamond streets is transformed into a public park; Powder House Hill, now a very unsightly place, is converted into a desirable public viewpoint.

TOWN-PLANNING ACHIEVEMENTS

Walpole not only has adopted a comprehensive plan for its development but has made serious and successful efforts to carry it into effect. Since March, 1914, when the plan was adopted, notable steps in a definite program have been made. It was first determined that all plans for new streets and other physical improvements must meet with the approval of the Town Planning Committee. This gave control to the committee, advancing it from the status of a merely consulting body.

Following this action several state laws were adopted, which were essential to local planning and development. These were:

(1) The Betterment Act, authorizing the planning of future improvements and the preparation of street plans establishing grades and building lines. This act prevents the evils of indiscriminate transportation extension and of ill-considered building projections.

(2) The Reserve Space Act, giving power to reserve planting spaces in streets, and so forth.

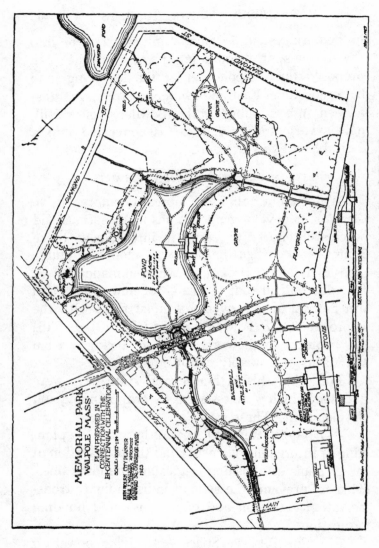

MEMORIAL PARK, WALPOLE, MASSACHUSETTS

Plan prepared in connection with the bi-centennial celebration of the town

This law allows street reserves to be made now in anticipation of eventual public use.

(3) The Concurrent Jurisdiction Act, giving to the town equality of jurisdiction with the county, as regards through roads and bridges.

(4) The Tenement-House Act, prohibiting the erection of " three deckers " (multiple dwellings of three stories).

By using the powers accorded to them by these state acts, the town immediately safeguarded itself against many future depredations, made possible great improvements, and lodged added authority and responsibility for these improvements with its Town Planning Committee. It was further resolved to devote one thousand dollars a year for five years to complete the town survey, so that full information would always be available for the improvements to be effected. In 1926 a new charter providing for the city manager of the " town engineer " plan of government was inaugurated, and at the same time zoning regulations were adopted.

On the basis of the town plan the following items represent achievement:

(1) Widening of the principal town thoroughfares — East Street, Main Street, and the automobile route from Boston to Providence.

(2) Better road rearrangements at Lewis's corner, an important but inconvenient intersection, which provides a small park.

(3) Streets surveyed and laid out: Common, High, Plain and Peach streets.

(4) Extensions of East and Common streets planned.

(5) Establishment of the parkway system begun by acquiring thirty-five acres for Central Park, in the center of the town, for a future civic-center playground and park. The town hall and Stone School are in this area, and a swimming pool maintained by the Boy Scouts.

(6) Purchase of park lands for South Walpole, adding a park area of nineteen acres to the high school, and the development of the playgrounds.

(7) Additions to the school playgrounds in all the villages.

(8) Enlarging and development of the Plimpton School grounds in connection with the Town Forest. Improvement of the Bird School grounds.

(9) Acquisition by gift of Mr. George Plimpton of the Walpole Town Forest as a wild park, providing a bird and game sanctuary and protection for the water supply.

(10) Purchase of one hundred and five acres of watershed for waterworks.

(11) New charter adopted (1924).

(12) New system of street paving from its gravel banks.

(13) Planting of trees each year on watershed.

(14) Construction of Memorial Bridge as a feature of Memorial Park; dedicated to the Soldiers, Sailors and Nurses.

(15) New swimming pool, gift of Mr. Philip R. Allen.

(16) Adoption of the Zoning By-Law providing for
use districts (industrial, mercantile, general
residence and one-family residence), and
regulating the height and area of buildings.

The movement in town planning in Walpole has
been the incentive for a unification of all social
forces for community betterment, and proposals
are on foot for vigorously carrying out many more
of the recommendations of the Town Survey and
Town Plan. Few better examples than Walpole
could be given of the advantages of town planning,
for no other small Massachusetts town has accomplished so much towards its improvement, based
upon a definite plan and program.

IV

AN INDUSTRIAL CITY BUILT TO ORDER

Kingsport, Tennessee

Kingsport, Tennessee, is in various respects one of our most remarkable American examples of modern city planning. It began as a new town. Its site, though hardly a wilderness, was an out-of-the-way agricultural region, remote from the world's activities. In 1912 the only human habitations there were two farmhouses. As late as 1915, only a few months after the outbreak of the World War, when it had started to grow in an entirely different way from the course destined for it, it was merely a small agricultural community of about nine hundred inhabitants. In four years more it had become a flourishing city of more than ten thousand people.

PURELY A MATTER OF BUSINESS

Yet, unlike so many new populations of phenomenal development that originated about that time, when armies of industrial workers were massed at various points to meet urgent demands, it was not at all a " war-baby." Kingsport became what it was simply because a new railroad, built through an undeveloped region, needed traffic. So a city was built for the sake of making business for

50

KINGSPORT

Sidewalk without roadway between groups of houses

KINGSPORT

The community house

Courtesy of Wurts Brothers   *Clinton Mackenzie, Architect*

KINGSPORT
Golf and Country Club

Courtesy of Wurts Brothers   *Clinton Mackenzie, Architect*

KINGSPORT
The Kingsport Inn

the railroad. It could have made no business, however, had the makings of business not been on hand.

The story of it all reads like a romance. In its origin Kingsport was much the sort of town that, early in the eighteen-nineties, often came into being in western Canada, when the great railway undertakings were pushing their way along the prairies and over mountain ranges, across the continent and up into the north. The railroad in question here was the Carolina, Clinchfield and Ohio, running from Spartanburg to Elkhorn City through a region in southeastern Tennessee where population was sparse and construction was costly even for that day. Fortunately the country was replete with natural wealth: coal, timber, a great variety of minerals, including sand, clay, limestone, silica, feldspar and kaolin, and other desirable raw materials. There was an excellent water-supply. It was a good agricultural country, though little developed.

Transportation had been lacking to make these things available. But all these materials were valuable for working up into a diversity of manufactured products. With the railroad built, this was made locally possible; it was manifest that, with industries once established, profitable tonnage for the railroad would be produced, while the needs of the town built as the seat of these industries would assure other new business.

The little agricultural community that with the

coming of the railroad had sprung up indicated that Kingsport was the proper site for this town. The land was favorable for building — a wide and winding valley of remarkable natural beauty, coursed by the Holston River. Important industries immediately began to establish themselves here, attracted by the favorable conditions. First came a large producer of Portland cement, building up very speedily an extensive business. Others followed, alive to the value of the clay fields and other sources of raw materials. The prospective development assured by these activities promised to be so rapid and extensive that both the railroad company and the heads of the industries decided that continued growth ought to be carefully prepared for. They had the good sense and the good taste to see that this should be done as thoroughly as possible. So the services of a town planner and of an architect were enlisted.

Fortunately the community was still in its early stages; the revision and extension of the inadequate scheme prepared by the railroad's engineers proved easily practicable to a degree that gave the town a new and substantial basis for intelligent growth. The result was the development of one of the best-planned industrial communities in the annals of modern town planning — remarkable by reason of the harmonious coöperation of several independent agencies in an achievement that may well be called ideal in the quality of their respective fruitions:

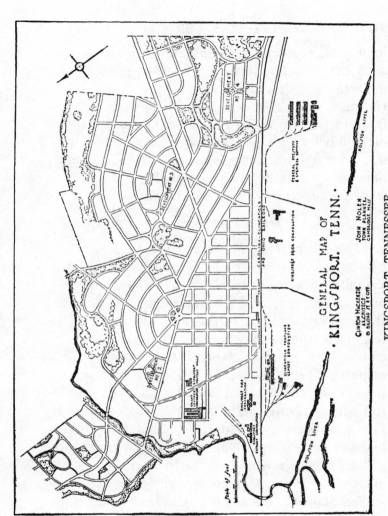

KINGSPORT, TENNESSEE
General plan, showing all main features

industrial, economic, hygienic, civic, cultural and æsthetic. It was primarily a business proposition, undertaken with a common-sense view to profitable returns. With such enlightened perception as to the directions in which true self-interest lay, these other advantages were added thereto as by-products, derived from development along intelligent lines as essentially as the by-products that come from the processes of modern chemistry.

THE DEVELOPMENT

This harmonious coöperation was made possible by the organization of an effective instrument for the purpose, in the shape of the Kingsport Improvement Corporation. This organization has stood at the head and front of all the basic activities and is responsible for the town. Chartered as a commercial venture, it has succeeded phenomenally in all respects. It started right. In it were represented the various business interests mainly concerned, the railroad company and the leading industries. It began its operations with a plan that farsightedly looked to the future. The plan laid down courses of wholesome growth along the lines of least resistance. Looking to community well-being, it forestalled the evils that modern industrial developments otherwise bring in their train as surely as neglected puddles breed mosquitoes.

The Kingsport Improvement Corporation owns most of the real estate; it builds, rents and sells

Grosvenor Atterbury, Architect

KINGSPORT

Church on the circle near the head of Broad Street

Grosvenor Atterbury, Architect

KINGSPORT

Top of hill in "The White City," high-school tower in the background

KINGSPORT
Railroad station

KINGSPORT
Looking down Broad Street across circle toward railroad station,
Kingsport Inn at the left

houses; it runs a central power-plant; it established an inn, constructed a golf course and developed the industries. Local administration rests with a council of five representatives, elected by the citizens every four years. The city charter was designed with the intention of achieving the most efficient results, by the Bureau of Municipal Research established by the Rockefeller Foundation. Under its provisions the council chooses the mayor directly from one of their number and the mayor appoints a city manager with complete control of city work and employees. The manager need not be a resident of the city or state when chosen. The school board, consisting of three men and two women, is appointed by the mayor.

The schools are organized according to the admirable system that originated at Gary, Indiana, generally regarded as a model of its kind. Physical training is an essential feature; to this end each school has four acres of playground in charge of a special instructor.

PUBLIC HEALTH AND UNIVERSAL INSURANCE

A community kept in good health by proper physical training for the young, and by the dissemination of popular knowledge of hygienic principles, prospers correspondingly by reason of enhanced earning capacity. A person well and strong is a public asset; a sick person is a public liability. In this regard, Kingsport is unique. A city hospital, thoroughly equipped, is managed by the municipality; it has accommodation for forty patients. In

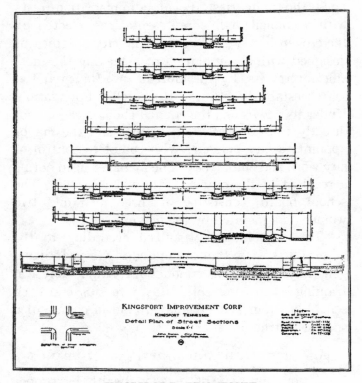

KINGSPORT, TENNESSEE

Detail of street sections, ranging in width from 36 feet to 100 feet

the matter of public hygiene particular stress is given to the importance of preventive measures.

Kingsport's distinction comes still further from employing a type of effort for public health over and above the usual and customary measures. " Group insurance " has for some time been an established practice. In this way it is not uncommon for all the workers of an industrial or commercial organization to be insured. But Kingsport offers the first instance whereby the group principle has been applied collectively to all the workers of a city, male and female — with life, health and accident policies covering them individually, all taken out under an arrangement with a single great insurance company. This is done without previous physical examination.

Practically all the business of Kingsport is conducted by ten large industrial concerns: the Kingsport Hosiery Mill; the Kingsport Extract Corporation; the Kingsport Tannery, Incorporated; the Clinchfield Portland Cement Corporation; the Kingsport Pulp Corporation; the Kingsport Press; the Kingsport Stores, Incorporated; the Kingsport Farms Corporation; the Kingsport Brick Company; the Kingsport Utility Company. To these must be added the municipality, itself an employer. In order to include the city employees in the scheme of blanket insurance, special legislation had to be obtained.

All these undertakings are represented in the Kingsport Improvement Corporation, whose president and moving spirit is J. Fred Johnson. Of the conclusion reached by Mr. Johnson and his indus-

trial associates, A. M. Kingman says:[1] " These
men decided that Kingsport should be as nearly an
ideal manufacturing city as human agencies could
make it. They realized that living conditions
greatly affect the morale of a town, and that general contentment and the elimination of worries go
far toward producing the spirit so necessary to the
accomplishment of good work. Men who are wor-
ried because they have sick children at home, and
men and women who cannot make ends meet because they have lost wages through sickness or accident, are prone to become discontented and make
trouble. Improper housing, insufficient amusement,
lack of care in illness, poor food — all these things
tend to lower industrial efficiency. Mr. Johnson
and the men working with him saw that Kingsport
alone could not provide the means of making itself
the city they want it to be. So they decided on the
insurance plan, whereby, in reality, they formed a
partnership with the life-insurance company for the
purpose of bringing Kingsport up to their expec-
tations.

" Each employing corporation sent out to its
employees a statement setting forth the general
plan of the insurance. This statement announced
that an arrangement had been made with the Metropolitan Life Insurance Company of New York
for life, health and accident insurance for each
employee who was at work on the previous July 1,

[1] Writing in *Business* (August, 1920).

Clinton Mackenzie, Architect

KINGSPORT
Part of hill-top group

Lola Anderson, Landscape Architect

KINGSPORT
House garden

Courtesy of Wurts Brothers　　　　　*Clinton Mackenzie, Architect*

KINGSPORT

Houses fronting on "The Oaks" Park, built in 1924, costing $2,100 each

Courtesy of Wurts Brothers

KINGSPORT

"The Oaks" Park screening the Borden Mill from the houses

the insurance becoming automatically effective from that date. The entire cost of this insurance was borne by the employing corporation."

The insurance company regards the Kingsport undertaking as of great value in demonstrating what may very widely be done. " We propose to show the nation," it says, " what it is possible to accomplish in the preservation of health and life in an intelligent community when the proper steps are taken."

HOUSING ACTIVITIES

The administration of housing activities by the Improvement Corporation has produced results that make Kingsport, in the quiet beauty and charm of its residence sections, compare favorably with some of the celebrated model communities in England. Mr. Clinton Mackenzie, the architect, has made his work seem a natural outgrowth of the plan. The dwellings range in size from three to eight rooms. A six-room house is rented at twenty-five dollars a month. A man may buy his home for a moderate cash payment, with subsequent installments through a period of fifteen years. The Improvement Corporation sells the houses at cost, plus six per cent. The prevailing price for years was in the neighborhood of twenty-five hundred dollars. The purchaser gets a finished house with tastefully planted grounds. A trained woman landscape gardener gives all her time to the planting of shrubs and trees. The highest-grade houses, designed for the higher-salaried employees, cost between nine and ten thousand dollars. This means more than this amount in value, owing to the production of so much of the building material in the neighborhood. In some of the houses, as an experiment, the kitchen has been located in the front; the mother can thus keep an eye on her children at play outdoors and enjoy the sight of what is passing; it is also convenient for the delivery of supplies.

Of Mr. Mackenzie's work, Mr. Charles C. May says:[1] " The range of house types is very great, as is the variety and freedom of architectural style. There are several types of small cottages, even three-room bungalows, and from them all the way up to the pretentious two-story, porched house, with six good-sized rooms; there are Colonial farmhouse types, there are numbers of units which are independent of local tradition, and there are several cottages in which an ingenious, restrained use of vertical battened boards, together with an overhanging second story, gives a look which is reminiscent of the Tyrol."

CONSTRUCTION MATERIALS LOCALLY PRODUCED
COÖPERATIVE TEAMWORK

The extensive production of Portland cement at Kingsport has greatly reduced local building costs. The city has wide concrete sidewalks and

[1] Writing in the *Architectural Forum.*

Allen Dryden, Architect

School building

Clinton Mackenzie, Architect

Part of hill-top group of houses

Clinton Mackenzie, Architect

Part of hill-top group

Clinton Mackenzie, Architect

Oak Street houses

KINGSPORT

Clinton Mackensie, Architect

Clinton Mackensie, Architect

Houses on Watuga Street

Six-room houses on Oak Street, built in 1921,
costing $4,000 each

Clinton Mackensie, Architect

Clinton Mackensie, Architect

Group-houses on Shelby Street, opposite Kingsport Inn

KINGSPORT

several miles of broad, concrete-paved streets. The cost of this concrete pavement was only $1.35 a square yard. Other locally produced building materials are proportionately cheap.

Under a scheme of coöperative teamwork, devised by experts, an enormous prevention of industrial waste has been effected. One factory supplies another. The industrial alcohol plant, the dyeworks and the pulp mill all get their needed lime from the cement works. The tannery supplies the harness factory with leather; the tannery gets its needed extract from the extract plant, which turns its chips over to the pulp mill. Building materials are supplied to all the local industries by the cement and brick works; the Utilities Company supplies power and water. The Dye Company supplies the Hosiery Company with dye and the Pulp Company with bleaching powder. Furthermore, expansion plans for new industries have been worked out: a fertilizer plant to utilize the regional deposits of potash and phosphate and the tannery refuse; a packing-house to stimulate cattle raising and produce fertilizer material. The wood-alcohol plant's charcoal is to be used in a charcoal iron furnace.

The Kingsport Press has established its full right to the title of book manufacturer. It depends for its employees almost wholly on the native population, who have been drawn from their mountain homes. The plant has had a remarkable development. Closely associated with it are a pulp mill and a paper mill, to the advantage of all. The press today has a daily capacity of seventy-five thousand hand-bound books.

A most gratifying outcome of all these activities that have built Kingsport into an almost ideal industrial city is the intelligent and public-spirited interest in community affairs shown by the exceptionally capable working population, which realizes that it has a stake of its own in it all.

THE COMMUNITY AND THE PLAN

The region where Kingsport stands lies thirteen hundred feet above sea level, in a fertile agricultural country. The climate is equable. The site is equally well adapted to good residential and industrial life, under urban as well as rural conditions. The white population is at present entirely native American, of what is commonly termed Anglo-Saxon stock. Neither inter-racial nor international difficulties have yet presented themselves to complicate the social and political scheme of the community.

The plan gives due consideration to the colored population, which, being uncommonly high-class and industrious, is esteemed accordingly. Appreciating the value of the colored element in the local labor situation, Kingsport aims to counteract the tendency to migrate to the North, by developing its colored section in marked contrast to the squalid " Nigger-town " districts so common in Southern

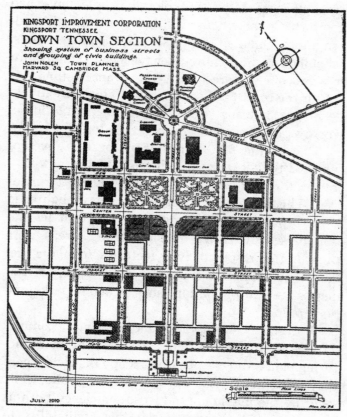

KINGSPORT, TENNESSEE

Plan of down-town section, showing system of business streets and grouping of civic buildings

63

communities. Here the colored people have had comfortable, new houses built for them, with modern improvements. In this section the playgrounds, schoolhouses and churches have been planned for in ways commensurate with the advanced standards set for the rest of the community. This attractively developed housing area assures its population a worthy place in the social organization.

One of the first steps taken for the development of the site was the division of the new city into well-recognized zones for the several forms of use. This was done according to the enlightened modern practice now recognized by recent legislation in several states of the Union. Areas were thus allotted respectively to factories and industrial plants, to wholesale trade, to retail trade, to residences, and to public buildings, schools, parks and playgrounds.

Industrial development and housing accommodations were the two main factors. The manufacturing plants thus far located occupy districts where they cause the least annoyance for the public, while securing the maximum industrial efficiency both as regards transit accommodation and availability to the homes of the workers. The residential tracts are kept away from the smoke, dust, noise and danger of the industrial plants. In general, the broad streets with good paving for vehicular and pedestrian movement proclaim something unusual in workmen's surroundings. Each street, planted with shade trees, offers to the section where the working classes live a restful seclusion that is commonly a feature of only the higher-class residential districts of an industrial community.

V

A VILLAGE FOR FACTORY WORKERS

KISTLER, PENNSYLVANIA

IN what might be termed the heart of the Alleghanies, on the banks of the Juniata River, is Kistler, an industrial housing project with many points of interest. It realizes an industrial village of which its promoters had dreamed, where the highest working efficiency would be reached with the best home surroundings for the worker. It was primarily intended for the unskilled worker. Of the alien element, the Slavonic is the prevailing nationality.

DEVELOPMENT

In 1918 the Mount Union Refractories Company, who own and operate a large brick-making plant at the foot of Mount Union in Pennsylvania, decided to build a new model village to house its work-people. A town planner was secured to make a survey of the locality and prepare a housing development scheme on modern planning lines. There are some seven hundred employees; Mount Union, the nearest town, is one and one-half miles to the west. The district is very hilly; it is agricultural, and is coursed by the Juniata River with well-wooded banks. The site itself is about sixty acres in extent, and has a triangular shape, determined by the river, the Pennsylvania Railroad (Harrisburg-Altoona main line) and adjacent agricultural land. The boundaries being unalterably fixed on two sides, it was necessary to devise a scheme which would make the most of both factors. The railroad, running high above the property, is carried over the Juniata at a height of sixty feet above the regular water level. The river runs at the edge of the development for half a mile; a strip about one hundred feet wide, ten feet above normal river level, is so low-lying that the spring freshets put it under water. Surveys showed two terraces, the first ten feet above the river, and the other twenty-five feet. The lower terrace, annually flooded, was saved from erosion only by a thick planting of trees. The buildings on the town site, a brick farmhouse, a stone spring-house and a barn, were all retained for use. The community was placed on the opposite side of the river from the Works, the dwellings being thus freed from dirt, dust and noise.

STREET PLAN

The central point of the plan may be said to be Kistler Green, although the design has really no definite axis. There is rather a decentralization of the community life than a concentration at any par-

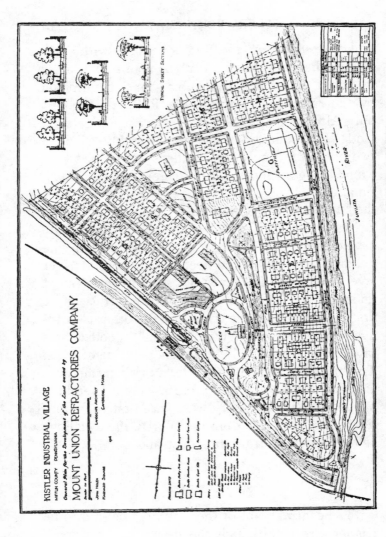

KISTLER INDUSTRIAL VILLAGE, PENNSYLVANIA

General plan for the development of the land owned by the Mount Union Refractories Company

ticular part. It has been taken into consideration that three vital things affected the settlement: first, the access to the Mount Union Refractories Works; second, the railroad station; third, the street connections at the south end. Of them all, the Works connection is unquestionably the most important; this is effected by the Mount Union bridge. From this particular point, actually the apex of a triangle, Kistler stretches out southward; convenient and quick access can thereby be had to all parts. Riverside Road has eight street connections which run southeast from Park Road, a parallel street. Park Road and Nolen Street are the two main arteries leading into the development from the south. State Street, parallel to the railway, gives access from a proposed railway station. The open spaces, well chosen, provide ample recreation area for all residents. The railway embankment on the one hand and the river on the other prevent through streets from east or west outside the development; should expansion in the future warrant such streets, they can be carried out with the minimum of difficulty, provision having been made for such a contingency. An attractive design is that made for the vicinity of the proposed railway station, where a semicircular park will be formed in combination with Penn Park on the opposite side of State Street. The south side of Penn Park, in quadrant shape, forms a shopping quarter for the community.

The width of streets plays an important part in all the newer town-planning work. The controlling motive is to avoid unnecessary street paving and expenses, and to give the individual lot owner as large a lot as possible.

At Kistler, the street widths range from forty to seventy feet. In two typical examples — the forty-foot street and the seventy-foot street — the divisions show the relative importance of the streets in the development design. The forty-foot street has a roadway of eighteen feet, a planting space of six feet on each side, and sidewalks five feet wide. The seventy-foot street has two roadways sixteen feet wide, separated by a central parking strip twenty-two feet wide. The sidewalks are four feet wide, with a four-foot planting space next to the roadway. The property line, or rather the restriction which safeguards the relation of the houses to the street, has been fixed at fifteen feet from street to house. This set-back makes a width of seventy feet between houses in a forty-foot street, and one hundred feet in the case of the seventy-foot street. While there is ample recreation area provided, it has been thought a good thing to leave for the time being several of the secondary streets in grass, the small amount of traffic making it possible to use them as play spaces for children.

KISTLER: MOUNT UNION REFRACTORIES COMPANY
Park entrance to works

KISTLER: MOUNT UNION REFRACTORIES COMPANY
Community Hall

KISTLER: MOUNT UNION REFRACTORIES COMPANY
Playground

KISTLER: MOUNT UNION REFRACTORIES COMPANY
Street Scene

WOODED AND PARK FEATURES

A glance at the plan will show the large amount of open area retained. Much of this is covered with natural woods such as willow, locust, sycamore, persimmon and black and white oak. The retention of this growth has been an important feature of the work. The river embankment is reserved as a park, its north end devoted to a children's playground and picnic grounds. The south end is to have a boat-landing on the river, and also a playground intended to be a completely equipped athletic field when finally developed, with field house, baseball diamond, and so forth. The terrace on the east side of Park Road is reserved as Juniata Park, and is a good framework for the oval setting of Kistler Green. The terrace is steep, but, cultivated with native shrubs, forms a striking feature in the village scene.

HOME SITES AND BUILDINGS

The street blocks average in size about three hundred feet by two hundred feet; the house lots, about forty feet by one hundred feet deep. Houses have been built for nearly two hundred families. Almost without exception the sites throughout the development are regular in shape, arranged to accommodate both the single house and the group type. There are two hundred lots, or a proportion of five to the acre. The houses now built are largely of frame construction of varying character, in de-

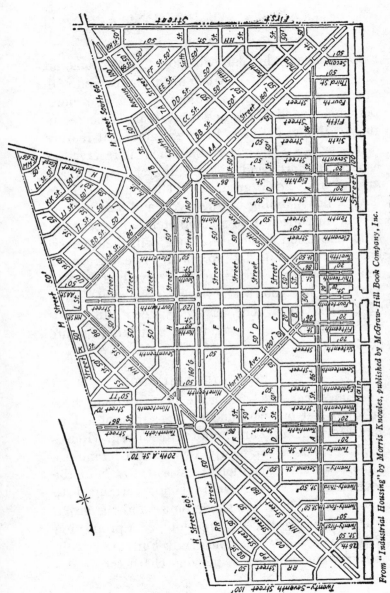

From "Industrial Housing" by Morris Knowles, published by McGraw-Hill Book Company, Inc.

OJIBWAY, NEAR WINDSOR, CANADA

Street plan of the Ojibway project of the Canadian Steel Company

tached and semi-detached quadrangles. From four to eight rooms are provided, with baths and porches.

The principal public building is the community hall, transformed from the old barn, remodelled. Eventually, schools and so forth will be erected at points of vantage in choice of site and vista. The rising ground from Park Road, though partially cutting off the area to the west of the community hall and stores, is traversed by footpaths and steps which are most useful to the pedestrian.

COMMUNITY WELFARE

Considerable attention has been given by the Mount Union Refractories Company to plans for the welfare of the little community, which is so inseparably connected with its interests as an industrial enterprise. It has endeavored not only to provide good houses in suitable surroundings, but also to cultivate a spirit of citizenship and social life among the inhabitants. The population being so largely foreign in its make-up, there is distinct necessity for a lead to be given in the direction of Americanism. This is done in a much better way than by exhortation — by the provision of something tangible, in the form of good living conditions, which more nearly expresses the ideals of this country. There are few places in this country where the problem of low-cost housing, primarily for the unskilled worker, has been better solved for the employer and employee alike. Those who believe that housing is something more than an incident in the life of the worker will welcome the growing appreciation which is being manifested in securing suitable and healthful homes. The example of Kistler in this regard is distinctly heartening. It has already attracted the attention of persons concerned with industrial welfare.

VI
AN OLD SEACOAST TOWN
Cohasset, Massachusetts

Cohasset, rural and individual, with narrow, crooked streets, eccentric in gradient and scenic in their vistas, is a survival of old-time New England community life. It is situated just a little way in from where the broad Atlantic sweeps into Massachusetts Bay, on a tiny harbor of its own. The influences that have guided it in its long history are practically identical with those that have governed scores of other such localities along the New England coast.

THE COMMUNITY VISION

As long ago as 1892, Mr. J. B. Harrison, as an official investigator for the Board of Trustees of Public Reservations of Massachusetts, pointed out the great lack of public open spaces in the state. Mountain-tops, sea-beaches and many sections of exceptionally picturesque countryside were rapidly passing into private control. Not only were the people being shut away in many cases from scenes of natural beauty; in the end the scenery itself was often destroyed to satisfy the interests of selfish owners who wished to develop it either for resi-

75

dential uses or for industry. Cohasset, less than an hour out of Boston by rail, is largely a section of fine country estates, good automobile roads, woodlands and long-distance views over land and sea. Its famous and historic Jerusalem Road, bordering the open sea on the South Shore, corresponds to the equally celebrated North Shore Drive along the Cape Ann coast.

The population of all the South Shore region has increased and become more residential, with exceptional attractions for the tourist and pleasure-seeker. Largely for these reasons, public-spirited local residents have been looking for some program of safeguarding the future town. Cohasset has as yet no local authority which could accept the responsibility of public lands; it has not even adopted the Massachusetts Park Act; the Harrison report of twenty-eight years ago stands today as a fairly reasonable summary of the position. There are no building regulations in force, and, although private enterprise has not as yet spoiled the town in the sense of indiscriminate and inappropriate construction, there are decided indications that the present state of affairs is not beneficial. Not only is it necessary to frame regulations to reduce the fire hazard and insure healthful homes, but proper control of streets and houses means an increasing regard for the æsthetic features of the town. In this connection it is pleasing to record the adoption of a regulation prohibiting " three-decker " houses.

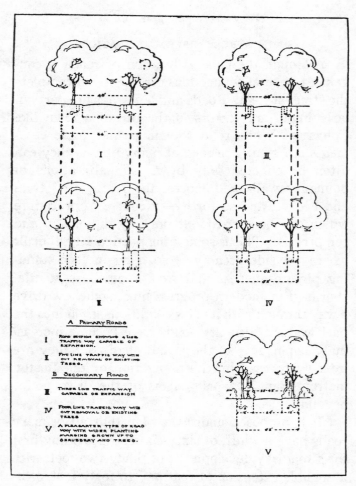

COHASSET, MASSACHUSETTS
Primary and secondary road cross-sections recommended

SOME STREET RECOMMENDATIONS

Although the general location of roads is convenient, several connections are needed to complete the street system. Roads and highways are particularly important factors in the life of a town like Cohasset. While road widenings and grade easements are greatly needed at many places, they can often be effected only by drastic alterations of boundary walls and fences, the removal of trees and hedges, and so forth — a course of procedure which can be carried out only by diplomacy and compromise. This is something particularly difficult where wayside scenery is so fixed in long-standing picturesqueness and well-groomed residential charm. But modern progress must somehow drive a way through with its new conditions, even into the back waters. Primary roads have become increasingly important; in the Cohasset district they are intensively used by the population of the Boston metropolitan area, as well as of the districts far beyond.

It is proposed under the plan that all primary roads have a width of sixty-six feet, providing first for a roadway development of thirty-two feet, with a possible extension of roadway to forty feet without the removal of existing trees. Examples of such roads are North Main and South Main streets, Jerusalem Road, Atlantic Avenue, Margin and Summer streets. Secondary roads, defined as local traffic streets, are constantly increasing with further settlement. These have to be treated not only on their own merits, but in many cases as potential

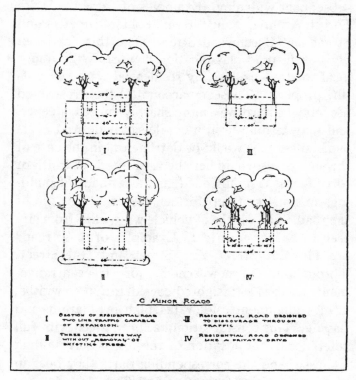

COHASSET, MASSACHUSETTS
Minor road cross-sections recommended

primary roads. They are laid out with a width of fifty-two feet. In two instances the roadway is shown at twenty-four feet, with different treatments of the planted margins; in another instance the

roadway has a width of thirty-two feet. In no case
would trees necessarily be interfered with by any
subsequent widening. Examples of these roads are
Forest Avenue, King Street, Sohier Street, Pond
Street and Beechwood Street. The third and last
division in road classification comprises the minor
local roads — exclusively residential ways to abut-
ting property. These, on account of their restricted
use, may be narrower, more sharply curved, steeper,
and may terminate in a cul-de-sac if desired. Circumstances that would be detrimental in the case of
through roads would here be warranted. A width of
forty feet is recommended, and a set-back of buildings of not less than thirteen feet on each side of
the road. The widths of vehicle ways vary from sixteen to twenty-four feet. Examples of these roads
are Pleasant Street, Ash Street and Hill Street.
Throughout the new scheme for street arrangements there is a farsighted consideration of widths,
grades, alignments, sidewalks, planting margins and
paving. This consideration has been given with full
reference to the location of the towns surrounding
Cohasset and the corresponding parts they bear in
making provision for use and traffic.

ROAD IMPROVEMENT

A plan has been made for changes in the neighborhood of the railway station. This would re-
arrange the roadway so that an attractive planting
space would center on the porte-cochère of the sta-

COHASSET

St. Stephen's, the church of the carillon

COHASSET COMMON AND ST. STEPHEN'S CHURCH

Before and after pictures, showing the improvement resulting from
the removal of old houses and stores

tion. The roadway and sidewalk lines along North Main and South Main streets are also proposed for revision. At the Osgood School on Elm Street, a better roadway character is suggested. Traffic considerations have also been regarded at Gulf Island in widening a road and defining a separate sidewalk — a proceeding of some difficulty, possible only by blasting on one side and carrying a hanging path over the stream on the other side. But some such radical changes are necessary on the score of safety for traffic, if for no other reason. The same state of affairs exists at the grade crossing from Spring to Summer streets.

In the recommendations for road improvements attention is drawn to the need of planted margins on many of the streets of Cohasset. It is not suggested that these margins should be uniform, but a varied treatment of grass, trees and shrubs would considerably enhance the town's appearance. The old difficulties of overhead wires and poles receive attention: it is urged that there be a gradual construction of underground conduits. Not only would this be a distinct æsthetic gain; the disastrous ice storm of November 28, 1921, has shown it to be a necessity. The telephone company has already eliminated poles for a short space in the center of the village. The sightliness of the streets would also be increased by the adoption of a more artistic type of furnishing. This would cover lighting standards, signposts, fountains, and so forth.

The whole scheme of road improvements in Cohasset has been studied with a view to convenience of traffic, together with beauty and picturesqueness. The retention of open spaces will serve traffic and other purposes and be an agreeable foreground for buildings, but they need proper definition and maintenance.

TOWN FEATURES

In spite of the removal of the Guild Hall, the fire house is not now in a position which harmonizes with the town's development. It obstructs what would otherwise be an uncommonly fine view. Its removal and a rearrangement of the road lines would be most advantageous, especially as the intersection where it stands is one of the most important in Cohasset. The plaza at the railroad station could be much improved by a redesign involving a planting of trees and shrubs that would make a worthy setting for an important public utility. There is a fine realization of improvement here in connection with the Tilden lot, recently acquired. The junction of South Main Street and Spring Street is now of a very indefinite character. This could be improved by acquiring the land opposite the public library and then replanning the locality. This would provide a triangular space as a sightly location for a monument or fountain. At the intersection of Elm and South Main streets an unnecessary expanse of paving could be reduced to

COHASSET

Common, showing old town hall and churches

Charles M. Baker, Architect

COHASSET

Sketch for new town hall

COHASSET
Bathhouse, Sandy Beach

COHASSET
Characteristic roadway

advantage. Throughout the town some definite improvement of the setting of the public and semi-public buildings is needed. All future buildings should be erected with a view to making the most of their surroundings in connection with an ordered street plan.

RECREATIONAL PROPOSALS

As the growth of Cohasset is intimately associated with its attractiveness as a residential town and its popularity with pleasure-seeking summer dwellers, the subject of parks, reservations, shore improvements, pleasure spots and bathing facilities plays a considerable part in any study of its future. Deplorable as it is that so much has been neglected in this direction, much can still be done at little expense before a more permanent complexion has been given to the neighborhood. Without question parts of the shore, both rock and beach, the stream valleys and the rock-bound hills should be publicly owned and kept permanently open for public use. There are different types of seashore in Cohasset which should be preserved now. The most important is the beautiful beach of fine, white sand, one thousand feet long, outside of Little Harbor. This has already been set aside for public use and a community bathhouse built, through the initiative and generosity of the Sandy Beach Association.

The whole question of the shore reservations is vital to the interests of the town as well as the public in general. Sandy Beach, Little Harbor, Kimball's Point, James Brook and other brooks, Sunset Rock and other rocks are natural features that should be in public hands. In a concerted plan

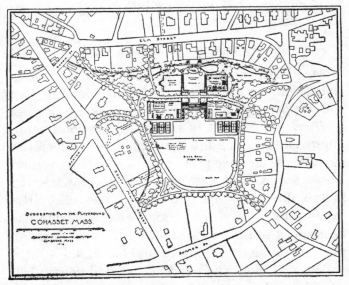

COHASSET, MASSACHUSETTS
Suggested plan for playground

for such public acquisition, playground facilities of an organized character should be provided. The triangular area bounded by Elm Street, South Main Street and Summer Street offers possibilities in this direction. Laid out as an athletic field and playground for men, women and children, this would be of real community value. A field house equipped with assembly hall and gymnasium would provide a good rendezvous for winter activities. Such a scheme would also result in a great property improvement in the center of the town, and would open up low-lying land which at the present time is of small use to its owners.

ACCOMPLISHMENTS

What has already been accomplished at Cohasset shows the enlightened public spirit of the Cohasset Men's Club and other organizations, which took the initiative in enlisting the services of a town planner to prepare a comprehensive scheme of improvements, and then followed this up with detailed plans for the carrying out of various projects. Later, in 1917, came the organization of the Cohasset Improvement Association, Inc., which now functions so satisfactorily.

The record of achievements of Cohasset is a notable one. As a result of the activity of these public-spirited groups, three triangular open spaces at street intersections have been given to the town; also a tract of about eighty acres of woodland near North Main Street, the gift of Henry A. Wheelwright. The sites of the Osgood School and the public library were also contributed, the library building itself being a bequest. The acquisition of Sandy Beach has already been referred to. In addition to the beach, a parallel tract of land has been acquired. One of the most valuable and conspicu-

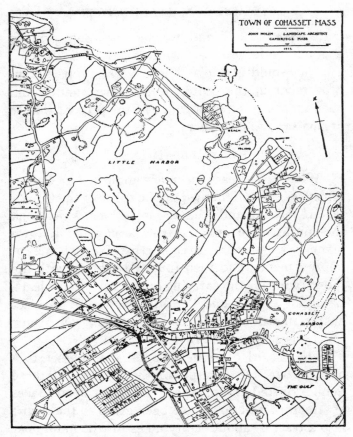

COHASSET, MASSACHUSETTS

Map of town, showing situation and main features

ous improvements has been the purchase of the land that adjoins Cohasset Common and St. Stephen's Episcopal Church. This has been added to the common, and its landscape improvement carried out. What were known as the St. John Stores were removed, so that a fine and unobstructed view of St. Stephen's Church is afforded. In this church there has been installed a notable carillon of bells. Concerts are given in summer by the famous Belgian *carillonneur*, Kamiel Lefévere. The bells themselves were the gift of Mrs. Hugh Bancroft, daughter of Mr. C. W. Barron, in memory of her mother. At Cohasset station an unsightly barn building on an adjoining lot on the Tilden estate has been removed, and the area reconstructed so as to afford an agreeable view at the railroad approach to the town. Other changes were made in the neighborhood of the station. Fourteen acres of land on the easterly side of King Street, near the Black Rock station, have been presented by Mrs. Hugh Bancroft to the Federation of Bird Clubs of New England, to be maintained as a reservation for wild life. The Whitney Woods Associates have laid out and maintained excellent riding paths through the woods surrounding Turkey Hill, thus stimulating horseback riding and an annual horse show. The town lands which have been in the hands of the authorities for many years, such as the common, Harbor Green, and so forth, have been improved, and the harbor and channel have been dredged by the government, largely at the expense of local funds. The improvement of the Golf Club grounds and the laying out of private grounds over Turkey Hill have been not merely to private advantage, but of some public benefit in enhancing the attractiveness of Cohasset.

Individualism in residential towns, particularly those which also attract as centers of summer and vacation pleasures, can well afford to subordinate itself to the common welfare. Sometimes our unselfishness may serve to our personal advantage. Homogeneous neighborhoods, attractive housing, plenty of space for every one, are all easier to obtain by forethought and planning. In the long run, prosperity and popularity go to the locality that moves in time to preserve its natural attractions, combining public welfare with the best interests of the individual.

VII

A WAR EMERGENCY PROJECT
Union Park Gardens

Union Park Gardens is an outcome of the World War — of those eventful days when America was straining every nerve to match her forces effectively against the enemy across the seas. The Emergency Fleet Corporation, the driving force of the United States Shipping Board, was confronted with the problem of housing the thousands of workers engaged in the shipyards. All ordinary housing facilities had broken down; no new houses were being erected to fill the breach. This condition arose from dearth of labor for building, excessive cost of materials and labor, and absence of adequate transportation for supplies. The emergency demanded everywhere a complete community coöperation. At Wilmington, Delaware, a company was organized to meet the requirement. Options were secured on several available and suitable sites; finally one was decided upon, at the intersection of Union Street and Lancaster Avenue, on the outskirts of Wilmington. The site stands fairly high, at an elevation considerably above the town. It contains about fifty-eight acres of rolling country. The district is well wooded, and to the south is a stretch of park land. Lancaster Avenue and Union Street are the boundaries on the north and east, respectively. On the west lies Cathedral Cemetery; southwesterly is the main highway to Baltimore and Washington.

RESIDENTIAL ENVIRONMENT

Many otherwise desirable residential areas are spoiled by the encroachment of cheaper property on their outskirts — property ugly in appearance, temporary in construction and housing a totally different type of resident. To obviate this drawback, property adjacent to Union Park Gardens was purchased for the safeguarding of this development. Commonplace buildings standing on the north side of Lancaster Avenue and vacant land on the east side of Union Street were capable of being thus dealt with, and were included in the complete scheme. These inclusions were of much moment. Not only has the Liberty Land Company thereby been able to safeguard the increased property values of Union Park Gardens and prevent contiguous undesirable occupancy; it has been able to design both sides of Lancaster Avenue and Union Street in harmony with the general layout. Any plan which neglects to take into account the artificial environment of the site, as well as the natural characteristics, really fails in a fundamental way.

Ballinger & Perrot, Architects

UNION PARK GARDENS
Grant Avenue from Sycamore Street

Ballinger & Perrot, Architects

UNION PARK GARDENS
Intersection of Grant Avenue and Linden Street

Ballinger & Perrot, Architects

Intersection of Harrington Street and Sycamore Street

Ballinger & Perrot, Architects

View on Harrington Street

Ballinger & Perrot, Architects

Linden Street from Grant Avenue

Ballinger & Perrot, Architects

Apartment houses at Lancaster Avenue and Grant Avenue

UNION PARK GARDENS

GENERAL SCHEME OF PLANNING

The scheme aims at creating a self-contained garden suburb for the adjacent city of Wilmington. The relationship to Wilmington has always been kept in view in the design; some of the present city streets are continued through the tract, and transportation by street car on Union Street and Lancaster Avenue is entirely a part of the general city plan. The essential of an industrial suburb is realized by bringing the workers' homes within ten minutes' ride of the plants where they are employed. The Pusey and Jones Company, the Harlan plant of the Bethlehem Shipbuilding Corporation, and the American Car and Foundry Company are all within this radius.

The elements of the plan are, first, the houses and apartment buildings; second, the community building, school and stores; third, the provision of recreation areas. For the present these elements have not been carried out, although forethought has been exercised in the provision of sites which may be available for such eventualities. Police, fire and school services are now within easy reach of the development. It was not found necessary to reserve extensive areas for park purposes, since the development bounding the property on the south was devoted to just such uses. The Wilmington Park Commission has started to lay out the continuation of Grant Avenue through the park land adjacent to Union Park Gardens. The community center

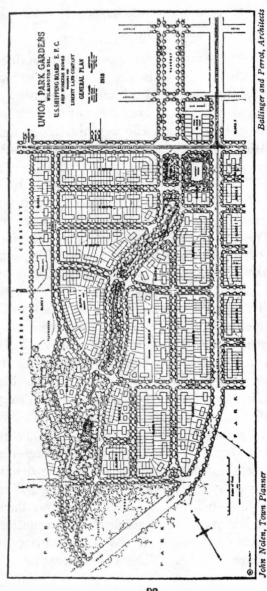

John Nolen, Town Planner

Ballinger and Perrot, Architects

UNION PARK GARDENS, WILMINGTON, DELAWARE

General plan for ship-workers' homes, designed for Liberty Land Company, United States Shipping Board E. F. C.

was fixed at the intersection of Union Street and Lancaster Avenue. This decision was based upon the proximity to Wilmington, the transportation on the two roads and the desirability of keeping the heavy traffic away from the subsidiary streets. From this point the area dedicated to park land becomes a kind of spine for the residential tract. Throughout the design an effort has been made to assure privacy for the houses by street arrangements which would not attract through traffic. The group-houses have been located as near as possible to the transportation lines, and the semi-detached houses are in locations farther away — an arrangement which gives the lesser-paid workman living in a group-house (minus an automobile) the just claim to transit facilities.

STREET PLAN

The street plan of Union Park Gardens gives two curved streets across the tract from each direction; all the other streets are straight. There is no vital alteration of the land surface; unnecessary street widths are avoided; the blocks, though of varying dimensions, are not of inconvenient size and shape. In spite of an inevitable connection with the checkerboard plan of Wilmington and a consequent joining up of streets, there has been ingeniously evolved a plan not only practical but highly attractive. It has variety without complexity. The lots in no case are of unusable irregularity.

The simplicity of the plan also gives a great advantage in the surveying and partitioning of the land.

The main artery, Grant Avenue, runs from east to west through the tract, the roadways proper being on either side. At the intersection of the more important thoroughfares open spaces make interesting viewpoints; at the village-green intersection of Grant and Lancaster avenues this gives a most appropriate setting for the community and apartment buildings there situated. The traffic divisions on Grant Avenue give twenty-foot roadways on either side of a central parkway varying in width from sixty feet to one hundred and twenty feet, a seven-foot planting strip and a six-foot sidewalk on the property side only. Lancaster Avenue and Union Street (Lincoln Highway) are both eighty feet wide, having thirty-six-foot roadways, fourteen-foot planting strips and six-foot sidewalks, with two feet between sidewalks and property lines. The secondary streets are forty and fifty feet in width, having roadways of twenty and twenty-four feet respectively, and five-foot and seven-foot planting strips on each side, with five-foot sidewalks. No alleyways are provided, the Wilmington authorities giving no assurance that cleaning, lighting and removal of ashes and garbage could be made in such alleys, owing to insufficient appropriations as well as to the city ordinances, which limit such service to streets alone. (Union Park Gardens is now within the limits of Wilmington, and has all the city con-

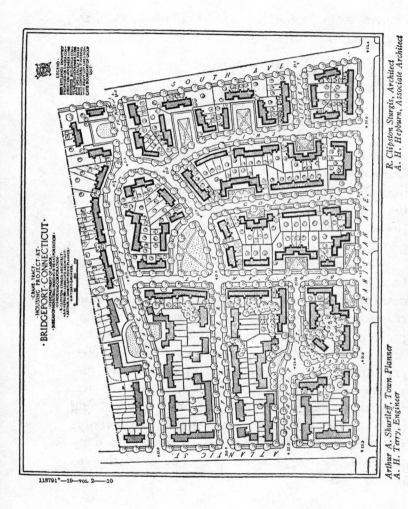

Arthur A. Shurtleff, Town Planner
A. H. Terry, Engineer

R. Clipston Sturgis, Architect
A. H. Hepburn, Associate Architect

BRIDGEPORT, CONNECTICUT

Crane Housing Project. Plans prepared for United States Housing Corporation

veniences, including the collection of ashes, garbage, and so forth.)

LAND DIVISION

The project provides for five hundred and six
houses; three hundred and ninety-nine are group-
houses, one hundred and ninety-four semi-detached,
and three detached. Space is allowed for apartment houses, stores, community buildings, a school
and a playground, and a few lots remaining may be
built up later. The school site calls for an adjoining playground for ball and tennis; two reservations unsuitable for residences are made into allotment gardens.

An analysis of the proportion of land devoted
to various purposes shows 54.5 per cent for residential use; 14.5 per cent for the future school and
playground, community buildings and parks; 31
per cent for streets. The density of housing, calcu-
lating five hundred and fourteen families in separate houses and forty families in apartments, dis-
tributes 15.83 families to the net acre over the total
of thirty-four acres. This intensification of housing
is due to the use of the group-house; only twenty-
four per cent of the land is actually occupied by
the buildings, seventy-six per cent consisting of
open-lot area.

HOUSE SITES

There are no uniform dimensions for the lots.
The intermediate group-houses between parallel

streets average from sixteen to twenty feet in frontage and from ninety-five to one hundred feet in depth. End plots of this same depth have a somewhat greater frontage, to allow a definite distance between groups. This distance has been fixed at sixteen feet, but as much as eighteen feet has been secured. Lots for the detached and semi-detached houses have a frontage of from thirty to fifty feet, with a varying depth. The distance between houses on opposite sides of the street is eighty to one hundred feet on the narrower streets, and ninety to one hundred and ten feet on the wider streets, according as the minimum twenty-foot or the maximum thirty-foot set-back is used. The distance between the rear of the houses runs from ninety to one hundred feet. In front, behind and on each side of the houses, an abundance of light and air is thus provided. The lots that were left have been sold and built upon with a type of house similar to those that were erected by the government. Seventy per cent of the residents own their homes, and there is a great community spirit. A local body called " Union Park Gardens Improvement Association " has been formed.

LANDSCAPE TREATMENT

In the landscape design considerable attention has been devoted to the connection between house location and street plan. The aim has been to obtain good vista effects, not only at junction points

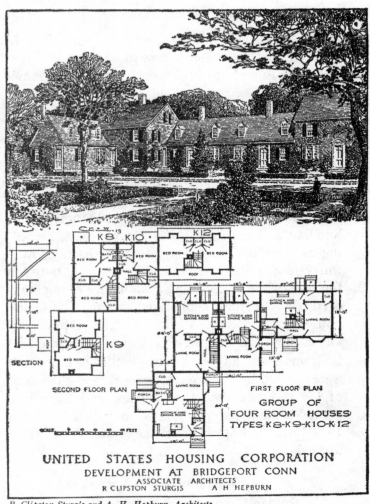

R. Clipston Sturgis and A. H. Hepburn, Architects

BRIDGEPORT, CONNECTICUT

Plans for group of four-room houses

but along straight streets, by an irregular arrangement of the building line of the houses. This street effect has been heightened in many cases by the preservation of existing trees and the natural beauty of foliage. In the planting spaces of the streets are hardy trees; on Grant Avenue, both trees and shrubbery. The lawns before the houses are unobstructed by either fences or hedges and give a good setting to the property.

Union Park Gardens is today one of the most attractive suburbs of Wilmington. It compares favorably with other " war housing suburbs " and, with the exception of Yorkship Village (Camden, New Jersey), has been praised as the best low-cost example of community planning and development in the Philadelphia region.

VIII
A HIGH-CLASS RESIDENTIAL SUBURB
MYERS PARK

MYERS PARK, adjoining Charlotte, North Carolina, is a new suburb created along distinctive lines, designed aright from the first, and influenced only by the best practice in modern town planning. Taking the wide area of America, with its great cities and urban development, the number of characteristically beautiful suburbs, specifically designed as such, is small. Roland Park, Baltimore; Forest Hills, New York's Long Island suburb; the Country Club district of Kansas City, Missouri; Twin Peaks district, San Francisco; Palos Verdes, near Los Angeles; and some of the newer developments in Florida — for example, San José, a suburb of Jacksonville, or the new town of Venice on the west coast, south of Sarasota — these are among the few and are widely known. Among the lesser-known instances of suburban planning is Myers Park. From certain points of view, it should be properly classed with the better-known examples.

DEVELOPMENT

Myers Park is situated close to the city of Charlotte, being about one and one-half miles south-

100

MYERS PARK

Airplane view, showing extensive development carried out in less than a decade

MYERS PARK

Airplane view, showing general suburban development, including J. B. Duke estate

easterly from the center of that town. It originated
in 1912 under the auspices of the Stephens Company, with Mr. George Stephens as its controlling
head. A great need was arising in Charlotte for
homes of a high character amid surroundings of natural beauty. Charlotte was growing fast. Then it
had something around thirty-five thousand inhabitants; now, with its suburbs, there are over seventy-five thousand. Myers Park answers well the
question of civic expansion. The business public of
Charlotte has gained an invaluable asset by the
planning and building of Myers Park, and since
its ultimate financial success was assured from the
first, it is an object lesson to less forward-looking
communities.

NATURAL SETTING

Imagine a gently rolling countryside covered
here and there with beautiful groves of oak and
pine. Set into this landscape a tract three miles in
length and varying in width from a few hundred
feet to one mile! Such is the site of Myers Park, as
it runs from its entrance at the lower end to the
full width of the ridge between Sugar and Briar
creeks. It is a typical Southern landscape of the
Piedmont country. In its residential adaptation
this quality has been utilized to the full. The plan
developed from this environment admirably fits the
topography. Avoiding both unnatural checkerboard streets on an undulating surface and mean-

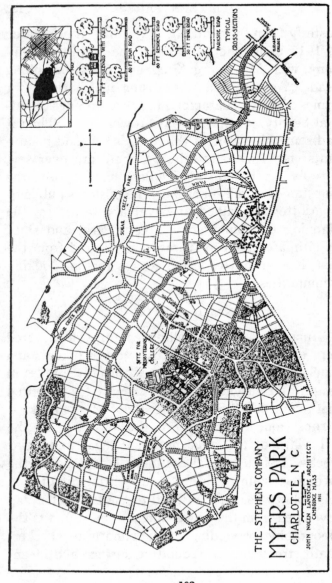

MYERS PARK, CHARLOTTE, NORTH CAROLINA

A residential suburb of a thousand acres, developed for the Stephens Company, Charlotte, North Carolina

ingless curved streets, it adjusts the home to the landscape in a way that assures æsthetic harmony.

In such a problem the street plan is the predominant element; its treatment in high-class residential tracts demands the satisfaction of a sense of seclusion together with means for easy and convenient access to the broad world. This is achieved not alone by gentle curves of the street lines, for continued interest and variety, but by marked variation in street widths. Not every street is a carrier of general traffic; some merely lead to the home. While need of through circulation is amply met, the quiet byways receive corresponding attention in planning that respects their privacy. A main boulevard carries the car line out from Charlotte; with ample roadway it takes good care of the ever-expanding motor traffic incidental to better-class property. The connection with the city is good; the loop of the boulevard at the extreme end provides transportation no farther than two blocks away from any lot in the development.

STREET TREATMENT

The streets vary in width from forty to one hundred and ten feet. The roads along the park areas are forty feet in width, with a five-foot sidewalk and fifteen-foot planting space on one side only, and a motor drive of twenty feet. The fifty-foot minor roads have a roadway of twenty-four feet, with eight-foot planting spaces and five-foot

sidewalks on each side. The sixty-foot roads that
front the residences except on main roads and
boulevards have a drive of twenty-four feet, thir-
teen-foot planting spaces and five-foot sidewalks.
The larger arteries are the eighty-foot main roads
and the one-hundred-and-ten-foot boulevards. The
eighty-foot type has a drive of thirty-two feet,
eighteen-foot planting spaces and six-foot sidewalks. The boulevard is divided for purposes of
traffic on lines similar to those of European examples. Down the center a reserved space is devoted
to the two tracks of the street-car service; this
width includes planting strips on both sides, with
rows of trees. The actual vehicular traffic is carried
by drives on each side of the reservation for car
tracks; on one side there are planting spaces fourteen feet wide and sidewalks five feet wide. These
arrangements, conceived after much study, represent very desirable improvements in street design.
The paving throughout is bitulithic, or concrete,
the curbs and sidewalks being of concrete. The
arboreal effects are achieved by shade trees, the
willow, oak, tulip, plane and elm predominating.

THE BEAUTY OF THE TREE

The development of Myers Park has been distinguished by the unusual attention given to tree
planting. Since it takes time for nature to reach
maturity, many new residential areas are glaring
in their rawness. The experiment of transplanting

Courtesy of Air View Photo Service

MYERS PARK

Airplane view of Queens College and street layout in vicinity. Polo field in upper left corner

A STREET SCENE IN MYERS PARK

big trees has been carried out in Charlotte with
much success. Of one hundred trees, with trunks
from six to twenty inches in diameter, planted the
first year, only one has died, and that was from
an understood neglect. The full exposure to the
southern sun demands shady avenues; houses and
grounds likewise need shade. Trucks, specially
made, have removed large trees and replanted them,
bringing early into the suburb a sense of age and
stability which could be obtained in no other way.
The transformation effected has been remarkable.
The streets have been planted with full-grown trees
and the grounds of many of the homes have likewise
been systematically planted. Native trees of a long-
lived variety have been used; they were removed
by the method employed with success originally on
the Duke estate at Somerville, New Jersey. Though
the cost of transplanting is naturally high, owing
to the care and subsequent handling involved, it
has been found possible to minimize the expense
considerably by wholesale operations in which the
estate-owners and the home-owners have coöper-
ated. The example is well worth imitation by those
having the care of residential areas, as well as by
landscape architects in laying out new tracts.

RESIDENCE LOTS

To plan a residential area in a shape that
respects the lay of the land obviously necessitates
blocks of irregular shapes and sizes, and conse-

quently varied building lots. At Myers Park this has been the case throughout. It has led to individuality in home-making, the variations producing no incongruous results. The lot minimum is one half an acre, with a frontage of no less than one hundred feet and a depth of two hundred feet. The

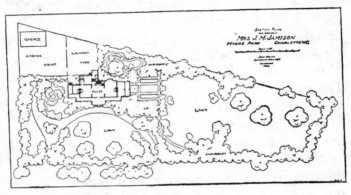

CHARLOTTE, NORTH CAROLINA

An example of plans prepared for private places in Myers Park

estate restrictions, which apply to every house, demand a set-back of the building line; this is used as lawn and approach, while flower and vegetable gardens are provided for in the rear. The Stephens Company, in developing the property, holds the view that all land in excess of requirements for residences not only is a burden on the owner in its purchase but remains still a burden in the expense and care required for its proper maintenance. This view is undoubtedly right, provided a happy mean is struck between congestion and waste, as in this instance. The company, having no wish to cramp the home, has encouraged the creation of landscape effects and the cultivation of open space. To this end the services of a landscape architect have been made available to all lot buyers, so that the general landscape design may be harmoniously developed under expert control.

The native plants of North Carolina have long been considered by botanists as unsurpassed in variety and beauty. The flora is largely that of the transition from North to South, with many varieties of the best of each. While the heat of the South precludes generally the fine lawns one sees in the North, there is a very luxurious growth of tree and shrub and vine. The attractiveness of Savannah, Atlanta and other Southern cities shows the possibilities of developing a distinctive Southern style of residential landscape architecture.

SAFEGUARDS AGAINST INCONGRUITY

Myers Park is a restricted residential section operating under a development company with the coöperation of the various land buyers. It was realized that so far as possible the estate must be built up along regular lines and assured of a certain permanency of character. The only way to do this was by safeguards against nuisances and haphazard development, with consequent property depreciation. At the same time the restrictions should

attract desirable clients, with eventually an en-
hancement of land values rather than a depreciation. The minimum building price of residence was
fixed originally at four thousand dollars, while in
some blocks it was put at a higher figure. The fluc-
tuating cost of building construction since the war
has made this minimum grotesque; as a matter of
fact, residences costing ten to twenty times that
figure have been erected. Other restrictions are the
fixing of building or set-back lines at distances varying from forty to eighty feet, and the fixing of side
lines at fifteen or twenty feet. The outbuilding,
bane of so many subdivisions, is restricted to seventy-five feet or more from the street line; none can
be erected before the residences themselves are
built. Fences cannot be built in front of the houses;
they are limited in height and material, where
erected at sides and rear. All the various utility
signs and conveniences are artistically designed in
the best interest of the community.

PARKS

It is now a recognized axiom of modern real-
estate practice that open areas pay. A conspicuous
instance is on record as regards Madison (Wisconsin) Park and Pleasure Drive Association. The
average gain in value in Madison was found to be
at least one hundred per cent. Similar conditions
resulted in the neighborhood adjacent to Keney
Park in Hartford, Connecticut.

MYERS PARK
Former home of George Stephens of the Stephens Company

MYERS PARK
Queens Road looking northeast from Queens College corner, at the
intersection of Radcliff and Selwyn Avenues

MYERS PARK

A street intersection. Streets have been fitted to the topography, and the large native oaks carefully preserved

At Myers Park it has been found that the assured beauty of the community and the pleasures derived from park lands have been an additional inducement to the home seeker to settle there. When there is a real community effort to achieve beauty it reflects itself in the desire of individuals to make the most of their home surroundings. The high-class residences with well-kept lawns, the tasteful gardens with terraces, pergolas, fountains, sculpture and inviting outdoor allurements, to say nothing of tennis courts, golf courses, and so forth, are to be seen throughout the park. A coördinated scheme of æsthetic effectiveness can be produced only by some such mutual coöperation.

SOME ARCHITECTURAL FEATURES

Myers Park is approached by three thoroughfares from the north, giving convenient access into Charlotte. One entrance has an architecturally designed gateway that serves as a waiting station for the street cars. Built of granite, it houses a central lodge over the car tracks. At various points on the main boulevard are waiting stations for car passengers.

In the heart of the park twenty-five acres of forest land are devoted to Queens College, an institution of advanced education for women, with some two hundred and fifty students. The spaciousness and beauty of the site promise to make the college one of the most attractive in the South.

The strong individuality of the college development, with its well-designed architectural features, has had a decidedly favorable effect on the types of residences, in developing an air of refinement and artistic appreciation.

Charlotte is called " the Queen City of the Carolinas," and Myers Park has a wide reputation as one of its civic assets. There is in the park a general appreciation of the benefits of a well-ordered social life. Only in settled communities where a sense of personal responsibility among the people prevails can a genuine social life manifest itself. The seclusion of the private house may be understood to represent the personal qualities of the individual and the family. But the street and the great out-of-doors assuredly stand for the brotherhood of man and its unity with all nature. Family life is spontaneous and primæval; social life is cultivated and typifies the progress of the race.

At Myers Park considerable attention has been given to a concerted program of community activities. The foundation of a Suburban Club, with a clubhouse and grounds, swimming pool and tennis courts, is intended to furnish the residents with a good social rendezvous. A nine-hole golf course is a valuable recreation feature. The feeling of good fellowship cultivated in this residential tract is a prominent factor in drawing the Charlotte city dwellers out into Myers Park, and an incentive to those farther afield to make it their home.

IX

A WHOLESALE MIGRATION FROM CITIES IN PROSPECT

Mariemont as an Example

It cannot be too strongly emphasized that the preparation of an adequate plan for a community requires far more than consideration of its embellishment with beautiful or imposing buildings. Especially in a community where architectural features of costly and elaborate character are assured in advance — for instance, in the establishment of a new county seat or a state capital — this matter of suitable planning must all the more be made the primary motive. Structures designed in advance, with the intention of planning the community particularly for their effective display, seem instead to prove in some unforeseen way actually ineffective when they and the plan come to realization. Logically, the building must be designed with reference to the plan rather than the plan studied with reference to the buildings it is to make conspicuous. The county seat, say, when rightly developed, should be planned according to the features of local topography, and with reference to existing or contemplated approaches and connections with other communities by highway, railway, or water. The

111

matter of climate should be taken into account — the prevailing winds, the seasonal temperatures, the direction of sunshine through the day, humidity or aridity. The planner should endeavor to shape his design according to the particular needs of a particular sort of community — its public building sites, its civic center, its open spaces to be developed as parks and playgrounds — all depending upon individual conditions. All these things being properly provided for, it may turn out that the styles of buildings that had been proposed for the place would be quite unsuited for it. Just as the architectural appearance of a building must be evolved from its plan, thoughtfully adapted to its purpose, rather than the plan shaped in accord with a handsome external design, so the style and shape of buildings to be erected in a town must depend upon the character of the town plan, out of which they should appear naturally to grow.

A REVOLUTIONARY MOVEMENT OUT OF THE CITIES

Some important factors that appear destined to enter into the development of new communities under population tendencies now under way were recently indicated by Mr. Roger W. Babson, the economist and statistician. Mr. Babson, it may be noted, is himself leading in a remarkable development for the beautiful Boston suburb of Wellesley Hills, where his important Statistical Institute (operated on a factory scale but with essential

Courtesy of Mattie Edwards Hewitt

School — Fechneimer, Ihorst & McCoy, Architects
Church — Louis E. Jallade, Architect

MARIEMONT COMMUNITY CHURCH AND THE MARIEMONT SCHOOL

Hubert E. Reeves, Architect

RESTHAVEN DEMONSTRATION FARM
NEAR MARIEMONT

Model dairy, cow stables, barn, and farmer's cottage

Edmund B. Gilchrist, Architect

MAPLE STREET CLOSE, MARIEMONT

Group housing, with varying set-backs, irregular roof lines and
building over the entrance

regard to the welfare of its high-grade employees)
has become a factor in shaping the civic character
of the community. His predictions therefore give
fresh emphasis to what is said in the introductory
chapter of this book regarding the prospective tendencies of population away from the great cities.

Mr. Babson looks for a revolution in real-estate
conditions for large cities. While, for a decade or
more, people have been crowding to the cities, he
now sees a reverse movement to the country about
to set in, promising " the greatest shifting in population since the institution of the railroad. Within
the next ten or more years the building of suburban
homes should rival the growth of the automobile,
good roads, the movies, the phonograph or radio!"

It is by very reason of these phenomenal inventions that Mr. Babson predicts a correspondingly
phenomenal suburban movement. With more than
ten million motor cars now in use in the United
States we have an average of one car to every ten
persons. Good roads, extending nearly everywhere,
are opening up millions of acres hitherto inaccessible. These facilities come opportunely as a relief
to the congestion of population in the large cities,
now becoming more and more intolerable because
of high rents and the tendencies to crowding in the
slums. " Wage earners," says Mr. Babson, " during
the last period of prosperity spent their money for
motor cars; in the next period of prosperity they
will buy country homes."

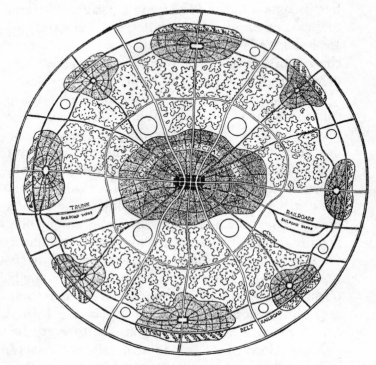

DIAGRAM OF SATELLITE TOWNS

Diagram illustrating a theory of satellite towns; designed by Robert
Whitten. Drawn primarily to show the use of open development strips
in metropolitan planning, it serves to illustrate several other possible
improvements

All this indicates a leveling-up process — the lifting of the masses to higher planes, socially and economically. Country life is rapidly undergoing a transformation from the old-time conditions of dreary isolation. The factors comprised in the great inventions mentioned above make for convenience, comfort, and joy of living, and almost imply the annihilation of distance. " The motion picture," says Mr. Babson, " has put the local town hall on a par with the city theater. The motor truck is giving the rural or suburban dweller nearly the same freight and express facilities as has the city. Motor bus lines are covering routes which never could be served by trolley cars. Automobiles are bringing the schoolhouse and the village to within a few minutes of the country home. Chain stores are carrying to every community the same efficient merchandising as the city dweller enjoys. Last, but not least, radio . . . gives to suburban homes the finest city lectures and music."

This prospective development is providentially coincident with the culmination of the evils that must drive workers from the cities by the thousands. " Congestion of dwelling house space and high rents long have been brewing discontent. For more than five years now these conditions have existed. Rebellion on the part of the rent payer is reaching the point of explosion. Almost any kind of change would be attractive. Once the average city worker realizes that with a few hundred dol-

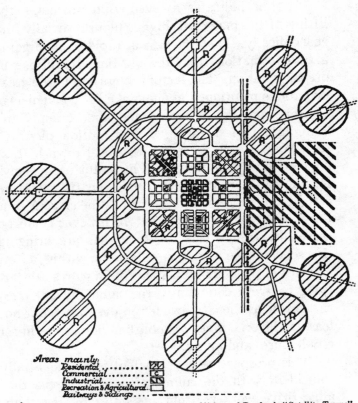

Areas mainly:
Residential ....
Commercial ....
Industrial ....
Recreation & Agricultural ....
Railways & Sidings ....

By permission of J. M. Dent & Sons, Ltd., publishers of Purdom's "Satellite Towns".

A METHOD OF ZONING

Diagram suggesting a method of zoning a new town and dividing it into distinct areas separated by open spaces; designed by Raymond Unwin

lars and a flivver he can get a house of his own with all the land he needs, the chances are two to one he will move."

It is a prospect that spells duty as well as opportunity: the opportunity of the worker to escape the oppressive urban surroundings that have been keeping him under, body and soul; the opportunity of investors to profit by anticipating this certain tendency; and with these the duty of all who have the public welfare at heart, to see that the movement of the workers out to the land is rightly organized and directed, that they are advised wisely, and guarded against the cupidity of those who would debase this tendency, for the sake of sordid speculations, to the workers' harm.

In the rural neighborhoods of many a city instances of such perversion of wholesome aspirations may be seen in beautiful landscapes despoiled, mutilated, scarred, and either abandoned or covered with shacks. Sites for settlement have been hastily adjusted to scrambled misplanning, without regard to intelligent growth. This sort of urban overflow is like that of a rising flood breaking a dike at its weakest point and spreading uncontrolled over the adjacent country, greatly to its damage.

The inevitable movement away from the cities, being foreseen, must accordingly be rightly prepared or organized, directed into the proper channels of escape, and conducted to suitable areas made ready for its reception. Herein lies a splendid task for constructive workers of foresight and capacity, as well as a remunerative field for sagacious investors.

A great opportunity lies in the selection and securing of the sites thus to be occupied. A prime consideration is accessibility. Mr. Babson points out that the railroads in most cases followed the valleys and lowlands, which are not the best building locations. " Between these lines are miles of land much more desirable for building but which have been inaccessible to the commuter because men had no means of getting to the train. It is in these areas between the railroad lines and within a radius of fifteen or twenty miles of the cities, which the motor car and good roads have opened up, that the most spectacular development in new building should take place!" Furthermore, we are told that the conditions cited " indicate that the coming readjustment in real estate will be more like a revolution!"

The terms " spectacular " and " revolution " employed by an economist accustomed to weigh his words suggest that the movement will proceed on an unprecedented scale. It follows that corresponding activities for taking care of it will be demanded. Hence preparations of the sort heretofore undertaken — such, for instance, as the establishment of garden cities (as in England) and the development of model suburban communities — extensive as they may have been, are of minor character in com-

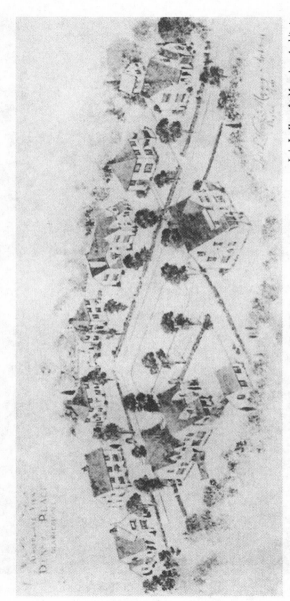

MARIEMONT

Airplane drawing of Denny Place

MARIEMONT
Dogwood Park

MARIEMONT
Garden in Dale Park

parison with what must be undertaken if the opportunities presented are to be adequately dealt with.

A COMMENSURATELY VAST SCALE ORGANIZATION OF THE MOVEMENT REQUIRED

If the movement away from the cities assumes
the formidable aspect of a hegira (and the magnitude of recent modern developments like the automobile and the radio makes this appear quite
likely), then it is immensely important that it be
organized and directed accordingly. The only comparison that can justly be made, it would seem, is
with the colossal character of the emergency housing movement attempted in connection with the
World War. Industrial communities were intelligently and admirably planned, and building operations were undertaken with extraordinary prompti-
tude and efficiency, to take care of the sudden and
peremptory movement of workers concentrating at
numerous industrial and shipping centers all over
the country. We have now in prospect a correspondingly great tendency of the workers away
from the cities, an emergency that happily has reference to the constructive demands of peace time
rather than to the destructive requirements of a
devastating war.

With the Armistice these vast housing preparations, nation-wide, came suddenly to an end. We
may now picture these operations as resumed.
They will be prosecuted with like energy into an

indefinite future and carried to great consummation. They not only will transform suburban countrysides into smiling garden cities and towns, but will react also with rejuvenant beneficence upon the cities themselves, purging them of their slums and changing them into institutional centers for the radiation of metropolitan activities out over the land — replanned for the new day and architecturally worthy of it all.

To construct the future thus in imagination may be only to foresee it in its actuality. The task calls for preparations on a scale comparable with the building up of the most gigantic business and industrial undertakings of the day. And in the promise of remunerative results, so conceived and executed, they should be as vast in achievement and rich in fruition as anything that has come from those gigantic and far-reaching affairs. The moment appears to be near. So let us say with Whitman:

> When the materials are prepared and ready,
> then the architect will appear;
> The architect will appear without fail.

MARIEMONT: AN ANTICIPATORY EXAMPLE

As an anticipatory example of this future, a development near one of our large cities is of exceptional interest. It has been planned with a most painstaking thoroughness. It provides an extensive housing of industrial workers of various economic grades under conditions that fairly deserve the

MARIEMONT
Houses in Maple Street Close

MARIEMONT
Apartments and shops in the Dale Park neighborhood center

Ripley & LeBoutillier, Architects

Houses on Chestnut Street

Courtesy of Mattie Edwards Hewitt   Kruckmeyer & Strong, Architects

Maple Street Close

MARIEMONT

Charles F. Cellarius, Architect

Group housing on Beech Street

Courtesy of Mattie Edwards Hewitt   Richard Henry Dana, Architect

Chestnut Street four-house group

term of ideal, so completely are considered the factors that assure comfort and convenience of living, together with a rational enjoyment of life. The conditions to be realized make for healthful existence with opportunities for community well-being, bringing therewith the corresponding welfare of the individual.

Mariemont is the name of the new town which in a near future will come into being as a garden suburb of Ohio's second great industrial city, Cincinnati. In its conception Mariemont follows in general the example set in the creation of Letchworth and other garden cities in England. Although its establishment is due to an enlightened enthusiasm for doing something worth while, cherished by a public-spirited lady of large means, the project is intended to justify itself along business lines followed with all efficiency. The beneficent aspects are incidental to the practical and business-like basis upon which the enterprise has been projected.

Mrs. Mary M. Emery of Cincinnati is the founder of this town; its name, Mariemont, is conferred in honor of the beautiful seaside estate of Mrs. Emery at Newport, Rhode Island. Mrs. Emery's attention was first attracted to the desirability of such a project through her experience with extensive industrial undertakings in which she had proprietary interests. She became convinced that workers need primarily to live in comfortable and attractive homes amid a favorable environment if

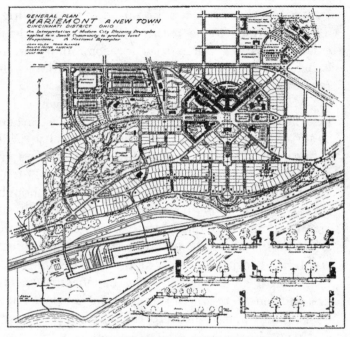

MARIEMONT, A NEW TOWN

General plan of a new town in the Cincinnati district covering a tract of about three hundred and sixty-five acres, providing for a village green and public buildings, stores and places of amusement, school sites, playgrounds and parks, and complete and attractive housing accommodations for wage earners of different economic grades

they are to develop a high working efficiency, and that this efficiency is affected by their opportunity to realize their best as human individuals apart from their work.

For many years, Mrs. Emery cherished the desire for the practical application of this truism. As long ago as 1915, working through competent representatives, notably Mr. Charles J. Livingood, she began the gradual purchasing of land in a region near Cincinnati favorably situated for the purpose. This work had to proceed cautiously to avoid the cupidity of speculators, who otherwise could easily have thwarted the project so far as the selected locality was concerned. Now that it is accomplished and the elaborate plans agreed upon, the work of construction will be energetically carried through with all the celerity of modern methods. A few years should see Mariemont well realized — the most enlightened feature of the industrial district of Cincinnati.

The site has an area of about three hundred and sixty-five acres, located on the main line of the Pennsylvania Railroad as it runs into Cincinnati. Mariemont, adjoining Madisonville and Plainville, is only about two miles from the chief manufacturing suburbs, Oakley and Norwood. With such an environment and such a location on the main line of a great railway, no site could be more favorable in the way of convenience. Happily the site had remained open country in an unspoiled rural state.

Its level topography made it easy for economical development.

The close connection with Cincinnati makes the theaters, institutions of art and learning, parks, and great retail stores of the big city at any time accessible. Mariemont itself, however, is to be self-contained; for ordinary shopping, recreation, schools and other features incidental to a well-equipped community there will be no occasion to go out of town. As planned, the population will be five thousand at the outset, with opportunities for a growth as high as ten thousand when called for. In planning for such communities it is felt that the latter figure should be the maximum; this being reached, like communities can be projected as desired.

The plan has been studied with particular reference to convenient circulation. Communication from point to point is to be as direct as practicable. The location of the main streets has been determined with regard to the general highway system of the Cincinnati district. At the attractive civic center radiating streets converge. Here, either in spacious grounds or grouped about the village green and the plaza-like central open space, are to stand the town hall, the theater, the public library, the post-office, the hotel and other buildings of monumental architecture, surrounded by the compact business center — approached by direct ways from all sections of the town. Church sites are provided

Charles F. Cellarius, Architect

MARIEMONT
Dale Park fire station

Fechheimer, Ihorst & McCoy, Architects

MARIEMONT
Mariemont School, Dale Park section

MARIEMONT

Typical views in Dogwood Park

for in various quarters where they will be accessible, their architecture displayed to advantage, and the congregations undisturbed by noise and heavy traffic. The schoolhouses are adjacent to ample space for play and sports. A fine athletic field is to be equipped with a stadium. There are inviting parks of various types, public tennis courts, a bathhouse, a gymnasium, a lagoon, and reservations for public enjoyment along the bluffs overlooking the river.

The main property has an area of about two hundred and fifty acres; in the river-bottom lands are seventy acres, and the hospital group contains about twenty-five acres. About one half the acreage is devoted to lots, one quarter is in public areas, and one quarter in streets which vary in width from forty to eighty feet. Fifty acres are in parks alone, and twenty additional acres are in other public open spaces. There are allotment gardens located at convenient points.

The dwelling layout for this community of wage earners allows for a population density not exceeding six or seven families for the acre. Even the humblest class of workers is assured comfortable and attractive living conditions. There are group-houses, apartments, and semi-detached and detached houses, according to individual requirements.

The detached houses stand in lots ranging from fifty by one hundred and twenty feet to eighty by one hundred and twenty feet. For the group-houses the normal lot size is twenty by one hundred feet. The greatest of care has been exercised to secure fine architectural design combined with harmonious variety. The community picture will thus be assured protection against the defacements that come from indulgence in individual whims and the willfulness of bad taste. The houses are mostly of brick or other permanent material, avoiding the tendency to shabbiness inherent in surfaces of wood, which demand constant repainting, and also making use of local stone and materials. Electricity and steam heat will be furnished from a central plant.

A feature of the project is a sort of annex to the main plan, with about twenty-five acres specially provided by Mrs. Emery for the accommodation of pensioners, but with facilities for caring for patients own extensive industrial and other personal interests. Here they will be assured restful retirement in pleasant cottage homes of their own. In this section there is to be a hospital, for the benefit of the pensioners, but with facilities for caring for patients belonging also in Mariemont proper. There will also be a convalescent home and a workshop.

A real-estate undertaking, the Mariemont Company, has been organized to carry out the project. The individual ownership of homes is contemplated; the workers will be given favorable terms for purchase.

MARIEMONT
CINCINNATI DISTRICT, OHIO

STATISTICAL STATEMENT

DATA HEREWITH IS BASED ON A TOTAL OF 253.58 ACRES

LOTS	ACREAGES		PERCENTAGES		LOTS
HOUSES	111.52		43.97		Number of House Lots
STORES & APARTMENTS	10.04		3.97		**759**
Total		121.56		47.94	Houses per net acre
SEMI-PUBLIC PROPERTIES					**6.81**
GARAGE	.89		.35		
FILLING STATION	.07		.03		Average Lot Area
HOTEL	.87		.34		**.15 acres**
BANK	.37		.15		
CHURCH	.55		.22		Normal Lot Sizes
CHURCH & CEMETERY	1.00		.39		Detached
CHURCH	.76		.30		50 ft. × 120 ft.
					80 ft. × 120 ft.
Total		4.51		1.78	Semi-Detached
PUBLIC PROPERTIES					30 ft. × 100 ft.
POST OFFICE	.83		.33		
TOWN HALL	1.88		.74		Group
FIRE STATION	.32		.13		20 ft. × 100 ft.
PUBLIC MARKET	1.19		.47		
LIBRARY	.97		.36		Northwest Section
COMMUNITY BUILDINGS	2.57		1.01		Density per net acre
SCHOOL & STADIUM	8.59		3.37		**11.09**
SCHOOL	1.00		.39		
PARKS & PLAYGROUNDS	51.76		20.45		
Total		69.11		27.25	
STREETS					**LENGTH OF STREETS**
FORTY FOOT	10.00		3.95		40' WIDE 2.2 MILES
FIFTY FOOT	22.84		9.02		50' " 3.7 "
SIXTY FOOT	12.39		4.87		60' " 1.7 "
EIGHTY FOOT CARLINE	8.01		3.15		80' " .7 "
150 FOOT SPECIAL	5.16		2.04		150' " .3 "
Total		58.40		23.03	Total 8.6 MILES
TOTAL	253.58	253.58	100.00	100.00	

John Nolen City Planner
Philip W. Foster Associate
Cambridge Mass.

MARIEMONT, CINCINNATI DISTRICT, OHIO
Statistical statement, showing acreages and percentages devoted to lots, semi-public properties, public properties, and streets

As a method for achieving the " home of his own " ideal, the tenant-proprietor idea, as exemplified in the plan of certain model-town undertakings in England — as in the case of the Ealing Tenants, Limited, at Ealing, near London — has not yet obtained a foothold in America. " Every man his own landlord " is the basic principle. The idea originated in Germany in the shape of a scheme for common ownership by the occupants of large apartment houses; in England it was adapted to the community ownership of a whole village. In New York City a similar plan obtains in the common ownership of fine apartment houses by individual occupants of ample means.

In brief, the English plan is for the formation of a coöperative company with shares; this company builds the houses of the village; the occupants in paying their rent to the company pay up gradually on their shares; this being accomplished, the individual owns in shares the equivalent of the house he occupies, although the title to the property remains with the company. Undesirable occupancy is thus prevented. If for any reason a person wants to withdraw (as in having to move away because of health or business), the company buys back his shares and finds a new purchaser and occupant for the premises. This procedure avoids the hardships that arise when a house owner, obliged to move elsewhere, may have to part with his home at a sacrifice.

This tenant-proprietor idea has been proposed in connection with various model-homes projects in America, but has not yet found favor; the individual, when not a tenant pure and simple, usually wants to own his home outright. He has not learned to appreciate that the tenant-proprietor plan accomplishes with greater flexibility practically the same end, while it also gives him a proprietary interest in the real estate of the entire community. This, it is claimed, promotes a public-spirited interest in community affairs.

The Mariemont Company intends to give the residents the opportunity to purchase its shares. This generally carried out would accomplish a similar end. In Germany many municipalities build houses for their public employees. Others, like Ulm, build houses which are sold to citizens on favorable terms that assure to the city a return of its outlay. The purchasers have the privilege of selling back to the city, should occasion arise. Possibly an organization like the Mariemont Company might find a way to adopt a similar plan. By reserving the right to repurchase on occasion it might assure the character of occupancy and keep away undesirable people from the community.

The organization of the great housing undertakings that seem destined to be a feature of the future will doubtless take various shapes and be a subject for much instructive experimentation. However this may be done, it is important to see that whatever is done is well done, and to keep vigilant guard against perversions, whether willful or ignorantly inadequate, of what promises to be one of the most beneficent movements of the age.

DALE PARK SECTION OF MARIEMONT
Showing the plan in detail, with the assignments to the various architects

It follows as of equal importance that the greatest of pains should be taken to assure the maintenance of the standards set in the planning and construction of model communities. In the first place, the standard must not be set too high for the types of humanity who are to live in them. The individuals comprising America's heterogeneous, foreign population bring different grades of household needs and outdoor tastes, according to the habits of the countries from which they come, as well as according to individual training and inclinations. Some are cleanly and others are not. Some take naturally to gardening and others do not.

It is not enough to provide American standards of housing without some due consideration of the population which is to inhabit it, or else misunderstanding and disappointment will occur all round. For example, even the Italian peasant worker in the field lives gregariously in tenement houses in the village. To keep our new, well-planned neighborhoods fresh and neat, some forethought, care, and even help must be expended in order to adapt the foreigner's different viewpoint to our standards of living. Neglect, misuse and ruin are contingencies to be guarded against if possible. It would seem that this aspect of the case has hitherto been little considered, doubtless for the reason that the prospective population have been regarded according to the terms with which we are most familiar, those of the intelligent middle class, both of America and of northern Europe. For those others, who are given as far as possible the opportunity for the expression of the best of their national life, and who still violate fundamentals of health

and beauty, some sort of paternal community regulations will be necessary. The inhabitants of a
model town, if not fitted for the sort of living that
is meet for their environment, both domestic and
communal, should be even more by sympathetic
precept and example lifted to that level.

X

NEW COMMUNITIES PLANNED TO MEET NEW CONDITIONS

THE REQUIREMENTS FOR THE NEW TOWN

THERE are two main divisions of city planning directly connected with the better distribution of population: one is the replanning and rebuilding of existing towns and cities; the other is the laying out and construction of new communities, either what are known as " satellites "[1] of existing cities, or complete and separate new towns in new locations, what are termed in England " garden cities."[2] The town-planning problem is not whether our efforts shall be given either to the replanning of existing cities, or to the laying out of new communities of the two classes mentioned above. If

---

[1] " By a satellite town is therefore meant a town in the full sense of the word, a distinct civic unit with its own corporate life, possessing the economic, social and cultural characteristics of a town in these present times, and, while still maintaining its own identity, in some sort of relation of dependence upon a great city. The term does not mean a village, because a village is essentially not a town; neither does it mean a suburb or any form of community which is absorbed, or in process of absorption, into another community. The word ' satellite ' is used in a pseudo-astronomical sense: that is to say, of a body that is under the influence of a more powerful body but physically distinct."
—*The Building of Satellite Towns*, by C. B. Purdom.

[2] " A Garden City is a town planned for industry and healthy living; of a size that makes possible a full measure of social life, but not larger; surrounded by a permanent belt of rural land; the whole of the land being in public ownership or held in trust for the community."—*Town Theory and Practice*, by C. B. Purdom.

there is to be a better distribution of population, both of these solutions must be employed to the full and both must go on concurrently.

Illustrations could readily be given of dead cities, of cities that have ceased to be, but the civilizations that these cities represent have gone with them. Illustrations might also be cited of towns and cities that, through changes in industrial, economic or other conditions, have become less important, less populated. This is the case, for example, with mining towns, and with other towns built as a means of utilizing natural resources, which in time are exhausted. But cities, generally speaking, are permanent, and will remain permanent through the ages. Cities are not only permanent in the fact that they continue to exist, but are largely unchangeable in all of their main features. A review of the form of cities in this country or in other countries will bring to mind the comparatively small changes that have taken place in them. Furthermore, a review of American cities for the last twenty-five years, the period of most active modern city-planning work, will show that, notwithstanding substantial improvements and fine achievement in many directions, the form of these cities remains much the same. A study of Chicago and St. Louis, of Detroit and Flint, of San Francisco and Los Angeles, or of other cities that have a proud record of vigorous progress in modern city planning, would illustrate the point that under the most favorable

KINGSPORT, TENNESSEE

General view, showing progress in construction work, with reservations of land for
the future expansion of the business center

C. E. Howard, Architect

Marshall R. Lawson, Architect

Typical residences in the new town. Mr. Howard's was the most worthy of note in the Art Jury award of 1925

Pierpont & Walter S. Davis, Architects

A typical residence

Pierpont & Walter S. Davis, Architects
Winchton L. Risley, Architect for additions

La Venta Inn

PALOS VERDES, CALIFORNIA

circumstances, and the most energetic efforts, the replanning and rebuilding of existing cities must be done in most instances from a very conservative and limited point of view.

Is there anything comparable to the unchanging character of cities from the city-planning point of view? Consider how little alteration is made in the plan of a city even when a great conflagration, earthquake, or flood occurs, sweeping all buildings and improvements from the land. London, Boston, San Francisco, Baltimore, Galveston and Dayton are examples of this point. Almost everything else that mankind has produced, except art and things of great beauty, is periodically destroyed and modified to meet the new conditions and new requirements of civilization. Indeed, very little remains even of cities except their general plans, by which is meant the location of streets and the distribution of the main organic parts of the city—the location, for example, of the principal features, both public and private. But these general plans, these principal features, remain much as they were originally.

If it can be demonstrated that old cities are not well adapted to the new conditions, and if they are so unsuitable for their present purposes, and if they cannot be changed very much, why cannot such cities be scrapped? The answer is: first, they have certain great advantages of location with reference to harbors or railroads or topography or raw materials or agricultural products, and so forth; secondly, the vested interest of individuals and corporations or of the whole body of citizens represents too great an investment of capital in land and improvements. Probably most of the finest sites for concentrated urban population are now occupied, representing an investment of wealth, both tangible and intangible, that involves a tremendous responsibility for efficient use and conservation. Whatever can be done to ameliorate in any degree the incompatibilities produced by the combination of age and progress in great cities is worth consideration and trial. A lack of public spirit or foresight in the past is no excuse for present inertia. There is always, even for the most complete and compact of localities, as the Old World well realizes, an evolving future to be faced and provided for.

New communities, large and small, are constantly coming into existence, either casually or deliberately. There are substantial reasons why the increase in population, which in the United States amounts to over a million a year, cannot and should not be taken care of entirely in or immediately around existing cities, or in many instances even in the neighborhood of existing cities. So far as new communities are concerned, the main point of the town-planning movement is to make action more deliberate, to plan and build towns and cities by intention, with knowledge and skill and understanding. The problem is different from the replanning of existing cities in that it need not be approached

HAMPSTEAD GARDEN SUBURB, ENGLAND

WELWYN, SECOND GARDEN CITY, ENGLAND

MOUNTAIN LAKE PARK, NEAR LAKE WALES, FLORIDA

MYAKKA RIVER VIEW, VENICE, FLORIDA

so conservatively. These new towns should express new standards and new ideals, and be an attempt to meet in new ways the modern conditions of life and the peculiar opportunities that these conditions and resources offer.

There are two reasons of major importance for building new communities. The first is to take care of territories that are from time to time opened up for settlement; and the second is to meet modern requirements and standards by new planning.

There are a number of causes for the opening up of new territory, obviously, such as the extension of railroads and the main highways, and the construction of new harbors and canals. The transcontinental development and the settlement of the Middle West, the Northwest, California and the Southwest can be traced to this cause. Many of the recent settlements in Florida, also, are the result of railroad extensions, especially the Florida Western and Northern (Seaboard Air Line), but lately constructed across the state; or of highway extension, such as the Dixie Highway and the Tamiami Trail.

The occupation of new lands, as a result of the discovery of gold or oil or other minerals, or of new agricultural or industrial products, has been widely operative in the past. There are still further developments to come from the establishment of new industries due to new inventions, of which the automobile, the airplane and the radio are present examples. The construction of a series of industrial or manufacturing plants distributed more or less over the whole country, such, for example, as the United States Steel Corporation, the General Electric Company, and Sears, Roebuck & Com-

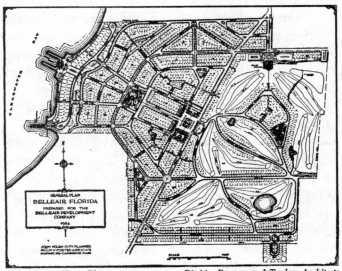

John Nolen, Town Planner   *Ritchie, Parsons and Taylor, Architects*

BELLEAIR, FLORIDA
General plan of Belleair, Florida, near Clearwater

pany, various automobile companies and railroad repair shops, fosters the growth of fresh communities. The drainage and irrigation of unused land by the reclamation service of the government, or similar work carried through by private enterprise, opens up still further tracts for habitation. The building of islands, as in Florida, is the actual creation of new land for occupation, giving opportunity for new planning and construction on original lines. The increasing use of resort communities for winter or summer occupation, and the possibilities of their development and enjoyment because of the accumulation of surplus wealth seeking investment, in addition to tourists looking for health and recreation, inspired Mr. Babson, the economist, to speak aptly of " going-away winters " as a new industry. There are various other miscellaneous reasons leading to the formation of new communities, such as the establishment of new colleges or other educational institutions, and so forth.

May we not add another cause for new towns? There is a limit to the size of cities. What this limit is may be open to discussion, it is true, but human capacity to organize and govern, or at any rate the law of diminishing advantages in cities in proportion to cost (like the law of diminishing returns in agriculture), will sooner or later fix a limitation to the size of existing cities and compel new populations to establish settlements elsewhere.

It is not only because new territories are opened up that new cities should be planned and constructed; changes have come in the requirements of urban living. There is good reason in modern municipal needs and standards for the laying out and construction of " satellite " towns, or more independent and complete new towns and villages, to take care of the overflowing population, rather

GENERAL Town-Plan of Welwyn Garden City shewing Road and Rail Communications, Shops, Public Buildings, etc.

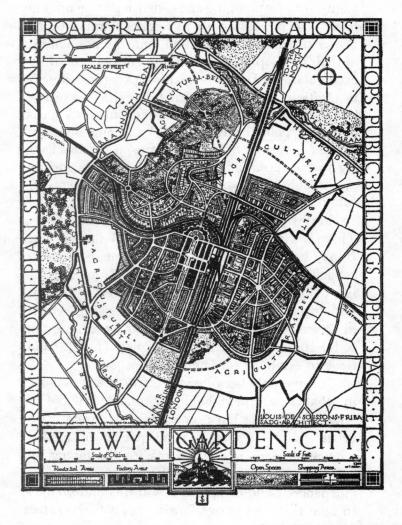

Reproduced from " The Building of Satellite Towns," by C. B. Purdom, published by J. M. Dent & Son, Ltd. (1925).

than to overtax the rigid outlines of our present cities by still further strain.

The operative forces that demand new planning are found both objectively in the material aspects and organization of the city, and subjectively in the life of its inhabitants. The very equipment of a modern city actually requires a city planned differently from one fifty years ago, or at least such changes give advantages and economies whenever new planning is employed. The modern city is evolving an expert policy in filling its needs when it considers the placement of the steam railroad and its other means of conveyance, whether trolley car or motor vehicle. The elevator and steel construction for buildings have produced new aspects and possibilities presenting new problems. There has been progressive invention in municipal utilities and in city engineering, such as in pavements, sidewalks and street lighting.

Municipal sanitation and sanitary standards have gone forward amazingly, with better methods of city water supply and disposal of wastes. The effect is shown in the lowering of the death rate from about 20 per 1,000 in 1880 to 12.3 per 1,000 in 1923. Economic changes and the consequent raising of the standard of living are expressing themselves in urban conditions as the result of the increased per capita wealth, which in 1850 was only three hundred dollars and is today over three thousand dollars.

The material changes are reflected and further influenced by changes in the life of the people inhabiting the modern community. New habits and tastes animate the city dweller. Home life is different from what it was a century ago. The apartment house has come into existence, with greater and greater dependence upon cafés and restaurants. The servant problem has arisen. A need of nature has developed. Country clubs have become a necessity. It is only in the last seventy-five years that public parks and playgrounds have come to be an integral part of a city's layout, producing wild reservations, bathing beaches and provision for winter sports. All sorts of expansions of community efforts for education and recreation are taking place, from the greatly increased spaces for schools to experiments with community clubs both public and private. So quickly has the usual citizen accepted the automobile, the moving picture and the radio, that he hardly realizes that his full use and enjoyment of these pleasures are dependent upon public coöperation and planning.

Especially important are these changes in leisure and its use, and the new ideas with regard to outdoor games and sports and physical education generally. The working-day fifty years ago was two or three hours longer than it is now, the Saturday half-holiday was unknown, and Sunday was regarded as primarily a day for religion and rest. No existing city, large or small, practically finds it pos-

WELWYN GARDEN CITY

400 ft

In the Hertfordshire Highlands

Twenty-one miles from Kings Cross

The New Town for Residence & Industry.

IT is not good to waste two hours daily in trains buses and trams to and from the workshop, leaving no time nor energy for leisure or recreation.

AT Welwyn Garden City a mans house will be near his work in a pure and healthy atmosphere

He will have time & energy after his work is done for leisure & recreation

REPRODUCED FROM THE PAGES OF "PUNCH" SUMMER NUMBER, 1920.

By permission of J. M. Dent & Sons, Ltd., publishers of Purdom's "Satellite Towns"

sible to provide today adequate open areas for its well-recognized requirements. The problem of properly employing the new leisure depends directly upon new planning to provide adequate and suitably organized areas for the new ideals of recreation.

Except in remote sections the old simplicity and charm of American villages and towns has largely disappeared, and a new form of urban beauty has not yet taken its place. The Victorian period of architecture and the planning standards of our own Civil War time are still too much with us, but there are many hopeful and unmistakable evidences of a transition stage. No longer are we satisfied with crass and crude uglinesses. We may tolerate them but we take no pride therein. Different standards of beauty inspire our times from those of the preceding generation. We are pioneering in an up-to-date civic art. We are gradually breaking away from the old, gradually taking on the new. This stage is naturally an awkward one and not generally characterized by beauty. The amenities of city life have been sadly sacrificed. New town planning, new forms of architecture and landscape architecture, new engineering should unite more and more, as there is now an opportunity to do, in a harmonious expression of new city ideals. It has recently been written of one of the most practical, progressive and successful builders of a new city on the East Coast in Florida: " One thing he has already

Yesterday

Living and Working in the Smoke

To-day

Living in the Suburbs—Working in the Smoke

To-morrow

Living & Working in the Sun at WELWYN GARDEN CITY

By permission of J. M. Dent & Sons, Ltd., publishers of Purdom's "Satellite Towns".

done and it is the biggest part of that accomplishment which I undertook to write about; he has proven that the practical can be romanticized and that 'beauty draws more than oxen.' He has showed in the hearts of his fellow men a deeper respect and a truer reverence for loveliness than they ever had before."

New towns cannot for one reason or another be planned, perhaps, to meet all of these enlarged requirements, but under normal circumstances very much more successful provision can be made in planning new towns than in the replanning of existing cities. The difference, after all, is much like the success with which old buildings constructed fifty or more years ago, as compared with new construction, could be revamped now to meet the needs of a modern office building or a metropolitan city hotel. Furthermore, the new communities can and should be planned not only to take care of present requirements, but also to anticipate those of the future which we can now, in some measure at least, forecast, permitting frequently an easier conversion of city territory to different uses and changed conditions.

WHAT SHOULD THE NEW TOWN OR CITY BE LIKE?

1. The new town or city should have the right location, the right site geographically. This is a matter of primary importance, and is related closely to national, state and regional planning. It should

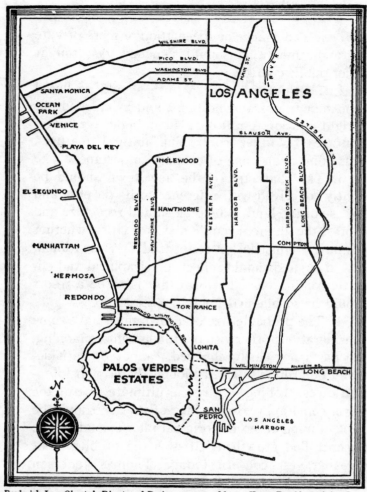

Frederick Law Olmsted, Director of Design   Myron Hunt, President of Art Jury
              Charles H. Cheney, City Planner

PALOS VERDES, CALIFORNIA
A complete and perfected plan of community development

not be left to chance or speculation or mere private aggrandizement. It should somehow be brought under public control.

2. The local plan for a town should be based upon topographical conditions, and be worked out in right relation to railroads, main highways, water frontages or other controlling natural features. This point is also one of primary importance.

3. The character of the new town should be rightly conceived with reference to its purpose and the use of the land. The plan should recognize and express the different requirements of cities, whether primarily industrial or residential or recreational, and so on, and should reflect topographical and climatic conditions. The town that is to be a resort should be so planned for its greatest success.

4. The probable size of a town must have some consideration; otherwise the fundamental planning, the parts not easily changed, cannot be satisfactorily determined. Even though there is no intention of controlling rigidly the ultimate size of the town, some approximate idea of its size should be kept in mind when the original plan is made. The uncontrolled growth of cities is the problem that gives gravest concern today. Thomas Jefferson long ago said that " great cities are great sores." One of the most striking illustrations that could be given is a quotation from Ferrero in his volume entitled " Ancient Rome and Modern America," in which he says: " The disease which killed the

Roman empire was in fact excessive urbanization. Neither the attacks of barbarism from outside, nor those of Christianity from within, would have prevailed against its might and its massive weight, if the strength of the Colossus had not been already undermined by this internal cancer." Whatever the estimate of the size of a town or city may be, whether it be twenty-five thousand or two hundred and fifty thousand or more, in the planning of new communities there should be some notion of size, but there should also be an elastic element to provide, so far as possible, for error in forecasting, in either overestimating or underestimating the size of the town.

It would seem worth while in the discussion of this subject to consider some of the essential physical features of a town or city. Even a brief summary of the essential features from the planning point of view will bring to mind the considerations that should control and influence new planning and the degree to which such considerations could have weight in new planning as compared with the revision of old planning.

Take, for example, the railroads, and consider the situation in existing cities, and how little can be done to bring about railroad changes, and even then the great cost and difficulty involved. The problems of the railroads would include the location of rights of way, separation of grades, the reduction in number of crossings by local streets, the location of passenger and freight stations, adequate platforms for the use of passengers, the unification of rights of way, the relation of railroads to industrial property, the coördination of rail and water transportation, and so forth, and so forth. It is difficult to revise such matters as these in an established city, but in new planning a proper and convenient layout could readily be secured.

This contrast of the railroad is equally true of waterfronts, whether for industry or recreation. The logical division of the waterfront for the use of industry and recreation has been a source of controversy and conflict in many existing American cities. San Diego in California is an apt illustration. In new planning, a satisfactory line and policy could be established with comparative ease. The same situation exists with regard to other waterfront problems.

The most striking comparison, perhaps, of new towns and existing cities could be made with regard to streets and main thoroughfares. In new cities the selection of locations for major streets, and the fixing of their width, alignment and grade, involves no great difficulty beyond the technical skill of the engineer and designer necessary to an understanding of the requirements. In an existing city, on the other hand, the changes in the major streets necessary to take care of modern requirements are a more and more baffling problem, and one that has not yet been fully solved in any American city of

importance. The seriousness of the traffic problem
is shown in the mortality figures. According to a
statement recently issued by the National Automobile Association, based on tabulations made by
the National Automobile Chamber of Commerce,
19,828 persons were killed in automobile accidents
in 1925.[1] This figure shows an increase of ten per
cent over that for 1924.

The contrast of new and old in cities could be
applied readily to other subjects, as, for example,
public buildings and their grouping, schools and
the selection of open spaces. The latter is one of the
most far-reaching factors in rendering modern city
life wholesome and happy. It involves the setting
aside of natural features for parks and recreation,
the distribution throughout the city area of play
space, and the establishment of neighborhood and
recreation centers for children and adults.

A well-known legal authority, one versed in
city planning, has said that what finally remains
and is most permanent in a city is " the determination of the legal quality of the various land areas
for various purposes." It is quite obvious that by
the proper application of skill to the planning of
new areas, combined with easily determined restrictions and early zoning, it is possible to fix this legal
quality of land in a much more satisfactory manner
than is possible with an existing city where condi-

[1] One automobile out of every 923 killed a person during the year
1925.

tions are already firmly established and more or less unchangeable.

Housing, a matter of supreme importance, has not been given as much attention by city planners in the United States as in other countries, and there are some good reasons for this difference. Furthermore, the housing standards in many American communities, both large and small, are not as high as they should be. Here again there is the contrast between the potentialities of the two situations. In the planning of new communities it is feasible from many points of view to apply successfully housing standards that are much higher than in existing cities, especially the large cities. In such matters as the size of lots and the provision of light, air, sunshine and an agreeable environment, the contrast is obvious, as also in the securing of neighborhood recreation and other essential facilities for family and social life, more particularly the requirements of children.

Must the control of the location of towns and cities be left to accident or to the sporadic promotion of the owners of property, as, for example, is now the case in Florida, as it has been in other states in periods of great activity, or could such development be regulated and controlled in any way by the governing public authorities? Would national planning and regional planning give opportunities to regulate reasonably the location of future towns and cities? No definite answer can be given at the present time to these questions, but, at any rate, some of the practical ways in which the development of new towns could be initiated and to some extent more wisely directed can be indi-

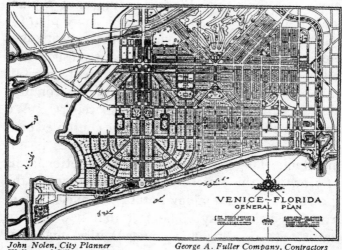

John Nolen, City Planner
Walker and Gillette, Architects

George A. Fuller Company, Contractors
Black, McKenney and Stewart, Engineers

VENICE, FLORIDA

Town-site plan, part of a larger regional plan, prepared for the Venice Company and the B. L. E. Realty Corporation

cated. The Federal government has had a great opportunity in the past, especially in connection with the reclamation service, and still has considerable opportunity, to influence favorably the location and development of new communities. The Farm Communities Association, recently organized, working in connection with the Federal government, or with some of the state governments, could develop well-ordered and well-located villages and towns in the country — " farm cities," as they are sometimes called, making new centers of agricultural life. There should be plans for states as well as for cities. Florida should have a plan. The State of New York has undertaken to plan for its future through the services of the Housing and Regional Planning Commission, one of its chief purposes being to secure a more efficient distribution of population. The chairman of this commission recently stated in a published report: " We have come to the conclusion that the continued concentration of population in our big cities is not inevitable. There are opportunities for better forms of growth in this state. We can choose to guide the growth of the state along natural channels, but in a more efficient way. The fact that new uses of nature are opening new opportunities, makes it essential that we take advantage of these to redirect the current of growth before the mold is again set."

The railroads have been instrumental in past years and will probably be more so in the future in establishing and developing new towns of all classes —commercial, industrial, residential and resort.

Industrial corporations of national dimensions, such as the United States Steel Corporation, the General Electric Company, and also groups of smaller industries working together, which is even better, have it in their power to inaugurate in many

BEACH ON THE GULF OF MEXICO, VENICE, FLORIDA

AIRPLANE VIEW OF VENICE, FLORIDA

One year's progress in town building. The project is owned and directed by the Brotherhood of Locomotive Engineers

places new towns, well located and planned to meet the new conditions of modern life, especially modern industrial and labor conditions, combined with proper housing.

There is an endless opportunity for limited dividend companies, working along the lines represented by Letchworth and Welwyn, the garden cities of England, or by the Hampstead garden suburb, or by Mariemont, Ohio, and other new towns in this country.

A movement for the planning and building of new towns, like its fellow movement for the replanning of existing cities, is dependent upon public opinion. In the formation of public opinion to stimulate, encourage and support these various forms of action leading towards new town planning, should be mentioned the National Conference on City Planning, the American City Planning Institute, the National Housing Association, the Federated Civic Societies, and the various other national, technical and popular groups concerned with this and related subjects. Mention should also be made of the various " foundations," and the financial help that they could give to a more thorough study of this subject and to actual demonstrations of the advantages of applied better methods.

Considerable influence could also be contributed by the new technical town-planning knowledge that is constantly being developed at the universities and special schools working in this field, such as Har-

vard University and the various other universities
and educational institutions in this country, the
University of Liverpool in England, and higher art
and technical institutions throughout the world.

Attention should be drawn to the International
Federation for Housing and Town Planning. This
Federation can be especially useful because of the
great value of the international exchange of ideas
and experience, and the generous, public-spirited
pooling of the results of research, invention, study
and experiment in planning new communities to
meet new conditions in modern life.

The new order of community life such as is
here roughly and briefly depicted as being possible
in the planning of satellite towns, garden cities or
farm cities, under whatever name they may appear,
ought to include more of the things that make life
worth living: decent homes; children well fed, with
fit bodies and active minds; sunlight not obscured
by a dense canopy of smoke; reasonable quiet; and,
above all, safety from danger and disease. In these
new cities we could, if we would, add much to the
decoration and adornment of life and its legitimate
amusements and recreations. We could help to better physical and æsthetic conditions, giving new
towns and cities more color and individuality. We
could have a wider enjoyment of music and art.
We could secure ample playgrounds, tennis courts,
parks, beaches and forest reserves. Indeed, by
building anew we could raise the whole plane and

standard of the common life, physical, mental and æsthetic, and at the same time, by good planning, actually lessen the cost of developing and maintaining cities, by reducing local taxes, because of the more practical ways in which provision could be made for the requirements of railroads and highways, of business and other economic factors upon which the wealth and therefore the welfare of cities finally rests.

APPENDICES

APPENDIX A

List of the more important printed reports by various town planners and other publications on the replanning of towns or small cities, land subdivision and suburban development, and the laying out of new towns.

This list is not intended to be complete. An effort has been made, however, to have it representative as to types of work, geographical distribution of places, and town planners. For the purpose of this list, the small city has been defined as being a place, usually, of not more than fifty thousand population. Because of their influence upon new town planning in the United States, a few references to English garden cities have been included.

ALTON, ILLINOIS
  The Advancement of Alton. C. M. Robinson. 1914.
ALTUS, OKLAHOMA
  Preliminary Report. L. P. Jenson. 1910.
ASHEVILLE, NORTH CAROLINA
  Asheville City Plan. John Nolen. 1925.
AUBURN, MAINE
  Text of the City Plan for Auburn, Maine. M. H. West. 1919.
  Lewiston (Maine) Journal, April 14, 1920.
AURORA, ILLINOIS
  A System of Parks for Aurora. M. H. West. 1918.
BAGNIO, PHILIPPINE ISLANDS
  Report of D. H. Burnham and Pierce Anderson. 1905.
  Philippine Commission Report, 1905; and plan, Philippine Carnival Circular, 1911.
BANGOR, MAINE
  Bangor City Plan: The Burnt District. W. H. Manning. 1911.
BERKELEY, CALIFORNIA
  Report on a City Plan for the Municipalities of Oakland and Berkeley. Werner Hegemann. 1915.

159

BILLERICA, MASSACHUSETTS
The Billerica Town Plan. W. H. Manning. 1912–1913.
Landscape Architecture, April, 1913.

BOULDER, COLORADO
The Improvement of Boulder, Colorado. F. L. Olmsted.
1910.

BRISTOL, CONNECTICUT
Local Survey and City Planning Proposals for Bristol,
Connecticut. John Nolen. 1920.

BROOKLINE, MASSACHUSETTS
Annual Reports, Brookline Planning Board. 1914–1916.
Report of Brookline Planning Board on Proposed Zoning
By-law. F. L. Olmsted and A. C. Comey, advisers.
1922.

CALGARY, ALBERTA
A Preliminary Scheme for Controlling the Economic
Growth of the City. T. H. Mawson and Sons. 1914.

CHAMPAIGN-URBANA, ILLINOIS
Notes for a Study in City Planning in Champaign-Urbana.
1913 and 1914 Classes in Civic Design, University of
Illinois. 1915.
Prepared under direction of Professor C. M. Robinson.

CHATTANOOGA, TENNESSEE
Plan and Report Outlining the General Features of a Park
System. John Nolen. 1911.

CLIFFSIDE PARK, NEW JERSEY
Zoning Ordinance and Building Code. Herbert Swan.
1921.

COLUMBIA, SOUTH CAROLINA
The Improvement of Columbia, South Carolina. Kelsey
and Guild. 1905.

COLUMBUS, GEORGIA
City Plan, Columbus, Georgia. John Nolen. H. J. Walker
and J. R. Hartzog, associates. 1925.

CRANSTON, RHODE ISLAND
Cranston Zone Plan. Robert Whitten. C. F. Fisher,
associate. 1923.

DECATUR, ILLINOIS
The Decatur Plan. M. H. West. 1920.

DOVER, NEW JERSEY
Town Planning for Dover, New Jersey. A. C. Comey.
1913.

DUBUQUE, IOWA
Report on the Improvement of the City of Dubuque, Iowa.
C. M. Robinson. 1907.

DUXBURY, MASSACHUSETTS
The Action of the Town of Duxbury Concerning a Zoning
By-law, and the Report of the Committee Appointed
to Consider, to Report and to Recommend. C. W.
Eliot, 2d, consultant. 1925.

EAST ORANGE, NEW JERSEY
Building Zones. G. B. Ford and E. P. Goodrich, consultants, 1920.
City Plan for East Orange. Technical Advisory Corporation. 1922.

ELGIN, ILLINOIS
Plan of Elgin. E. H. Bennett. 1917.

ELKHART, INDIANA
Planning Projects for Elkhart, Indiana: Report on Planning Proposals Based on Planning Survey, with a Supplement on Zoning. John Nolen. P. W. Foster, associate. 1923.

EVANSTON, ILLINOIS
Zoning Ordinance. Harland Bartholomew. 1921.

FITCHBURG, MASSACHUSETTS
Preliminary Study of the Thoroughfare System of Fitchburg. A. C. Comey. 1915.
Annual Reports, Municipal Development Commission.
1913–.

GARDNER, MASSACHUSETTS
Recommendations for the Development of the Town of
Gardner, Massachusetts. The Planning Board. Kilham,
Hopkins and Greeley, consultants. 1921.

GLEN RIDGE, NEW JERSEY
Plan for the Borough of Glen Ridge, New Jersey. John
Nolen. 1909.

GRAND CANYON, ARIZONA
A Plan for the Development of the Village of Grand Can-
yon, Arizona. United States Department of Agriculture,
Forest Service. F. A. Waugh. 1918.

GREENVILLE, SOUTH CAROLINA
Beautifying and Improving Greenville, South Carolina.
Kelsey and Guild. 1907.

162 APPENDIX A

HAMILTON, OHIO
The City Plan of Hamilton, Ohio. Harland Bartholomew. 1920.

HAMPSTEAD, ENGLAND
Co-partnership in Housing — Being an Account of the Three Hampstead Tenants' Societies from the Formation of the first in May, 1907. By E. B.
Foreword by Raymond Unwin.
Town Planning and Modern Architecture at the Hampstead Garden Suburb. Raymond Unwin and M. H. Baillie Scott. 1909.
The New Hampstead Garden Suburb: Its Recent Extension and New Development. F. C. Brown.
Architectural Review, November, 1912, pp. 126 ff.

HIGHTSTOWN, NEW JERSEY
R. V. Black. 1922.
Town Plan and Preliminary Draft of a Zoning Ordinance.

ITHACA, NEW YORK
Report to Accompany Study for a System of Reservations for Ithaca. W. H. Manning. 1908.

JOHNSTOWN, PENNSYLVANIA
The Comprehensive Plan of Johnstown, a City Practicable. Henry Hornbostel, George Wild and A. Rigaumont. 1917.

JOLIET, ILLINOIS
City Plan of Joliet. E. H. Bennett and W. E. Parsons. 1921.

KALAMAZOO, MICHIGAN
City Planning for Kalamazoo: Preliminary Report on City Planning and Sewerage Problems. Harland Bartholomew and W. W. Horner. 1921.

KENOSHA, WISCONSIN
The City Plan of Kenosha. Harland Bartholomew and Associates. 1925.

KINGSPORT, TENNESSEE
Kingsport, Tennessee, Set up as a Model City Plan Town. John Nolen.
Architect and Engineer, August, 1920, pp. 120 ff.
The New Industrial City of Kingsport, Tennessee. Rexford Newcomb.
Western Architect, November, 1926, pp. 137 ff.

La Crosse, Wisconsin
  The Making of a Park System in La Crosse. John Nolen.
  1911.
Lansing, Michigan
  The Lansing Plan. Harland Bartholomew. 1921.
Letchworth, England
  Letchworth Garden City in Fifty-five Pictures. London,
  1911.
  The Significance of Letchworth. C. B. Purdom.
  The Health of Letchworth During the War. Norman Mac-
  Fadyen.
  The Lessons of Cottage Building at Letchworth. H. D.
  Pearsall.
  Testimony of Letchworth to the Garden City Idea. Re-
  port by Citizens.
    The above four articles were published in *Garden
    Cities and Town Planning*, September, 1918.
  The Progress of Letchworth.
  Coöperative Houses at Letchworth. Mrs. E. B. Pearsall.
  A Small Holding in Letchworth. W. G. Furmston.
  An American View of Letchworth. C. H. Whitaker.
    The above four articles were published in *Garden
    Cities and Town Planning*, August, 1920.
  Letchworth of To-day.
  Some Recollections of Letchworth Life. H. E. Hare.
    The above two articles were published in *Garden
    Cities and Town Planning*, June, 1923.
  The Building of Satellite Towns. C. B. Purdom. London,
  1925.
  Part 2: Letchworth, The First Garden City.
  Letchworth's Coming-of-Age.
    Garden Cities and Town Planning, July, 1926 (whole
    number devoted to Letchworth).
Little Rock, Arkansas
  Report on a Park System for Little Rock, Arkansas. John
  Nolen. 1913.
Longview, Washington
  The City Practical that Vision Built. G. E. Kessler and
  J. C. Nichols; Hare and Hare. 1923.
Madison, New Jersey
  The Improvement of Madison, New Jersey. W. H. Man-
  ning. 1909.

MADISON, WISCONSIN
Madison: A Model City. John Nolen. 1911.

MARIEMONT, OHIO
A Descriptive and Pictured Story of Mariemont, a New Town, " A National Exemplar." Cincinnati, 1925.
A Complete Residential Village Near Cincinnati. John Nolen. P. W. Foster, associate.
Architecture, September, 1926.

MONTCLAIR, NEW JERSEY
Montclair: The Preservation of Its Natural Beauty and Its Improvement as a Residence Town. John Nolen. 1909.

NEW BRUNSWICK, NEW JERSEY
The New Brunswick Plan. H. S. Swan and Associates. 1925.
Follows two special reports of 1924 on Civic Center and Raritan River Bridge, also incorporated in this report.

NEW LONDON, CONNECTICUT
General Plan of a Park and Playground System for New London. John Nolen. 1913.

NEWPORT, RHODE ISLAND
Proposed Improvements for Newport. F. L. Olmsted. 1913.

NEW ROCHELLE, NEW YORK
Zoning Ordinance of the City of New Rochelle. 1921.

NEWTON, MASSACHUSETTS
Annual Reports, Newton Planning Board. 1919–1921.
Including a special report upon a system of thorough-fares, parks and playgrounds, by A. A. Shurtleff, and a zoning plan and ordinance by J. R. Fox, with comments of J. W. Bartlett, city solicitor.

NIAGARA FALLS, NEW YORK
Parks and Playgrounds for Niagara Falls. Olmsted Brothers. 1917.
Published in multigraphed form, 1919.
Planning Problems of Industrial Cities: Niagara Falls as an Illustration. John Nolen.
National Conference on City Planning *Proceedings,* 1919, pp. 22 ff.

NORTH ADAMS, MASSACHUSETTS
Report on General Development Plan for North Adams, Massachusetts. John Nolen. 1925.

NORWOOD, MASSACHUSETTS
Report to the Citizens of the Town. A. A. Shurtleff. J. P. Fox, consultant on zoning. 1923.

PALOS VERDES, CALIFORNIA
The Benefit of Community Planning as Seen in the Development at Palos Verdes, California. C. H. Cheney. *House Beautiful*, August, 1926, pp. 146 ff.

PARIS, TEXAS
General City Plan for Paris. W. H. Dunn. 1915.

PASADENA, CALIFORNIA
Some Preliminary Suggestions for a Pasadena Plan. G. A. Damon. 1915.
Progress Report of the City Planning Committee. 1917.
The City Plans of Pasadena. H. W. Wadsworth. *California Southland*, May, 1923, pp. 7 ff.

PUEBLO, COLORADO
Pueblo Improvement Plan. I. J. McCrary. 1916.

QUINCY, MASSACHUSETTS
Annual Reports, Quincy Planning Board. 1915–1916.

RALEIGH, NORTH CAROLINA
A City Plan for Raleigh. C. M. Robinson. 1913.
City Planning: Act of Legislature Providing for Planning Commission. 1922.

REVERE, MASSACHUSETTS
Ordinance in Relation to the Laying Out of New Streets. 1916.

RICHMOND, CALIFORNIA
City Planning Recommendations for Richmond, California. Aronovici and Hayler. *Pacific Municipalities*, May, 1922, pp. 155 ff.

ROANOKE, VIRGINIA
Remodeling Roanoke. John Nolen. 1907.

SALEM, MASSACHUSETTS
First Annual Report, Salem City Plans Commission. H. P. Kelsey, chairman. 1912.

SAN JOSÉ, CALIFORNIA
The Beautifying of San José. C. M. Robinson. 1909.

SANTA BARBARA, CALIFORNIA
Major Traffic Street Plan, Boulevard and Park System for Santa Barbara, California. C. H. Cheney and Olmsted Brothers. 1925.

SANTA FÉ, NEW MEXICO
  First Annual Report, Board of Park Commissioners.
  1884–1904.
  Including report to Board of Park Commissioners. Olm-
  sted Brothers. 1903.
  The Plan for Proposed Improvements in Santa Fé. City
  Planning Board. 1913.
SARASOTA, FLORIDA
  Report on Comprehensive City Plan. John Nolen. 1925.
STILLWATER, MINNESOTA
  Plan of Stillwater. Morell and Nichols. 1918.
UNION PARK GARDENS, WILMINGTON, DELAWARE
  General Plan for Land Subdivision and Industrial Hous-
  ing. John Nolen. Ballinger and Perrot, architects and
  engineers. 1918.
  Union Park Gardens: An Industrial Housing Development
  at Wilmington, Delaware. W. E. Groben.
  Architectural Record, January, 1919.
WAKEFIELD, MASSACHUSETTS
  A Proposed Plan for Wakefield. A. C. Comey. 1925.
  A Proposed Zoning By-law. 1925.
  Zoning By-law Adopted November 16, 1925.
  Also printed separately.
WALPOLE, MASSACHUSETTS
  Walpole — Plan To-day for To-morrow. John Nolen.
  1914.
WATERLOO, IOWA
  The Well-Being of Waterloo. C. M. Robinson. 1910.
WATERTOWN, MASSACHUSETTS
  Report on Proposed Location for Town Hall, Together
  with Other Changes Suggested in Watertown Square.
  John Nolen. 1921.
WAYLAND, MASSACHUSETTS
  Brief Report and General Plan for Its Improvement as a
  Country Town. John Nolen. 1911.
  Abstract published in *The American City,* May, 1912,
  pp. 773 ff.
WELWYN, ENGLAND
  London's First Satellite Town. Sir Theodore Chambers.
  Garden Cities and Town Planning, May, 1920, pp. 95 ff.
  The Building of Satellite Towns. C. B. Purdom. 1925.
  Part 3: Welwyn Garden City, the First Satellite Town.

WESTERLY, RHODE ISLAND
  Report of the Town Planning Committee. Robert Whitten. C. F. Fisher, associate.
WEST HARTFORD, CONNECTICUT
  West Hartford Zoning. Robert Whitten. 1924.
WEST ORANGE, NEW JERSEY
  Building Zones. Technical Advisory Corporation. 1921.
WHEELING, WEST VIRGINIA
  Abstracts of Reports upon Several Phases of a City Plan for Greater Wheeling. Morris Knowles, Inc. 1920.
WHITE PLAINS, NEW YORK
  Building Zone Ordinance. H. S. Swan. 1920.
WICHITA, KANSAS
  A Comprehensive City Plan for Wichita, Kansas, 1923. Harland Bartholomew and Associates. 1925.
WILLIAMS BAY, WISCONSIN
  A Development Plan for Williams Bay, Wisconsin. J. L. Crane, Jr. 1923.
WINCHESTER, MASSACHUSETTS
  Report upon Mystic Valley Improvement. H. J. Kellaway. 1911.
  Report of Winchester Planning Board. A. A. Shurtleff. 1924.
  Reports of Town Officers, 1924, pp. 177 ff.
WOONSOCKET, RHODE ISLAND
  Woonsocket Zone Plan. Robert Whitten. C. F. Fisher, associate. 1923.
WYOMISSING, PENNSYLVANIA
  Wyomissing Park, the Modern Garden Suburb of Reading. Wyomissing Development Company. 1919.

APPENDIX B

Brief list of the most useful and available books and articles in English on town and city planning and related topics.

These books and papers have been selected primarily from the point of view of the material contained in this volume. The bibliography includes references bearing upon the replanning of towns and small cities, land subdivision, housing, the laying out of new towns, satellites and garden cities. Preference has been given to books containing records of achievement or methods of achievement.

ADAMS, THOMAS
Rural Planning and Development. Commission of Conservation, Ottawa, 1917.
Modern City Planning.
Supplement to the *National Municipal Review*, June, 1922.
A Forecast of the Regional Community of the Future.
American City, November, 1926, pp. 617 ff.
ADSHEAD, S. D.
Civic Design. An inaugural lecture delivered at the University of Liverpool. Liverpool, 1909.
Town Planning and Town Development. London, 1923.
ALDRIDGE, H. R.
The Case for Town Planning. A practical manual for the use of councillors, officers and others engaged in the preparation of town planning schemes. London, 1915.
AMERICAN ACADEMY OF POLITICAL AND SOCIAL SCIENCE
Public Recreation Facilities.
Annals, March, 1910.
Housing and Town Planning.
Annals, January, 1914 (entire number).
AMERICAN INSTITUTE OF ARCHITECTS
City Planning Progress in the United States. New York, 1917.

ARCHITECTURAL REVIEW, April, 1917.
Whole number devoted to low-cost housing in England and the United States.

ARONOVICI, CAROL
Knowing One's Own Community. Suggestions for social surveys of small cities or towns. American Unitarian Association, Boston.
Housing and the Housing Problem. Chicago, 1920.

ASHBEE, C. R.
Where the Great City Stands. A study in the new civics. London, 1917.

BASSETT, E. M.
Zoning.
Supplement to the *National Municipal Review*, May, 1920. Also National Municipal League, New York, 1922.
The Constitutionality of Zoning in the Light of Recent Court Decisions.
National Municipal Review, September, 1924, pp. 492 ff. Also reprinted.

BENTLEY, E. G., and S. P. TAYLOR
Housing, Town Planning, etc., Act, 1909. A practical guide in the preparation of town planning schemes. Foreword by Raymond Unwin. London, 1911.

BIRD, C. S., JR.
Town Planning for Small Communities. National Municipal League, New York, 1917.

CADBURY, GEORGE, JR.
Town Planning, with Special Reference to the Birmingham (England) Schemes. London and New York, 1915.

COOKE, M. L.
Our Cities Awake. New York, 1918.

DAVIDGE, W. R.
The Principles and Position of Town Planning. London, 1916.

DAWSON, W. H.
Municipal Life and Government in Germany. London, 1914.
Ch. 6, " The Planning of Towns," pp. 141 ff.

DE BOER, S. R.
Transforming the Business Centers of Pioneer Western Towns.
American City, November, 1926, pp. 690 ff.

DELANO, F. A., and OTHERS
City Planning Procedure. American Civic Association,
January, 1926.

ENGLISH HOUSING AND TOWN PLANNING ACT. 1909.

EVANS, F. N.
Town Improvement. New York and London, 1919.

FARWELL, P. T.
Village Improvement. New York, 1913.

FORD, G. B.
Digging Deeper into City Planning.
American City, March, 1912, pp. 557 ff.

FORD, JAMES
The Housing Problem. Harvard University, Department
of Social Ethics, Cambridge, 1911.
" Residential and Industrial Decentralization," in City
Planning (ed. John Nolen). National Municipal League,
New York, 1916.

GEDDES, PATRICK
City Surveys for Town Planning and the Greater Cities.
Edinburgh, 1911.
Cities in Evolution. An introduction to the town planning
movement and the study of civics. London, 1915.
Regional and City Surveys. Town Planning Institute,
Papers and Discussions, London, 1920–1921.

GEDDES, PATRICK, and VICTOR BRANFORD
The Making of the Future. London, 1917.

GRAY, C. P.
Capital Requirements of Subdivision Operation.
National Real Estate Journal, November 1, 1926,
pp. 17 ff.

HAVERFIELD, F. J.
Ancient Town Planning. Oxford, 1913.

HEGEMANN, WERNER, and ELBERT PEETS
Civic Art. New York, 1922.

HOWARD, SIR EBENEZER
Garden Cities of To-morrow. London, 1902.

HUBBARD, H. V., and THEODORA KIMBALL
Introduction to the Study of Landscape Design. New
York, 1917.
Ch. 11, " Land Subdivision for Residential Purposes,"
pp. 275 ff.
Also published in *Landscape Architecture*, October,
1917, pp. 23 ff.

HURD, R. M.
Principles of City Land Values. New York, 1903.
IHLDER, JOHN
Housing and the Regional Plan.
American City, November, 1926, pp. 636 ff.
JACKSON, H. E.
A Community Center: What it is and How to Organize it.
Department of the Interior, Washington, 1918.
JAMES HARLEAN
The Building of Cities. New York, 1917.
Land Planning in the United States for the City, State
and Nation. New York, 1926.
JULIAN, JULIAN
An Introduction to Town Planning. London, 1914.
KERN, R. R.
The Supercity: A Planned Physical Equipment for City
Life. Washington, 1924.
KIMBALL, THEODORA (Editor)
Municipal Accomplishments in City Planning and Pub-
lished City Plan Reports in the United States. Detroit
City Plan Commission, Boston, 1920.
Helps in Conducting Publicity Campaigns for Zoning.
Landscape Architecture, July, 1922.
Manual of Information on City Planning and Zoning,
including References on Regional, Rural and National
Planning. Cambridge, 1923.
KOESTER, FRANK
Modern City Planning and Maintenance. New York,
1914.
KNOWLES, MORRIS
Industrial Housing. New York, 1920.
LANCHESTER, H. V.
Talks on Town Planning. London, 1924.
The Art of Town Planning. New York, 1925.
LEWIS, N. P.
The Planning of the Modern City. A review of the prin-
ciples governing city planning. New York, 1916.
LOHMAN, K. B.
Small Town Problems.
American City, July, 1920, pp. 81 ff.
LOMMEL, G. E., and F. G. BATES
A City Planning Primer. Purdue University, Lafayette,
Indiana, 1925.

MacGarr, Llewellyn
The Rural Community. New York, 1922.
Mackenzie, Clinton
Industrial Housing. New York, 1920.
Mawson, T. H.
Civic Art. Studies in town planning, parks, boulevards and open spaces. London, 1911.
McMichael, S. L.
City Growth and Values. Cleveland, 1923.
McVey, F. L.
The Making of a Town. Chicago, 1913.
Mead, Elwood
How California is Helping People Own Farms and Rural Homes. University of California, Agricultural Experiment Station, Berkeley, 1920.
Moody, W. D.
What of the City? Chicago, 1919.
Munro, W. B.
Principles and Methods of Municipal Administration. New York, 1916.
Ch. 2, " City Planning," pp. 30 ff.
The Government of American Cities (3d edition). New York, 1921.
Municipal Government and Administration. New York, 1923.
Murphy, J. H., Edith E. Wood and F. L. Ackerman
The Housing Famine. New York, 1920.
National Conference on City Planning
Proceedings.
Published annually since 1910, and issued at New York.
Nettlefold, J. S.
Practical Housing. Letchworth, 1908.
Practical Town Planning. London, 1914.
New Townsmen
New Towns After the War. An argument for garden cities. London, 1918.
Nichols, J. C.
Real Estate Subdivisions: The Best Manner of Handling Them. American Civic Association, Washington, 1912.
Nolen, John
Replanning Small Cities. Six typical studies. New York, 1912.

NOLEN, JOHN   *(Continued)*

Some Examples of the Influence of Public Parks in Increasing City Land Values.
Landscape Architecture, July, 1913.

Land Subdivision and its Effects Upon Housing. National Conference on Housing *Proceedings,* 1915.
Also published in *National Real Estate Journal,* October 15, 1915, pp. 259 ff.

More Houses for Bridgeport. Bridgeport, 1916.

Planning Problems of Smaller Cities in the United States. National Conference on City Planning *Proceedings,* 1916.

City Planning. A series of papers presenting the essential elements of a city plan. New York, 1916.

" The Subdivision of Land," in City Planning. National Municipal League, New York, 1916.

A Good Home for Every Wage Earner. American Civic Association, Washington, 1917.

A Good Home for Every Wage Earner. United States League of Building and Loan Associations, Chicago, 1917.

The Effect of Land Subdivision upon Housing and Public Health. Washington, 1917.

Examples of City Planning in Small Places. National Conference on City Planning *Proceedings,* 1917.

The Housing Standards of the Federal Government. National Conference on City Planning *Proceedings,* 1918.

Industrial Housing. Better homes for less money. Cambridge, 1918.

The Industrial Village. National Housing Association, New York, 1918.

New Ideals in the Planning of Cities, Towns and Villages. New York, 1919.

Planning Problems of Industrial Cities. Niagara Falls as an illustration. National Conference on City Planning *Proceedings,* 1919.

Getting Action in City Planning. National Conference on City Planning *Proceedings,* 1921.

Industrial Village Communities of the United States.
Garden Cities and Town Planning (England), January, 1921, pp. 6 ff.

NOLEN, JOHN (*Continued*)

The Place of the Beautiful in the City Plan. Some everyday examples. National Conference on City Planning *Proceedings*, 1922.

Town Planning Tendencies in the United States. International Garden Cities and Town Planning Federation *Report*, London, 1923.

The Importance of Citizens' Committees in Securing Public Support for a City Planning Program. National Conference on City Planning *Proceedings*, 1924.

New Communities Planned to Meet New Conditions. National Conference on City Planning *Proceedings*, 1926.

Also a reprint.

Also in *City Planning*, April, 1926.

Planning Public Parks and Recreation Centers, in Home Building and Subdividing. National Association of Real Estate Boards, Chicago, 1926.

Town and Regional Planning in Relation to Existing and Potential Land Values. International Housing and Town Planning Congress *Report*, Vienna, 1926.

Also published in *National Real Estate Journal*, December 27, 1926, pp. 26 ff.

Town Planning and its Relation to the Professions Involved. American Society of Civil Engineers *Proceedings*, October, 1926.

Also a reprint.

NUSSBAUMER, N. L.

Subdividing Land in Foreign Countries.
National Real Estate Journal, October 18, 1926, pp. 24 ff.

OLMSTED, F. L.

How to Organize a City Planning Campaign. The Civic Press, New York.

City Planning. American Civic Association, Washington, 1910.

A City Planning Program. National Conference on City Planning *Proceedings*, 1913.

OSBORN, F. J.

Much Housing and No More Garden Cities. An accusation of failure.
Garden Cities and Town Planning (England), October, 1926, pp. 194 ff.

PARK, R. E., and E. W. BURGESS
The City. With a bibliography by Louis Wirth. Chicago, 1925.

PRAY, J. S.
The Survey for a City Plan. Conference of Mayors and other City Officials *Proceedings* (New York State), 1914.

PURDOM, C. B.
The Building of Satellite Towns. A contribution to the study of town development and regional planning. London, 1925.

ROBINSON, C. M.
Modern Civic Art, or the City Made Beautiful. New York, 1904.
The Improvement of Towns and Cities, or the Practical Basis of Civic Æsthetics. New York, 1913.
City Planning with Special Reference to the Planning of Streets and Lots. New York and London, 1916.

ROUTZAHN, E. G. and M. S.
Elements of a Social Publicity Program. Russell Sage Foundation, New York, 1920.

ROYAL INSTITUTE OF BRITISH ARCHITECTS
Transactions. London, 1911.

SENNETT, A. R.
Garden Cities in Theory and in Practice. London, 1905.

SHURTLEFF, FLAVEL, in collaboration with F. L. OLMSTED
Carrying Out the City Plan. New York, 1914.

SIMS, N. L.
The Rural Community, Ancient and Modern. New York, 1920.

SMYTHE, W. E.
City Homes on Country Lanes. New York, 1921.

SOCIOLOGICAL SOCIETY
The City Survey Preparatory to Town Planning. London, 1911.

TAYLOR, G. R.
Satellite Cities. National Municipal League, New York, 1915.

THOMPSON, F. L.
Site Planning in Practice. An investigation of the principles of housing estate development. London, 1923.

UNITED STATES DEPARTMENT OF COMMERCE, ADVISORY
COMMITTEE ON ZONING
    A Standard State Zoning Enabling Act.
    National Real Estate Journal, October 9, 1922, pp. 20 ff.
    Also a reprint. Washington, 1926.
    A Proposed Standard City Planning Enabling Act. Wash-
       ington, 1926.
    A City Planning Primer.
    American City, January, 1927, pp. 89 ff.
UNITED STATES HOUSING CORPORATION
    Reports
       Vol. 2: Houses, Site-Planning, Utilities. Washington,
          1919.
       Vol. 1: Organization, Policies, Transactions. Washing-
          ton, 1920.
UNITED STATES SENATE, COMMITTEE ON AGRICULTURE AND
FORESTRY
    Garden City Movement. Washington, 1917.
UNITED STATES SHIPPING BOARD, EMERGENCY FLEET COR-
PORATION
    Types of Houses for Shipbuilders. Washington, 1919.
UNWIN, RAYMOND
    Town Planning in Practice. An introduction to the art of
       designing cities and suburbs. London, 1911.
    Nothing Gained by Overcrowding. London, 1918.
    The Garden City and the Overgrown Town. International
       Garden Cities and Town Planning Federation *Report.*
       London, 1923.
    The Need for a Regional Plan. International Town Plan-
       ning Conference *Report.* Amsterdam, 1924.
    Methods of Decentralization. National Conference on
       City Planning *Proceedings,* 1925.
VEILLER, LAWRENCE
    Housing Reform. Russell Sage Foundation, New York,
       1910.
    A Model Housing Law (revised edition). Russell Sage
       Foundation, New York, 1920.
WATERHOUSE, PAUL, and RAYMOND UNWIN
    Old Towns and New Needs; also, The Town Extension
       Plan: being the Warburton lectures for 1912. Man-
       chester (England), 1912.

WAUGH, F. A.
Country Planning. American Civic Association, Washington, 1916.

WHITAKER, C. H.
The Joke About Housing. Boston, 1920.

WHITAKER, C. H., F. L. ACKERMAN, R. S. CHILDS and EDITH E. WOOD
The Housing Problem in War and in Peace.
Journal of the American Institute of Architects, Washington, 1918.

WILLIAMS, ANEURIN
Co-partnership and Profit-sharing. London, 1913.

WILLIAMS, F. B.
The Law of City Planning and Zoning. New York, 1922.

WOOD, EDITH E.
The Housing of the Unskilled Wage Earner. New York, 1919.

YEOMANS, A. B.
City Residential Land Development. Chicago, 1916.

ZUEBLIN, CHARLES
American Municipal Progress. New York, 1916.

PROJECT LIST

The following list is taken from a record of drawings compiled by John Nolen's office. The original list and most of the drawings are in the Nolen Papers at Cornell University. There is also a collection of Nolen's drawings at the University of Pennsylvania. There is no indication these projects were actually constructed, and some were abandoned after a brief consultation. Clients and locations that appear repeatedly indicate sequential, simultaneous, or enlarged projects. Dates indicate when Nolen's office began work on the projects; client names and project locations are given as they appear on his list. The project descriptions have been adjusted for consistency, and the list has been edited for typographical errors.

DATE	CLIENT	LOCATION	DESCRIPTION
1904			
Nov.	Fels and Co.	West Philadelphia, Pa.	Factory Grounds
Oct.	Ellicott, W. T.	Ardmore, Pa.	Private Place
1905			
June	Burnham, A. C.	Bailey's Island, Me.	Private Place
June	Stephens, George	Charlotte, N.C.	Private Place
June	Charlotte Park and Tree Commission	Charlotte, N.C.	Independence Park
Nov.	Russell, E. R.	Charlotte, N.C.	Private Place
Dec.	Abbott, F. C.	Charlotte, N.C.	Private Place

1906

Jan.	Brown, P. M.	Charlotte, N.C.	Private Place
Jan.	Kessler, M. L.	Thomasville, N.C.	Orphanage Grounds
Jan.	Harris, Wade	Charlotte, N.C.	Private Place
Jan.	Dotger, C. H.	Charlotte, N.C.	Consultation on Woodland
Jan.	Maxwell, W. C.	Charlotte, N.C.	Consultation on House Site
Mar.	Cromwell, A. J.	Charlotte, N.C.	Private Place
Mar.	Rodman, Col. W. B.	Charlotte, N.C.	Private Place
Mar.	Morrison, E.	Statesville, N.C.	Private Place
June	Birtwell, Miss	Cambridge, Mass.	Private Place
June	Taylor, C. S.	Haverford, Pa.	Private Place
June	Murphy, T. E.	Overbrook, Pa.	Private Place
June	Reinhold, H. L., Jr.	Ardmore, Pa.	Private Place
June	Dodsworth, L. A.	Charlotte, N.C.	Private Place
June	Griggs, Edward H.	Twin Mountain, N.H.	Private Place
June	Fels, Maurice	West Philadelphia, Pa.	Private Place
June	Weatherly Improvement Assoc.	Weatherly, Pa.	Monument Square Improvement
June	Dunn, R. A.	Charlotte, N.C.	Private Place
July	Univ. of North Carolina	Chapel Hill, N.C.	Design for Arboretum
July	Morristown Improvement Assoc.	Morristown, N.J.	General Consultation
July	Gresham, C. A.	Mount Airy, Ga.	Monterey Hotel Grounds
Nov.	Ellis, Rudolph	Bryn Mawr, Pa.	Hillside Garden
Nov.	Italian Cemetery	Forest Hills, Mass.	Planting Plan
Nov.	Hinkle, A. H.	Bar Harbor, Me.	Summer Place
Dec.	Mendoza, R. G.	Havana, Cuba	Private Place
Dec.	Baldwin, G. J.	Savannah, Ga.	Comprehensive Plan and Report

1907

Feb.	Westover Heights Co.	Lynchburg, Va.	Land Subdivision
Mar.	Hawley, F. O.	Charlotte, N.C.	Private Place
Apr.	Holt, F. S.	New Haven, Ct.	Pergola
Apr.	McLean, A. W.	Lumberton, N.C.	Private Place
Apr.	White, J. S.	Mebana, N.C.	Private Place
May	Savannah Park and Tree Commission	Savannah, Ga.	Complete Plan for Daffin Park
May	Robbins, O. A.	Charlotte, N.C.	Private Place
June	Charlotte Park and Tree Commission	Charlotte, N.C.	Vance Square
June	Charlotte Park and Tree Commission	Charlotte, N.C.	Cemetery Square
June	Charlotte Park and Tree Commission	Charlotte, N.C.	City Plan and Report
June	Williams College	Williamstown, Mass.	Planting Plan for Thompson Chapel
June	Davidson College	Davidson, N.C.	Consultation
June	Mallory, W. E.	Danbury, Ct.	Land Subdivision
June	Tompkins, D. A.	High Shoals, N.C.	Design for Village
June	Ellerbee Springs	Rockingham, N.C.	Report on Improvement of Summer Place
June	Craddock-Terry Co.	Lynchburg, Va.	Shoe Factory Grounds
June	Tompkins, Grace	Edgefield, S.C.	Private Place
Sept.	Ellis, Charles	Savannah, Ga.	Private Place
Nov.	Roanoke Civic Improvement Committee	Roanoke, Va.	Comprehensive Plan and Report
Nov.	San Diego Civic Improvement Committee	San Diego, Calif.	Comprehensive Plan and Report

1908

Feb.	Hollins Institute	Hollins, Va.	Location of Memorial Library and Improvement of Campus

Mar.	McCarthy, E. B.	Devon, Pa.	Small Country Place
Mar.	Bancroft, W. F.	Wilmington, Del.	Land Subdivision
Apr.	Rivermont Realty Co.	Lynchburg, Va.	Private Place
Apr.	Sackett, H. M.	Lynchburg, Va.	Private Place
Apr.	Shinkle, A. C.	Cincinnati, Ohio	Suburban Place
Apr.	Madison Park and Pleasure Drive Assoc.	Madison, Wis.	Landscape Architect Advisory
June	Waldo, C. H.	Newton, Mass.	Suburban Place
June	Wisconsin State Park Board	Madison, Wis. (Door County)	Landscape Architect Advisory
Aug.	La Crosse Park Commission (Hixon, J. N., Chairman)	La Crosse, Wis.	City Park System
Aug.	Gale, Zona	Portage, Wis.	Consultation on Town Improvement
Aug.	Cochrane, T. H.	Portage, Wis.	Private Place
Sept.	Smith's Agricultural College	Northampton, Mass.	General Plan
Sept.	Kanuga Lake	Hendersonville, N.C.	General Plan
Oct.	Montclair Art Commission Borough Improvement	Montclair, N.J.	General Plan and Report
Oct.	Citizen's Committee	Glen Ridge, N.J.	General Plan and Report
Oct.	Baptist Orphanage of Virginia	Salem, Va.	General Plans
Oct.	Henderson, G.	Paoli, Pa.	Private Place
Oct.	Ross, Howard D.	Wilmington, Del.	Land Subdivision and Private Place
Nov.	Brock, J. S.	Rockport, Mass.	Private Place
*	Wisconsin State Board of Control	Wales, Wis.	General Planting Plan, Tuberculosis Sanitarium
*	Wisconsin State Board of Control	Chippewa Falls, Wis.	General Planting Plan, Home for Feeble Minded Children

*	Wisconsin State Board of Control	Sparta, Wis.	General Planting Plan, State Public School
*	University of Wisconsin	Madison, Wis.	Landscape Architect Advisory
*	Fairhaven Land Co.	Madison, Wis.	Suburban Land Subdivision
*	Paine, E. W.	Oshkosh, Wis.	Private Place
*	Osborne, E. B.	Montclair, N.J.	Private Place

1909

Feb.	Reading Civic Assoc.	Reading, Pa.	City Plan, Mt. Penn– Treatment of Slope, Location of Public Buildings
*	Madison's Citizens' Committee	Madison, Wis.	City Plan and Report
*	Queen's University	Kingston, Ontario	General Plan and Advice
*	Montclair Board of Education	Montclair, N.J.	School Grounds
*	Olin, John M.	Madison, Wis.	Private Place
*	Lakewood Land Co.	Madison, Wis.	Land Subdivision

1910

May	Milwaukee County Park Commission	Milwaukee, Wis.	City Extension
May	Pabst Farm	Milwaukee, Wis.	Land Subdivision
May	Chattanooga Park Commission	Chattanooga, Tenn.	Park System
May	Capitol Commission	Madison, Wis.	State Capitol Grounds
July	Burnham, A. C.	Newton Centre, Mass.	Private Place
July	Playground Committee	Stoneham, Mass.	Playground (two sites)
Nov.	City of St. Paul and St. Paul City Club	St. Paul, Minn.	City Plan

Dec.	Main, John S.	Madison, Wis.	Land Subdivision
*	Round Top Land Co.	Madison, Wis.	Land Subdivision
*	Madison Park	Charlottesville, Va.	Land Subdivision
*	Krise, P. A.	Lynchburg, Va.	Private Place
*	Scranton City Improvement Assoc.	Scranton, Pa.	City Plan

1911

Feb.	Board of Trade and Civic Club	Lock Haven, Pa.	Town Plan
Feb.	Town of Lexington	Lexington, Mass.	Playground
Mar.	The Stephens Co.	Charlotte, N.C.	Myers Park, Land Subdivision
Apr.	Reinsch, Prof. P. S.	Blooming Grove, Wis.	Land Subdivision
Apr.	Johnson, Carl	Madison, Wis.	Private Place
Apr.	Goodnight, Prof.	Madison, Wis.	Private Place
Apr.	Village Improvement Society	Wayland, Mass.	Town Plan
Apr.	Chattanooga Estates Co.	Chattanooga, Tenn.	Highlands, Land Subdivision
July	Playground Commission	Cambridge, Mass.	General Plans for a Playground System, Construction Plans for Thorndike Field
Aug.	Tom[p?]kins, D. A.	Blowing Rock, N.C.	Private Place
Sept.	Municipal Art Society	New London, Ct.	Park and Playground System
Sept.	Committee on Parks of Chamber of Commerce	Sacramento, Calif.	Plan for Del Paso Park
Oct.	Milwaukee County School of Agriculture	Milwaukee, Wis.	General Plan
Dec.	Nickerson, Mrs. George W.	Stoneham, Mass.	Plan of Stoneham Square

1912

| Jan. | Men's Club | Cohasset, Mass. | Town Plan |

Feb.	City Planning Committee, Chamber of Commerce and Board of Trade	Erie, Pa.	City Plan
Mar.	La Monte, Miss Carolina B.	Bound Brook, N.J.	Westerly Gardens, Land Subdivision
Apr.	The Stephens Co.	Charlotte, N.C.	Plan for Presbyterian (now Queen's) College
May	City of Schenectady	Schenectady, N.Y.	City Plan
May	Board of Directors of City Trusts	Philadelphia, Pa.	Plan for Girard College Grounds
Oct.	The Stephens Co.	Charlotte, N.C.	Private Plans in Myers Park
Oct.	Jackson, J. F., and others	Milwaukee, Wis.	Milwaukee River, Land Subdivision
Oct.	Keokuk Industrial Assoc.	Keokuk, Iowa	City Plan
Nov.	Parkways Assoc., City of Little Rock and Pulaski County	Little Rock, Ark.	Park System and Civic Center
Dec.	Hopkins, J. A. H.	Morristown, N.J.	Selection of Site for High School and Sketch Plans

1913

Jan.	Dimmick, Mr. and Mrs. J.	Scranton, Pa.	Planting Plan, Church of the Good Shepherd
May	Longwood Improvement Assoc.	Brookline, Mass.	Local Street Improvement
May	Town of Walpole	Walpole, Mass.	East Walpole Playground
June	F. W. Bird & Son and others	East Walpole, Mass.	Neponset Garden Village, Land Subdivision
June	F. W. Bird & Son and others	Walpole, Mass.	Town Plan

July	Keokuk Industrial Assoc.	Keokuk, Iowa	Henry Rein Tract, Land Subdivision
July	Green, H. R.	Reading, Pa.	Dengler Hill, Neversink Mt., Land Subdivisions
Aug.	Ryrie, Harry	Toronto, Ontario	Land Subdivision (near Oakville)
Aug.	Belin, F. L.	Scranton, Pa.	Private Place
Sept.	Dennison Mfg. Co.	South Framingham, Mass.	Clark's Hill, Land Subdivision
Oct.	Allison, W. C.	St. John, New Brunswick	Private Place
Oct.	Bates College	Lewiston, Me.	General Plan
Nov.	McPeaks, F. J.	Watertown, Mass.	Land Subdivision
Dec.	Smith College	Northampton, Mass.	General Plan
Dec.	Ellsworth, J. E.	Erie, Pa.	Green Garden Terrace, Land Subdivision
Dec.	Board of Park Directors	Sacramento, Calif.	Park System
Dec.	Allison, W. S.	St. John, New Brunswick	Land Subdivision

1914

Feb.	F. W. Bird & Son	Walpole, Mass.	High School and other plans
Feb.	Civic Exhibition and Town Planning Competition	Dublin, Ireland	Advisory Expert
Apr.	City Plan Commission	Bridgeport, Ct.	City Plan
Apr.	Broadway Improvement District	Little Rock, Ark.	Street Plan
May	La Monte Estate	Bound Brook, N.J.	Land Subdivision
June	Irving Park Co.	Greensboro, N.C.	Land Subdivision
June	City Commission	Sacramento, Calif.	City Plans
Oct.	F. W. Bird & Son	Walpole, Mass.	Walpole Town Forest
Nov.	Bird, Charles Sumner	Walpole, Mass.	"Endean" Private Estate

1915

Jan.	Davidson College	Davidson College, N.C.	Campus Plan
Jan.	Charles Evans Cemetery	Reading, Pa.	Boundary Wall
Mar.	Nichols, J. C.	Kansas City, Mo.	Private Estate
Mar.	City of New London	New London, Ct.	Street System
Apr.	Crystal Spring Land Co.	Roanoke, Va.	Land Subdivision
Apr.	Nichols, J. C.	Kansas City, Mo.	Country Club District, Land Subdivision
May	Geneva Colleges	Geneva, N.Y.	General Plan for Hobart and William Smith Colleges
May	Coker College	Hartsville, S.C.	General Plan
June	Mt. Union Refactories Co.	Mt. Union, Pa.	General Plan for Industrial Village
Aug.	New London Park Board	New London, Ct.	Plan for Ocean Beach Park
Sept.	Latham, J. E.	Greensboro, N.C.	Land Subdivision and Industrial Village
Oct.	Everett City Planning Board	Everett, Mass.	Waterfront
Oct.	Elizabeth College (King, Dr. C. B.)	Charlotte, N.C.	Land Subdivision
Dec.	American Cast Iron Pipe Co. (Acipco)	Birmingham, Ala.	Land Subdivision and Industrial Village

1916

Jan.	Kingsport Improvement Corp.	Kingsport, Tenn.	Town Plan
Feb.	Waterbury Housing Co.	Waterbury, Ct.	Housing Report
Feb.	Town of Lincoln	Lincoln, Mass.	School Playground
Mar.	City of Durham	Durham, N.C.	Water Works Park

Apr.	City of Bridgeport	Bridgeport, Ct.	Housing Scheme and Land Subdivision
Apr.	American Brass Co.	Waterbury, Ct.	Land Subdivision and Housing Scheme
Apr.	Ellsworth, J. E., et al.	Erie, Pa.	Land Subdivision
Apr.	Kenosha Manufacturers Assoc.	Kenosha, Wis.	Housing Report
May	Elizabeth Realty Co. (Wriston Park)	Charlotte, N.C.	Land Subdivision
June	Kahkwa Park Realty Co.	Erie, Pa.	Land Subdivision
July	Brighton Mills (Allwood Realty Corp.)	Passaic, N.J.	Town Site
July	White, Gilbert C. (Rosemont)	Charlotte, N.C.	Land Subdivision
Aug.	American Metal Co. (Town of Langeloth)	Langeloth, Pa.	Town Site
Aug.	Bridgeport Housing Co.	Bridgeport, Ct.	Land Subdivision and General Advice (a. Ctt. Development, b. Fairfield Tract)
Aug.	General Electric Co.	Erie, Pa.	Land Subdivision (a. General Plan of Property, b. 16 acres, c. Municipal W., 30 acres, d. Lawrence Park)
Sept.	General Electric Co.	Schenectady, N.Y.	Communication and Extension Plan
Sept.	Akron Chamber of Commerce	Akron, Ohio	General City Plan, Housing Report and Civic Survey
Nov.	West Drew Land Co.	Chattanooga, Tenn.	West Drew Park, Land Subdivision
Nov.	Chase, Miss Helen E.	Waterbury, Ct.	Green Acres, Garden Village
Dec.	Reed, Carl M.	Erie, Pa.	Land Subdivision

1917

Feb.	City of Flint	Flint, Mich.	City Plan
Feb.	General Chemical Co.	Marcus Hook, Pa.	Overlook Colony, Industrial Village
Feb.	Charlotte Chamber of Commerce	Charlotte, N.C.	City Plan and Civic Survey
Mar.	City of Niagara Falls	Niagara Falls, N.Y.	City Plan
Mar.	Griswold, Marvin	Erie, Pa.	Grouping of Public Buildings
Apr.	Youngstown Sheet and Tube Co.	Youngstown, Ohio	General Plan and Industrial Housing
June	Washington and Lee University	Lexington, Va.	Davidson Park, Subdivision for Professors' Houses
July	Belmont Iron Works	Eddystone, Pa.	Small Subdivision
Aug.	State Institute for Blind and Deaf	Raleigh, N.C.	General Plan
Sept.	University of North Carolina	Chapel Hill, N.C.	General Plan
Nov.	Dawson Land Co.	Dawson, Colo.	General Plan, Town Site
Dec.	Chamber of Commerce	Wilmington, Del.	Housing Report

1918

Feb.	Miami Conservancy District	Dayton, Ohio	Consultation and Labor Camp Plans
Mar.	Dimmick, Mrs.	Scranton, Pa.	Sturges Park
Mar.	Board of Trade	Milton, Pa.	Housing Report
Mar.	Chamber of Commerce	Troy, N.Y.	Housing Report
Apr.	U.S. Shipping Board, Emergency Fleet Corp., Proj. 14	Wilmington, Del.	Union Park Gardens, Land Subdivision and Industrial Housing

Apr.	Sherwin and Griswold	Erie, Pa.	Sherwin Tract, Land Subdivision
Apr.	General Electric Co.	Erie, Pa.	Crowley Farm, Land Subdivision
May	Barney, J. Ross	Erie, Pa.	Chestnut Hill, Land Subdivision
June	Middleton Realty Co.	Middleton, Ohio	The Highlands, Land Subdivision
July	International Coal Products Corp.	Clinchfield, Va.	Town Plan
Aug.	U.S. Housing Corp. Proj. 404	Niagara Falls, N.Y.	Town Planner, Housing Project
Aug.	U.S. Housing Corp. Proj. 1635	Eddystone, Pa.	Town Planner, Housing Project
Aug.	U.S. Housing Corp. Proj. 2947	Ridley Park, Pa.	Town Planner, Housing Project

1919

Jan.	La Crosse War Memorial Commission	La Crosse, Wis.	Civic Survey, City Plan, Regional Survey, Regional Plan
Feb.	Keller, G. C.	Flint, Mich.	Woodcroft, Land Subdivision
Mar.	Chamber of Commerce	Janesville, Wis.	Civic Survey, City Plan, Regional Survey, Regional Plan
Mar.	St. James's Church	Cambridge, Mass.	Planting Plan
Apr.	DuPont Co.	Pontiac, Mich.	Industrial Housing Development
Apr.	DuPont Co.	Flint, Mich.	Industrial Housing Development
May	Cohasset Men's Club	Cohasset, Mass.	Town Plan
May	Warner, Mrs. Percy De F.	Waterbury, Ct.	Land Subdivisions

Aug.	Inspiration Consolidated Copper Co.	Miami, Ariz.	Industrial Housing Conference and Report
Sept.	Greenfield Tap and Die Co.	Greenfield, Mass.	Industrial Housing Development
Sept.	DuPont Co.	Penns Grove, N.J.	Industrial Village
Oct.	Modern Housing Corp.	Janesville, Wis.	Industrial Housing Development
Oct.	Modern Housing Corp.	Walkerville, Ontario	Industrial Housing Development
Oct.	Greenfield Tap and Die Co.	Greenfield, Mass.	Factory Park
Nov.	City of Bristol	Bristol, Ct.	Civic Survey, City Plan
Dec.	Carey Real Estate and Investment Co.	Hutchinson, Kans.	Land Subdivision

1920

Jan.	Davidson Realty Co.	Sioux City, Iowa	Land Subdivision
Jan.	Cincinnati Better Housing League	Cincinnati, Ohio	Housing Survey Consultant
Feb.	Armistead Corp.	Norfolk, Va.	Land Subdivision Consultant
Mar.	Wakefield High School	Wakefield, Mass.	Construction and General
Apr.	Olean Housing Corp.	Olean, N.Y.	Seneca Heights, Land Subdivision
Apr.	Tilton Seminary	Tilton, N.H.	Studies for Approach
Apr.	F. W. Bird & Son	Walpole, Mass.	Replan Neponset Garden Village
Apr.	F. W. Bird & Son	Walpole, Mass.	East Walpole Center
Apr.	F. W. Bird & Son	Walpole, Mass.	New School, East Walpole
May	Farm City	Wilmington, N.C.	Town Plan
May	McArthur, Arthur	Binghamton, N.Y.	Land Subdivision
June	Mt. Allison University	Sackville, New Brunswick	Consultation and Report

June	Planning Board	Flint, Mich.	Consultant, City Planner
June	Park Board	Flint, Mich.	Landscape Architect Advisory
June	City of Green Bay	Green Bay, Wis.	Civic Survey and City Plan
Aug.	Hendersonville, N.C., Finance Co.	Hendersonville, N.C.	Kanuga Town Plan
Aug.	Town of Cohasset	Cohasset, Mass.	Town Plan
Sept.	City of Elkhart	Elkhart, Ind.	Civic Survey and City Plan
Nov.	Mariemont	Cincinnati, Ohio	Town Plan

1921

Apr.	Planning Board	Watertown, Mass.	Plan for Center, School Grounds and Parks
Apr.	Alexander, Capt. S. B. (Camp Greene), Julia Alexander	Charlotte, N.C.	Land Subdivision
May	Lower Merion Township	Ardmore, Pa.	Plan for Center
June	Gerhard, Albert P.	West Philadelphia, Pa.	Land Subdivision
June	Board of Education	Flint, Mich.	School Ground Plans
Aug.	City of Springfield	Springfield, Mass.	Proposal for a Plan
Sept.	Park Commission	Spartanburg, S.C.	Civic Survey and City Plan
Oct.	Town of Torrington	Torrington, Ct.	Street Intersection
Oct.	Planning Board	Framingham, Mass.	Plan for Center
Oct.	Babson Institute Inc.	Wellesley Hills, Mass.	Group Plan
Nov.	McMurry, Josh	Forest City, N.C.	Swimming Pool and Children's Playground
Nov.	Saunders, B. H., Esq. (Hohokus)	Paterson, N.J.	Land Subdivision
Dec.	City Planning Commission	Asheville, N.C.	Civic Survey and City Plan

1922

Feb.	Jones, Miss Amelia	New Bedford, Mass.	Subdivision and School Group
Mar.	City Planning Board	St. Petersburg, Fla.	Civic Survey and City Plan
Apr.	Feidler, F. F., et al.	Erie, Pa.	Westminster, Land Subdivision
Apr.	Beaver Lake	Asheville, N.C.	Land Subdivision
Apr.	City of West Palm Beach	West Palm Beach, Fla.	Civic Survey and City Plan
May	Slater, Mrs. H. N.	Readville, Mass.	Estate Details
June	General Electric Co.	Schenectady, N.Y.	Athletic Field, Neighborhood Park
July	Grove Investments, E. W.	Asheville, N.C.	Land Subdivision
Aug.	Andover War Memorial Committee	Andover, Mass.	Memorial Location
Aug.	Clewiston	Clewiston, Fla.	Town Plan
Oct.	Thun, F.; Wyomissing	Wyomissing, Pa.	Regional Plan

1923

Jan.	New York and Environs	New York, N.Y.	Regional Plan
Apr.	Walpole Memorial Park; Allen, Phillip	Walpole, Mass.	Memorial Park
Apr.	Walpole Home Building Co.	Walpole, Mass.	Land Subdivision
May	Falmouth Board of Trade	Falmouth, Mass.	Street Widening
May	Mariemont	Mariemont, Ohio	Westover, Land Subdivision
May	Babson Park Co.	Babson Park, Mass.	Land Subdivision
May	Bird, Charles Sumner	East Walpole, Mass.	Construction Plans for Local Center
May	Planning Board	Haverhill, Mass.	Consultant on Civic Survey and Zoning

May	Planning Board	Lynn, Mass.	Program for City Plan
May	Coleman, G. W.	Wellesley Hills, Mass.	Seat and Marker Details
May	Wyomissing Park	Wyomissing, Pa.	Section 2, Land Subdivision
June	Planning Board	North Adams, Mass.	Consultant Services and City Planning
July	Planning Board	Auburn, Me.	Pettingill Park General Plan
Aug.	Falmouth Village Improvement Assoc.	Falmouth, Mass.	Shiverick Park General Plan
Aug.	Berkshire Heights, Mills, Nolan and Dellinger	Reading, Pa.	Land Subdivision
Aug.	Berkshire Heights, Thun, Impink and Janssen	Reading, Pa.	Land Subdivision
Oct.	Neighborhood Trust, Hill, O. W.	Wellesley Hills, Mass.	Land Subdivision
Nov.	Bird, Charles Sumner	East Walpole, Mass.	Plans for Francis William Park
Dec.	Planning Board	Wilmington, N.C.	Consultant Services
Dec.	Meinig, E. R.	Reading, Pa.	Oakbrook Industrial Village
Dec.	Olean Housing Corp. II	Olean, N.Y.	Seneca Heights, Land Subdivision

1924

Jan.	Schock, Clarence	Mt. Joy, Pa.	Consultant Services and Report
Jan.	Planning Board	Sarasota, Fla.	Consultant Services
Feb.	Meinig, E. R.	Reading, Pa.	Factory Grounds and Subdivision
Feb.	Township Commissioners	Lower Merion Township, Pa.	Zoning Advice
Feb.	Day, R. W., and Kelley, M. D.	St. George, Fla.	New Town

Mar.	Harbor Commission	San Diego, Calif.	Roseville Yacht Basin, Waterfront Civic Group
Mar.	Wyomissing Development Co.	Wyomissing, Pa.	Valley Park, Reichart Tract
Apr.	City of Sarasota	Sarasota, Fla.	City Plan
Apr.	Planning Board	North Adams, Mass.	City Plan
Apr.	Windsor Farms	Richmond, Va.	City Plan
May	Bird, Charles Sumner	East Walpole, Mass.	Development Plan, East Walpole Center
June	Woodcroft Corp.	Flint, Mich.	Consultant Services
June	City of San Diego	San Diego, Calif.	City Plan
July	Fall River Memorial Commission	Fall River, Mass.	Memorial Location
July	Belleair Development Co.	Clearwater, Fla. (Belleair)	Land Subdivision
July	Wyomissing Development Co.	Wyomissing, Pa.	Museum Location
July	Borough of Wyomissing	Wyomissing, Pa.	Zoning Study
Aug.	City of Columbus	Columbus, Ga.	City Plan
Aug.	Feidler, F. F., et al.	Erie, Pa. (Westminster)	Venice Pool Park
Sept.	City of Tampa	Tampa, Fla.	Planning Survey
Sept.	Albee, Dr. F. H.	Venice-Nokomis and Bay Point, Fla.	Land Subdivision
Sept.	Seaboard Air Line RR	Sebring, Fla.	Land Subdivision
Sept.	Belleview Hotel	Clearwater, Fla. (Belleair)	Land Subdivision
Sept.	Mariemont Co.	Mariemont, Ohio	Construction Plans
Oct.	Brooks, J. L.	Newagan, Me.	Land Subdivision
Oct.	Juniata Valley Realty Corp.	Mt. Union, Pa.	Country Club
Oct.	Seaboard Development Co.	Indian Town District	Town Development
Oct.	Albee, Dr. F. H.	Venice, Fla.	New Town

Oct.	Beach, Rex	Clearwater, Fla. (Belleair)	Land Subdivision
Oct.	Bird, Mrs. F. W.	Walpole, Mass.	Private Place
Dec.	Varn, C. G.	St. Augustine Beach	Land Subdivision
Dec.	Morrison, Cameron	Charlotte, N.C.	Private Place
Dec.	Ingoldsby, J. H.	St. Petersburg, Fla.	Maximo Estates, Maximo Shores, New Town Subdivision

1925

Jan.	City of Sarasota	Sarasota, Fla.	City Planning Report
Feb.	San Diego Park Commission	San Diego, Calif.	Balboa Park, General Park Plan
Feb.	City of Berkeley	Berkeley, Calif.	Consultant Services
Feb.	Marston, George W., San Diego	Presidio Hills, Calif.	General Park Plans
Feb.	Point Loma Estates	San Diego, Calif.	Land Subdivision
Mar.	Singer, Paris	Palm Beach, Fla.	Land Subdivision
Mar.	San Jose Estates	Jacksonville, Fla.	Land Subdivision
Apr.	City of Clearwater	Clearwater, Fla.	City Plan
Apr.	Broad Acres Corp.	Glens Falls, N.Y.	Land Subdivision
May	Clewiston, Ltd.	Clewiston, Fla.	Revised Town Plan
May	White, Col. W. L.	Floridale, Fla.	Model Poultry Farm
June	Board of Park Commissioners	Lowell, Mass.	Playgrounds
July	Reading, A. K.	Belmont-on-the-Gulf, Fla.	New Town
Aug.	Brotherhood of Locomotive Engineers Realty Corp.	Venice, Fla.	New Town
Aug.	Brown Development Co. of Michigan	Gainesville, Fla.	Land Subdivision
Aug.	Telfair Stockton and Co.	Jacksonville, Fla.	San Marco, Land Subdivision
Aug.	Buck and Buck	Jacksonville, Fla.	Lakeshore Estates, Land Subdivision

Sept.	Villa DeSoto Syndicate, Ind.	Sarasota, Fla.	Land Subdivision
Oct.	Alturas Development Co. (Stone and Webster)	Alturas, Fla.	New Town
Nov.	Tamiami City Corp.	Ft. Myers, Fla.	New Town
Nov.	Wayne Development Co.	Ft. Myers, Fla.	Orangewood, New Town
Nov.	Bird, Charles Sumner (Bird Club)	East Walpole, Mass.	Land Subdivision
Nov.	Wyomissing Development Co.	Wyomissing, Pa.	Land Subdivision

1926

Feb.	Bird, Charles Sumner, Jr.	East Walpole, Mass.	Athletic Field
Feb.	City of St. Petersburg	St. Petersburg, Fla.	Revision of City Plan
Mar.	Reading Tribune	Reading, Pa.	Location of Public Buildings
Mar.	Prescott, Mrs. Charles J.	Norwood, Mass.	Swimming Hole Planting
Mar.	Palmer (Esperanza)	Sarasota, Fla.	Hyde Park, Land Subdivision
May	Reading Lodge of Perfection	Reading, Pa.	Land Subdivision
May	Marston, George W.	San Diego, Calif.	Residence
July	Allen, Philip R.	Walpole, Mass.	Swimming Pool, Memorial Park

1927

Mar.	Titus, A. F.	Salem, Mass.	Land Subdivision
Mar.	City of Leominster	Leominster, Mass.	Bath House, Athletic Field
May	Edison, Mrs. Thomas A.	Ft. Myers, Fla.	Garden
June	Lowell Park Commission	Lowell, Mass.	Pawtucketville Memorial

June	American Glanzstoff Corp.	Elizabethton, Tenn.	Regional Plan, Community Housing
Sept.	City of Roanoke	Roanoke, Va.	City Plan
Nov.	City of Johnson City	Johnson City, Tenn.	City Plan
*	Bird, Charles Sumner, Jr.	East Walpole, Mass.	Regional Plan

1928

Feb.	Stamford Development Co.	Stamford, Ct.	Land Subdivision
Apr.	Wyomissing School District	Wyomissing, Pa.	Layout of School Grounds
Aug.	O'Connell Real Estate Trust	Worcester, Mass.	Land Subdivision
Nov.	City of Little Rock	Little Rock, Ark.	City Plan
Nov.	City of Lancaster	Lancaster, Pa.	City Plan
Nov.	Arkansas State Capitol Grounds	Little Rock, Ark.	Plan for Capitol Grounds
Nov.	MacArthur, Arthur	Binghamton, N.Y.	Replanning Moorelands

1929

Feb.	Regional Planning Federation of Philadelphia Tri-State District	Philadelphia, Pa.	Consulting Service
Feb.	City of Berkeley	Berkeley, Calif.	Consultation and Report
Feb.	Board of Park Commission	San Diego, Calif.	Report on Improvement of Highway Facilities, Torrey Pines Park
Mar.	Clewiston Co. Inc.	Clewiston, Fla.	Location of Airport Site
Mar.	Wyomissing Borough	Wyomissing, Pa.	Regional Plan
Apr.	Robinson, H. P.	St. John, New Brunswick	Private Estate
May	Allison, Walter	St. John, New Brunswick	Private Estate

May	McKenna, J. D.	St. John, New Brunswick	Private Estate
May	Tinsley, John	Worcester, Mass.	Plan for House Grounds
June	Hull, R. M.	Cambridge, Mass.	Plan for House Grounds
June	Town of Sharon	Sharon, Mass.	Reconnaissance Survey
July	City of Sharon	Sharon, Pa.	City Plan
July	Stevens Institute of Technology	Hoboken, N.J.	Improvement of Faculty Group and President's House Grounds, Camp Site
Sept.	Stone, E. L.	Roanoke, Va.	Land Subdivision
Sept.	Riverton Zoning Commission	Riverton, N.J.	Zoning Plan and Ordinance
Nov.	Clewiston Co. Inc.	Clewiston, Fla.	Plan of Canal Point Town Site
Dec.	Thun, Ferdinand	Wyomissing, Pa.	Land Subdivision
Dec.	Clewiston Co. Inc.	Clewiston, Fla.	Revision of the Town Plan

1930

Feb.	Zoning Commission	Winchester, Ct.	Zone Plan and Reconnaissance Survey
Apr.	Zoning Commission	Spartanburg, S.C.	Zone Plan and Zone Ordinance
Apr.	Franzheim, Kenneth	New York, N.Y.	"Wayside" Consulting Services
May	City Plan Commission	Dubuque, Iowa	City Plan
Aug.	Harriette F. Nevins Memorial Fountain	Walpole, Mass.	Memorial Fountain
*	Community Council	Reading, Pa.	Reconnaissance Survey

1931

| * | Community Council Berks-Reading Region | Reading, Pa. | Regional Plan |

*	Allsopp, Fred	Little Rock, Ark.	Plan for Allsopp Park

1933

Oct.	Dept. of Agriculture Division of Subsistence Homesteads	Reedsville, W.Va. (Arthurdale)	Plan for Subsistence Homesteads

1934

*	Dept. of Interior	Tygart Valley, W.Va.	Subsistence Homesteads
*	Dept. of Interior	Pender County, N.C. (Penderlea)	Farm City

*Indicates that no month was specified for this project.

INDEX